THE RHETORIC OF REVELATION
IN THE HEBREW BIBLE

OVERTURES TO BIBLICAL THEOLOGY

The Land
WALTER BRUEGGEMANN

God and the Rhetoric of Sexuality
PHYLLIS TRIBLE

Texts of Terror
PHYLLIS TRIBLE

The Suffering of God
TERENCE E. FRETHEIM

Reading Isaiah
EDGAR W. CONRAD

Battered Love
RENITA J. WEEMS

The Old Testament of the Old Testament
R. W. L. MOBERLY

Prayer in the Hebrew Bible
SAMUEL E. BALENTINE

Ministry in the New Testament
DAVID L. BARTLETT

Deuteronomy and the Death of Moses
DENNIS T. OLSON

The Collapse of History
LEO G. PERDUE

Prayer in the New Testament
OSCAR CULLMAN

Missing Persons and Mistaken Identities
PHYLLIS A. BIRD

Uneasy Neighbors
WALTER E. PILGRIM

The Torah's Vision of Worship
Samuel E. Balentine

*The Rhetoric of Revelation
in the Hebrew Bible*
Dale Patrick

EDITOR

WALTER BRUEGGEMANN
Columbia Theological Seminary, Decatur, Georgia

THE RHETORIC OF REVELATION IN THE HEBREW BIBLE

OVERTURES TO BIBLICAL THEOLOGY

Dale Patrick

FORTRESS PRESS

MINNEAPOLIS

To the Mount Angel Abbey Library

The Rhetoric of Revelation in the Hebrew Bible

Copyright © 1999 Augsburg Fortress. All rights reserved. Except for brief quotations in critical articles or reviews, no part of this book may be reproduced in any manner without prior written permission from the publisher. Write: Permissions, Augsburg Fortress, Box 1209, Minneapolis, MN 55440.

Scripture quotations from the New Revised Standard Version of the Bible are copyright © 1989 by the Division of Christian Education of the National Council of the Churches of Christ in the United States of America and are used by permission.

Cover image: Ghiberti's east baptistry door, Florence, Italy. Photograph © Roberto Soncin Gerometta. Used by permission.
Cover and book design: Joseph Bonyata
Typesetting: Peregrine Graphics Services

Library of Congress Cataloging-in-Publication Data
Patrick, Dale.
    The rhetoric of revelation in the Hebrew Bible / Dale Patrick.
      p. cm. — (Overtures to biblical theology series)
    Includes bibliographical references and indexes.
    ISBN: 0-8006-3177-3 (pbk. : alk. paper)
      1. Rhetoric in the Bible. 2. Bible. O.T.—Language, style.
I. Title. II. Series: Overtures to biblical theology.
BS1199.R5P37   1999
221.6'6—dc21   99-36969
                                              CIP

The paper used in this publication meets the minimum requirements of American National Standard for Information Sciences—Permanence of Paper for Printed Library Materials, ANSI Z329.48-1984.

Manufactured in the U.S.A.   AF 1-3177
02   01   00   99   1   2   3   4   5   6   7   8   9   10

CONTENTS

EDITOR'S FOREWORD

JAMES MUILENBURG, TEACHER TO MANY INCLUDING DALE PATRICK AND me, is commonly credited with revolutionizing Old Testament studies through his imaginative and exacting accent upon the cruciality of rhetoric. That impulse from Muilenburg is abundantly evident in Patrick's present book. The book follows Muilenburg in the effort to locate discourse in the life of the community—a genuine, lively transaction with an audience that takes the text seriously. Alongside Muilenburg, Patrick also gives some attention to the work of Yehoshua Gitay, who has pushed rhetorical study in the Old Testament in a somewhat different direction, namely, a focus upon the persuasive intent and force of the text. Patrick, however, does not linger over the work of Gitay, but seeks to articulate a hermeneutic that matches Muilenburg's dynamic sense of rhetoric.

Patrick's approach, informed primarily by J. L. Austen's theoretical work on the performative function of language, is concerned with a transaction between text and audience. Patrick asks how the biblical text "performs" for and in the midst of its reading audience. This suggestive enterprise has already been advanced in an earlier work by Patrick and his colleague, Allen Scult, *Rhetoric and Biblical Interpretation* (JSOTSup 8). By a continued focus upon the reading audience, Patrick deftly brackets out and moves beyond any "original audience," thereby skillfully leaping over the critical issues commonly linked to positivistic history. It is, then, the "second audience," the one now (contemporaneously) before the text. This move to the "second audience" is complex and problematic, because it is clear "even to the second audience" that the text has been primarily addressed to someone else and not to "us." It is, however, the written form of the text—reinforced by canonical claims enacted in the habit of continued reading and hearing texts long after the "original audience" is no more available or even identifiable—that makes this complex and difficult interaction both important and important to understand. It is the contention of such texts to press the second audience for a particular response to make them true.

vii

Freighted with careful theoretical foundations, Patrick takes up five clusters of texts to consider the persuasive force of the text as it addresses always again a second audience. The first three cases are of Moses—his call, the commands of Sinai, and the first commandment. The call of YHWH to Moses, saturated with promise, commission, and assurance, becomes a mediated call that is addressed to the reading audience. So also in his study of the commandments of Sinai, Patrick shows how the performance of command texts produces a relationship of command-obedience with the reader. In a most suggestive excursus on Emmanuel Levinas, Patrick probes the meaning of "obedient reason," so that the obedience appropriate to the commands of Sinai is not a blind, reactive obedience, but a response that is critical, thoughtful, and responsible, as well as responsive. More specifically, the first commandment generates a relationship with the one who commands, but Patrick is not insensitive to the potential for violence that is contained within the jealousy of YHWH's uncompromising command (on which see now Regina Schwartz, *The Curse of Cain*).

Patrick's final two cases offer a powerful dialectic that pervades the Old Testament text. In the fourth case concerning prophetic judgment, he undertakes a close and compelling exposition of Amos. He grounds his discussion in the sum of study concerning the prophetic "law-suit" (Westermann). He shows that Amos the "rhetor" is intent, in the final form of the text, to declare even to continuing generations that the old promises are null and void, that repentance is no option, and that the present audience is always again the one brought under judgment by the prophetic book. The intent of the book of Amos, as distinct from the eighth-century prophet, is to declare to a subsequent audience God's verdict that has been made anciently but continues to pertain. As the primary voice of the book of Amos expresses guilt, so the final promise of Amos 9 intends to effect a coming future for the second audience and situates that audience precisely between the verdict of guilt now enacted and the future only contemplated. This in-between status for the audience closely parallels the argument that I have made concerning the book of Jeremiah, so that the belated use of this literature is for the belatedly in-between.

The final case, that of the lament Psalms, forms a counterbalance to the prophetic judgment. In a suggestive probe of a "theory of lament," the prayers of complaint and protest indicate that monotheism of the Bible is not authoritarian or closed, but rather that, "from the other side, addressed to God as it is addressed to a reading audience," it uses prayer as an inversion of praise. The lament opens up the relationship that, without such protest, might be flattened into the prophetic judgment, as has often been the case in actual practice. The communal laments that likely arose in exile continue to address new audiences that continue in exile, still short of homecoming. I welcome this particular accent because it resonates with my own proposal that "exile" is an illuminating metaphor for current faith communities that continue to be a second audience.

In the end, Patrick is puzzled, which leads his own reading audience to ponder how it is that rhetoric functions as revelation. In his careful concluding analysis, Patrick urges that the text of Scripture must be read "whole." Thus, by a different route, with an accent on "wholeness" and "revelation," Patrick ends up with canon. His arrival there is not by reductionist theological themes nor by imposition of belated dogmatic categories, but from "the inside," by seeing how the text itself works and intends to work.

This most suggestive book is an important contribution to the new questions of scriptural authority, about how this book continues to "instruct and convert." The book is both a stunning indication of how decisively our work has changed with the breakup of the domination of historical questions, and an inviting recognition of how much work yet remains to be done. Patrick's peculiar gift is that he is able at the same time to employ remarkable theory—notably in his engagement with Nicholas Wolterstorff—and yet stay close to the text as befits Patrick's primary scholarly commitments. All around his work is the dazzling and abiding recognition that in this text is a "disclosure," defying and resisting our close explanations. Thus Patrick offers a theological hermeneutic to illuminate the way ancient revelation continues to be contemporary revelation. Patrick insists on close explanation; at the same time, however, he does not fail to notice that what is before us in the text steps always beyond us in power and in claim. It is revelatory, persuasive, and summoning to each new audience.

WALTER BRUEGGEMANN
Columbia Theological Seminary

ABBREVIATIONS

ANE	Ancient Near East
BDB	Brown, Driver, Briggs, *A Hebrew and English Lexicon of the Old Testament*
BZAW	Beihefte zur Zeitschrift für die alttestamentliche Wissenschaft
CBQ	*Catholic Biblical Quarterly*
GBS	Guides to Biblical Scholarship
HDR	Harvard Dissertations in Religion
IRT	Issues in Religion and Theology
JBL	*Journal of Biblical Literature*
JSOT	*Journal for the Study of the Old Testament*
JSOTSup	Journal for the Study of the Old Testament, Supplement Series
JSNTSup	Journal for the Study of the New Testament Supplement Series
LBW	*Lutheran Book of Worship*
OBT	Overtures to Biblical Theology
OTL	Old Testament Library
OTS	*Oudtestamentiche Studiën*
SBL	Society of Biblical Literature
SBLDS	SBL Dissertation Series
SBLMS	SBL Monograph Series
SBT	Studies in Biblical Theology
VT	*Vetus Testamentum*
VTSup	Supplements to Vetus Testamentum
WMANT	Wissenschaftliche Monographien zum Alten und Neuen Testaments
ZAW	*Zeitschrift für die alttestamentliche Wissenschaft*
ZThK	*Zeitschrift für Theologie und Kirche*

PREFACE

CONSIDER THE SAYING THAT AN AUTHOR WRITES THE SAME BOOK OVER and over again, whatever the subject. Taken literally, that notion is rather absurd. Readers might not notice, but publishers would not be fooled. Perhaps we should take it to mean that an author is trying to answer the same questions with the same habit of mind in book after book. A biblical scholar might even go back to the same passages.

The question that drives this theological essay emerged from my book published in the Overtures series a couple of decades ago—*The Rendering of God in the Old Testament*. In that book, I tried to devise a conceptual model of biblical God language, which took literally Karl Barth's observation that this language "renders an agent."[1] The Bible had long been compared in devotional literature to a drama and the God of Israel to a character, but theologians have invariably abstracted substance and attributes from this characterization. It was time, I argued, to develop a biblical theology that gave full weight to how the writers of the Hebrew Scriptures represent God for readers. In proposing this model, I allied myself with the literary turn in the interpretation of biblical texts.

What does it mean to "render an agent"? What distinguishes this type of language from abstract conceptualization is its presentation: the *persona*[2] is evoked as present to the reader. The biblical God carries on an inner dialog, he thinks and feels, and he projects his presence through speaking and acting. As a persona, God has a personal identity. The reader comes to recognize this identity through the divine name, a "biography," a characteristic disposition and style, as well as the attributes that distinguish YHWH as a deity.

The biblical God establishes his identity in interaction with creatures, primarily human beings. The authors of scripture employed artistic means to represent a human world in which God is an active participant. This representation was built upon the cultural assumptions of the ancient Near East that certain occurrences and outcomes are attributable to divine

---

1. *Church Dogmatics* II/1 (Edinburgh: T. & T. Clark, 1958), 271f.; cf. D. Kelsey, *The Uses of Scripture in Recent Theology* (Philadelphia: Fortress, 1975), 39–50.

2. I chose *persona* over *agent* because the latter suggests subordination in English; moreover, it is not a literary-critical term; I chose *persona* over *character* because the latter has too many different, and potentially ambiguous, uses.

agency. The rendering of YHWH as actor built upon the idea that the twists and disruptions of the expected course of events manifested divine intervention. God's motivation and purpose are known through verbal exchanges with humans. Biblical narrative is distinguished from that of the ancient Near East by its concentration of supernatural agency in YHWH alone. The singularity of God led to a sequential, cumulative story tending toward a final resolution of the conflicts and contradictions of history.

This model of Biblical God-language was offered to solve the breakdown of the reigning model of the Biblical Theology movement—"revelation in history." In graduate school I identified closely with this movement; I studied the theologies of W. Eichrodt, G. E. Wright, G. von Rad, and W. Zimmerli closely, and still count them my canon. Yet, as I was engrossed in efforts to repair the defects of one with the insights of another, Brevard Childs and James Barr mounted their devastating assault on the slogan and its hidden distortions of biblical literature and equivocations regarding history and revelation.[3] I decided to spend my first sabbatical as a postgraduate student of James Barr, and I came back from England with the idea of "bracketing out" historical and metaphysical reference, locating biblical theology entirely within the textual world.

The self-referential scheme that I had devised, however, made me rather uncomfortable. How was the imaginary world created by the artistry of the biblical text to be appropriated as a "real world" for the believer? The final two chapters of *Rendering* addressed this question. It was my thesis that all God-language within Hebrew Scripture referred to the persona already recognized in the tradition. Each new writing had to conform to this identity, and if it did so, it became a part of the tradition in which God is known.[4] The collectively sustained imaginary world of Yahwistic tradition was used to interpret the experiences of the present, and the interpreted experiences of the present modified the imaginary world. The people who lived within this tradition assumed that what I am calling their imaginary world was in fact the real world. For us, however, the disjunction is acutely felt.

The crisis came long before the modern age. When Jews encountered Hellenistic culture, and particularly Hellenistic philosophy, they were forced to approach theological questions from a radically different perspective. To be sure, Israelite wisdom had as anthropocentric a perspective as Hellenistic philosophy, but wisdom was an auxiliary mode of thinking within the biblical tradition, attaching generalizations to the God whose identity was known in the national story.[5] It was the Greek intellectual tradition that

3. B. S. Childs, *Biblical Theology in Crisis* (Philadelphia: Westminster, 1974); J. Barr, *Old and New in Interpretation* (New York: Harper & Row, 1966).

4. Based on Barr, *Old and New in Interpretation*, 89.

interposed speculative reason between the knower and the object of knowledge. Religious traditions had to be tested for rational consistency and moral validity.

Cultured Jews in Alexandria and elsewhere began to adopt Hellenistic philosophical thinking, which removed them from the dramatic world of the scriptural tradition. They sought to justify the latter by referring biblical God language to a metaphysical absolute defined by abstract reasoning. The anthropomorphic language of the Bible had to be reinterpreted and allegorized to fit the One beyond the many. The result was a conception of deity without emotions, without the capacity to interact with creatures, too perfect to change his mind, too transcendent and orderly to intervene in nature and history—in a word, without the prerequisites of a dramatis persona. Judaism and Christianity have had to live with an uneasy synthesis of dramatic persona and metaphysical concept since that fateful time.

Of all people, it was the atheist Ludwig Feuerbach who realized that the synthesis was filled with contradictions. The naive religious mind, according to Feuerbach, imagines God in very human terms.[6] When God reasons, it is human reason that is employed, only it is unlimited.[7] God's "moral standards" are the same as humans—God is good according to the norms that we apply to humans, only he is perfectly good.[8] God shares human emotions as well, especially love and the anger that arises from disappointed love.[9] For God to answer prayer, he must care about those who cry to him and be moved to compassion by their plight.[10] In revelation, God communicates knowledge of himself that humans are able to comprehend.[11] Philosophical theologians, embarrassed by the naive anthropomorphisms of their compatriots, reify and alienate God by "purifying" the concept of God and of piety.

5. The order and hierarchy of the Jewish canon warrants this inference. As a consequence, post-canonical wisdom acknowledged the greater authority of Torah by identifying it with wisdom: see L. Perdue's *Wisdom and Creation: The Theology of Wisdom Literature* (Nashville: Abingdon, 1994).

6. See his *Essence of Christianity*, trans. George Eliot (Amherst, N.Y.: Prometheus Books, 1989). If my argument is right, Feuerbach's "naive religious mind" is in fact consumate art and intellect.

7. Ibid., 33–43.

8. Ibid., 44–49.

9. Ibid., 50–58.

10. Ibid., 122–25.

11. Ibid., 207.

Only in later Judaism was Jehovah separated in the strictest manner
from man, and recourse was had to allegory in order to give the old
anthropomorphisms another sense than they originally had.[12]

According to Feuerbach, the more successful theologians are in distinguishing the being and nature of God from humans, the less satisfying God
is to the pious consciousness.

For Feuerbach, the humanity of God proved that God was in fact a projection of human powers, purified of the limitations of individual humans,
onto an objective being.[13] His metaphysical conclusion is not logically warranted, but it was persuasive to his skeptical nineteenth-century audience.
His proposal to redirect Christian religion from an alien being to essential
humanity was, however, never taken seriously because his effort to sacral-
ize everything was rightly experienced as a profanation of everything. What
humanity lacks as an object of devotion is *otherness*—holiness, majesty,
power, perspicuity, righteousness.

Feuerbach's argument, coupled with the impotency of his religion of
humanity, brings us to the threshold of a theological solution to the problem of the reference of biblical God language. I think that we can concur
with him that the God rendered in Scripture can be known because he
thinks thoughts a human in his position would think, experiences emotions a human would experience, and exhibits such moral traits as trustworthiness, justice, and mercy. YHWH is frequently accorded human titles,
and his status in the world requires human recognition. The inference is
warranted that the authors of Scripture employed mimetic imagination to
render God, and readers must exercise their imagination to encounter God
in the rendering. What Feuerbach's reductionism fails to appreciate is that
the rendering must carry a rhetorical force bestowed by the authority of the
One rendered.[14] The words and actions of YHWH depicted in the text
must convince readers that they are the revelation of a transcendent Other
before they can have efficacy.

An alternative to Feuerbach's reduction of God language to human projection is a model in which the human rendering of God is a vehicle of
God's accommodation to the capacity of the human mind and heart.[15] We
can regard the Old Testament as a persuasive discourse—a representation

12. Ibid., 198.

13. Ibid., 14.

14. The argument in the text does not refute Feuerbach's atheism; it only shows that his
reductionism cannot account for an essential element of religious language.

15. See *The Rendering of God in the Old Testament*. OBT (Philadelphia: Fortress, 1981) 135. On
the use of this argument through history, see S. D. Benin, *The Footprints of God: Divine Accommodation in Jewish and Christian Thought* (Abany: State University of New York Press, 1993).

of reality as a world under the sovereignty of its Creator.[16] It seals itself on the readers' minds and hearts by imparting power to live in hope, to take responsibility, to accept accountability, to rejoice in the reality of God. That this is so, and how it is so, is the subject of this monograph.

Just as I finished writing *The Rendering of God*, I found a new academic post at Drake University, and struck up a friendship with a member of the speech department, Allen Scult, who had written his doctoral dissertation on Hebrew Scripture as a persuasive argument. Under his tutelage, I learned to read narrative and histrionic texts as persuasive arguments. In the course of time, we team-taught a course on the hermeneutics of sacred texts and collaborated on a book applying rhetoric to biblical interpretation.[17]

Our understanding of rhetoric derives from the Aristotelian tradition, mediated by such contemporary rhetorical theorists as Chaim Perelman and Kenneth Burke. We defined rhetoric "as the means by which a text establishes and manages its relationship to its audience in order to achieve a particular effect."[18] To be effective, the speaker or author must make contact with what an audience believes and values, what its interests and concerns are, how it might resist or object, and so forth. Textual meaning is not self-contained, but has an input from the audience.

As interpreters of the text, we are members of the audience. We have no access to the rhetor's intention apart from the discourse that is designed to have a particular effect on us. We can circumscribe its likely import by reconstructing its setting in society and history, but our reconstruction is itself shaped by the force of the argument upon us. The interpretation of discourse as rhetoric requires, thus, a strategy for responding to the discourse to experience its power. Its power to "convict" us is its truth. We are, of course, to exercise our critical faculty, to be an audience capable of judging the truthfulness and justice of its appeal, but we cannot be so suspicious as to regard all persuasive power to be manipulative.[19]

After having conversed with Scult for a decade on how to detect the strategies of persuasion in discourse, I began to synthesize rhetorical analysis with J. L. Austin's speech-act theory.[20] Discourse not only persuades by what it says, but by what happens between speaker and addressee in the

---

16. I made that argument rather oddly on 117–31 of *Rendering*; the present book is meant as a replacement of those pages.

17. D. Patrick and A. Scult, *Rhetoric and Biblical Interpretation* (Sheffield: Almond, 1990).

18. Ibid., 12; see the footnote to the definition.

19. See "Rhetoric and Ideology: A Debate within Biblical Scholarship over the Import of Persuasion," with Allen Scult in *The Rhetorical Interpretation of Scripture: Essays from the 1996 Malibu Conference* ed. S. E. Porter and D. L. Stamps; JSNTS 150 (Sheffield: Sheffield Adacemic Press, 1999) 63–83.

20. See chapter 1.

saying. For my interests, it was Austin's class of statements known as performative utterances that stood out. These utterances, in various ways, put in force what they describe. I had already noted in *The Rendering of God* that YHWH speaks performatively in most of the discourse ascribed to him. That is, he commands, blesses, promises, names, censures, expresses feeling. It began to dawn on me that these performative utterances created the world they described. It is literally true in Genesis 1, when "God says, 'Let there be light,' and there was light" (v. 3). It is equally true when the Lord commands Abraham, "Go from your country and your kindred and your father's house to the land that I will show you. And I will make you a great nation . . ." (Gen. 12:1-2a). It is in performative utterances that the word of YHWH has the power to accomplish the divine purpose, like rain that waters the earth and brings forth vegetation (Isa. 55:10-11). Could it be that these performatives, which create the world for the characters of the text, also have performative force for the interpretive community that takes Scripture as its authority and authorization?

The argument of this essay will not be as sophisticated as many offerings of the litterateurs on the market today. The literary approach to biblical interpretation has unleashed an interpretive strategy that disregards or positively seeks to undo the rhetorical force of the performative utterances. These interpreters adopt what we might call a playful attitude to the texts of Holy Scripture. The text of Genesis portrays Abraham as a knight of faith; the playful interpreter inverts this pious reading: Abe and YHWH are playing a poker game in which the human can win if he pretends that his god is winning.[21] YHWH's alternation between benevolence and violent wrath must be due to a conflicted personality rather than the deliberate judgment of a just Judge.[22] These readings are intended to free the reader by means of humor from the rhetorical force of the text. The reader should learn to enjoy the text by inventing clever ways to overturn its pretenses. Shades of Voltaire.

It is a question of power and authority. The text makes such strong claims on the reader that it arouses a backlash. The literary turn in the past few decades of biblical scholarship provided an avenue for the aesthetic appreciation of Scripture, so it should not surprise us that it has become an avenue for establishing an aesthetic relationship to the text. The text becomes a mirror held up to its players.

What interpretive stance should biblical theology adopt toward the scriptural text? The rhetoric of the text sets the conditions for its audience to

21. P. R. Davies, *Whose Bible Is It?* JSOTS 204 (Sheffield: Sheffield Academic Press, 1995).
22. Jack Miles, *God: A Biography* (New York: Knopf, 1995).

receive it as truth. A divine commandment can only be interpreted and obeyed to know whether it is good and just. The promise of God can only be trusted and lived out to experience its fulfillment. The only audience that will have any existential interest in biblical theology will belong to a community that is willing to respond appropriately to the performative utterances of the biblical God. Biblical theology would seem to be a form of reflective thinking that accepts these rules of engagement and submits its findings to the judgment of the community that recognizes the authority of Scripture.

However, biblical theologians should be free from the dogmatic constraints of interpretive communities. The text is too multivalent to be captured by any one interpretive tradition. Moreover, religious communities often become wedded to time-bound and ethically dubious traditions of interpretation. In order for the text to speak with power and truth within the contemporary horizon, interpreters must be allowed to wrestle with it until it yields a blessing.

Biblical theologians are also responsible to the community of scholars, willing to be evaluated by scholars who recognize no authority but autonomous reason. The hermeneutics of suspicion has been the creative ferment of modern biblical interpretation, teaching the synagogue and church a realism about its claims and contents that the invested communities of interpretation would not have accepted until forced to. Biblical theology must stand up under the fire of skepticism for its own truth.

The germs of cc. 2 and 3–4 were published in two journal articles and an article in a Festschrift. The analysis of the interchange between YHWH and Moses at the burning bush (in c. 2) follows closely "The Rhetoric of Revelation" (*Horizons in Biblical Theology* 16, no. 1 [1994]: 20–34), but I take another tack on how the text has performative force for the reading audience. The thesis of cc. 3–4 was set forth in "Is the Truth of the First Commandment Known by Reason?" (*The Catholic Biblical Quarterly* 56, no. 3 [July 1994]: 423–41). I pursued one aspect of that thesis further in "God's Commandment" in *God in the Fray: A Tribute to Walter Brueggemann* (Minneapolis: Fortress, 1998), pp. 93–111. Chapters 3–4 represent the fruit of these articles, but not their formulation.

Portions of an earlier draft of chapter 2 were presented to interested faculty and students of the Graduate Theological Union in February 1987. I want to express my gratitude to Prof. Barbara Green for convening the session and to those who listened and responded. Despite the flaws in my presentation, those in attendance gave me valuable feedback that entered into an extensive revision of the chapter.

Many friends deserve thanks for reading and critiquing my chapters on divine commandment: William Morrow, James Watts, Martin Buss, Lowell

Handy, and Waldimar Janzen. Their remarks caught errors of fact, forced me to clarify positions, and charted me around some hostages to fortune. It is a delight to have friends who are willing to follow one's exploration of an idea that is unfamiliar and perhaps foreign to their ways of thinking.

Mary W. Patrick read through the whole manuscript just before I submitted it. She read it for how it read—for flow, clarity, coherence, and mood. At least one chapter and several other passages failed the test and were revised. The reader as well as the author owe her a debt of gratitude.

The book is dedicated to the Abbey of Mount Angel Library. Mary and I were visiting scholars at the library from July through December of 1996, and I continued through April of 1997. The library itself is a delight to inhabit, its holdings are sufficient, and the staff is friendly and supportive. Our life was sanctified by the offices of Midday Prayer and Vespers in the Abbey church, and Easter Morn was a truly transporting event. The seminary faculty and students included us in their social life. May the Abbey continue to prosper and witness to the spirit among the trees and farms of Western Oregon.

1.
OF RHETORIC
AND REVELATION

LET'S GET STRAIGHT TO BUSINESS. WHAT IS MEANT BY THIS TERM *RHETORIC*? It is an odd, old-fashioned word that has been rehabilitated in the last few decades. I hope to make the reader comfortable with it shortly by defining its scope and focus, and how attention to the rhetorical aspects of a text can be used in interpretation. The word *revelation* is also old-fashioned, but it has not lost its currency in religious discourse; its problem is that it can mean so many different things. The thesis of this book turns, at least in part, on what definition is appropriate to our texts.

We will be applying a particular theory of discourse to a set of texts of revelation in the Hebrew Scriptures. The term *Hebrew Scriptures* is a modern coinage.[1] The historic nomenclature is Torah, Prophets, and Writings (*Torah Nevi'im weKethubim*), abbreviated TaNaK, in the Jewish tradition, and Old Testament (or Covenant in some languages) in the Christian. All three names will be used in this book, depending on the fit of the context.

The Study of Rhetoric

We begin with a look at an example of a rhetoric situation, present a kind of ideal model of such a situation, and then bring in the various approaches scholars of rhetoric and biblical scholars have been proposing in recent years.

The ideal model for the era of classical rhetoric—the era that gave birth to reflection on and the teaching of the art of rhetoric—was a public speaker addressing an audience of peers. The teachers of rhetoric divided situations into three different kinds: (1) the judicial setting, where speakers sought to persuade judges that a particular defendant was innocent or guilty; (2) the

---

1. See C. R. Seitz, "Old Testament or Hebrew Bible," in *Word without End: The Old Testament as Abiding Theological Witness* (Grand Rapids: Eerdmans, 1998), 61–74.

1

deliberative setting, where speakers sought to convince a body of policy-makers to follow a particular course of action; and (3) ceremonial gatherings, where speakers praised the thing or person being honored.

In a general sense, *rhetoric* refers to how the speaker designs an address to attain its desired effect upon the audience. In the words of the influential eighteenth-century rhetorician George Campbell, rhetoric is "the means by which a discourse is adapted to its ends."[2]

One of the central unspoken conventions framing the transaction between rhetor and audience is the end to which the address is directed. A rhetorical transaction might be likened to a game in which a mutually understood "goal" is essential both to participating in the game and to appreciating it. The audience is either moved by the discourse of the rhetor to come to what the rhetor considers the right decision or attitude, or it is swayed by another side; thus is the game "won" or "lost."

The rhetor must make the decision or conviction he advocates a desirable one, that is, an outcome that the audience desires, by appealing to the audience's mind and heart. In many cases, the rhetor in a deliberative setting devotes much effort arguing that a particular course of action will have an outcome that all parties desire. For example, during the Cold War the consensus in the American body politic was that both "peace" and "freedom" were desirable ends. Conservatives and liberals debated whether a "tough," fear-inspiring policy or a nonprovocative, bridge-building one would attain the agreed-upon goals.

In simple terms, then, we are talking about a speaker who has a particular objective and adopts various strategies to attain it. "Strategies" cover everything including the quality of language, delivery, the ideas, organization, images, emotional appeals, and even the social position of the speaker. One of the reasons scholarship in rhetoric has exploded is the wealth of data to study in any given address.

An attentive reader will recognize that scholars studying ancient rhetoric have no access to the phenomena they study. Without tapes, or better videotapes, we cannot hear and see the speech. We do have texts that purport to have been delivered as addresses. With them we attempt to reconstruct the oral event. We can correlate the texts of speeches with manuals on rhetoric. The audience can be reconstructed from the addressee the speaker "constructs," checked against other texts and the fate of the address itself. If our object is to reconstruct classical rhetoric as the ancients understood it, we must follow this format.

---

2. From Campbell's *Philosophy of Rhetoric*, I/l, as reprinted in P. Bizzell and B. Herzberg, eds., *The Rhetorical Tradition* (Boston: St. Martin's, 1990), 749.

The Study of Biblical Rhetoric. Neither the Hebrew Bible nor the New Testament preserves the texts of oral addresses, at least not in what we might call a pure form. For those scholars of biblical rhetoric who understand their subject to be the discovery of the influence of classical rhetoric on biblical writings, it is imperative to show that the written works of certain authors— Paul and other letter writers in the New Testament—are close to oral address and employ the same basic strategies. As letters became the subject of rhetoric instruction in late antiquity, the argument gained some plausibility.[3]

The Old Testament presents more of a problem. We lack manuals of rhetoric and texts of speeches from the Ancient Near East and ancient Israel. Undoubtedly, certain occasions called for persuasive discourse. We have vivid accounts in the historical works of deliberation and debate over policy, and over guilt and innocence.[4]

The craft of persuading audiences must have been passed down orally, perhaps by apprenticeship. The historical interpreter must reconstruct the conventions shared by rhetor and audience from the evidence of the text. In a given passage, the implicit understanding that might have defined the point of the argument for its original audience is lost. If the text's rhetoric has been successful, however, then its power to lead us along the desired path continues and can help us in the recovery of its end and means. However, there will always be room for considerable disagreement among interpreters over the "original" situation and the import of the preserved discourse.

How can we speak of reconstructing the rhetoric of ancient persuasive discourses if we have none? What relevance is the art of persuasion to literature that was not designed for forensic or deliberative settings in life? Both ancient and contemporary hermeneutics find written as well as oral discourse to be aimed at persuading or reassuring as well as informing. The hermeneutical tradition Kathy Eden traces from Cicero, Quintilian, and Plutarch through Basil and Augustine to Erasmus, Melanchthon, and Flacius has regarded the composition of texts as conditioned by the same

---

3. The bibliography on the search for the application of rhetorical concepts and use of rhetorical techniques to Pauline letters is long. Near the head of the list would be G. A. Kennedy, *New Testament Interpretation through Rhetorical Criticism* (Chapel Hill, N.C.: University of North Carolina Press, 1984). See the following collections: D. F. Watson, ed., *Persuasive Artistry: Studies in New Testament Rhetoric in Honor of George A. Kennedy* (JSNTSup 50; Sheffield: Sheffield Academic Press, 1991); S. E. Porter and T. H. Olbricht, eds., *Rhetoric and the New Testament: Essays from the 1992 Heidelberg Conference*. JSNTSup, 90 (Sheffield: JSOT Press, 1993); and S. E. Porter and D. Tombs, eds., *Approaches to New Testament Study* (JSNTSup 120; Sheffield: Sheffield Academic Press, 1995); S. E. Porter and D. L. Stamps, eds., *The Rhetorical Interpretation of Scripture: Essays from the 1996 Malibu Conference* (JSNTSup 180; Sheffield: Sheffield Academic Press, 1999).

4. Perhaps the most vivid is the story of Absalom's counselors: 2 Sam. 16:20—17:14.

factors as public speeches.[5] Where the meaning of texts is the subject of debate, disputants tend to impute a rhetorical impulse to the texts and their authors. From Cicero on, interpreters have been counseled to reconstruct the intention behind the wording, discovered through textual and historical context, and to be guided by "equity" and charity in applying the general to the particular. When wording is ambiguous, interpreters have appealed to the artistic code that governed the genre of discourse. The interpreter's praxis is frequently compared to an odyssey through alien terrain on a journey toward home.[6]

The hermeneutical tradition traced by Eden was driven by the concern to determine *what* a text means, *what* doctrine a scriptural text teaches; interest in *how* it makes its appeal was subsidiary. Within the church, interpreters assumed that the human authors were inspired, so the literary context of each text was the whole of Scripture.[7] Each particular communication was fitted into the system of doctrine taught by Scripture as a whole. The interpreter did not presume to reconstruct how individual texts, or the Scripture as a whole, made truth claims effective through art and apologetics.[8]

The critical era has undercut the assumptions of this tradition, though its principles and concepts are certainly relevant.[9] The scriptural context has been eclipsed by constituent writings, the perennial message of a text has been eclipsed by its historical particularity, the historical reference of texts has been subjected to constant critique, and theology has become an investigation into the ideology of the authors and editors of the literature. The study of textual rhetoric must be reconstituted to fit, and perhaps challenge, this contemporary interpretive context.

A number of methods are being applied to the texts of Hebrew Scripture under the name "rhetoric." The turn to the rhetorical analysis of Old Testament texts was inaugurated by my teacher, James Muilenburg, in his SBL Presidential Address of 1968.[10] His objective, as stated in his title, "Form Criticism and Beyond," was to supplement the generic classifica-

5. K. Eden, *Hermeneutics and the Rhetorical Tradition: Chapters in the Ancient Legacy and Its Humanist Reception* (New Haven & London: Yale University Press, 1997).

6. This paragraph is a summary of the Introduction and first three chapters of *Hermeneutics and the Rhetorical Tradition*.

7. What constituted the scriptural context was defined differently, of course, by different religious communites.

8. Allen Scult, "Hermes' Rhetorical Problem: The Dilemma of the Sacred in Philosophical Hermeneutics, in *Rhetoric and Hermeneutics in Our Time* (New Haven & London: Yale University Press, 1997), 290–96, explains Augustine's reserve quite profoundly in the context of Heidegger's quest of the originary hermeneutical experience.

9. Eden methodically points out the dependence of Schleiermacher, Dilthey, and Gadamer on the tradition she traces; e.g., ibid. 91.

10. Published as "Form Criticism and Beyond," *JBL* 88 (1969): 1–18.

tions of form criticism with an identification of the artistic features that give a passage its individuality. He was convinced that structure corresponds to the content of the author's message. In rhetorical terms, his method was designed to identify the point an author is making.

Phyllis Trible divides the various methods that go by the name "rhetorical criticism" into two branches: those that carry out Muilenburg's attention to the structure of a passage, which she calls the study of the "art of composition," to be distinguished from the branch represented by Y. Gitay, which she names the study of the "art of persuasion."[11] She herself is an eminently successful and productive Hebrew Scripture scholar following and developing Muilenburg's method. The bulk of her work, and the scholarship of others practicing Muilenburg's method, has been on narrative texts, not prophecies.[12] Muilenburg himself analyzed prophecies, in particular Isaiah 40–55, and the same method was applied to Jeremiah[13] and some other prophetic texts. It turns out, surprisingly, that the same kind of structures, and the indices used to signal them, could be found in narratives, psalms, and even legal codes.

The study of the art of composition is virtually indistinguishable from poetics.[14] Indeed, in the hands of many compositional rhetorical critics, structure is an aesthetic phenomenon. The uncovering of structure does, nevertheless, serve the cause of regarding a passage as a unity, overriding the fragmentation of textual units by source criticism. Trible uses textual arrangement and deictic signals as an entrée into the message the text means to convey. True to the hermeneutics traced by Eden, Trible's study of how the text conveys its message yields what that message is.

Yehoshua Gitay represents the other wing of rhetorical criticism: rhetoric is the art of persuasion. Actually, he attends to the same stylistic features as the compositional critics, but outlines the structure in classical rhetorical terms: thesis, argument for it and against alternatives, ethos, and pathos. He has restricted his analysis to prophetic texts because, of all biblical literature, they have the earmarks of oral addresses designed to persuade.[15] Gitay's method rests upon the assumption that the types and

11. P. Trible, *Rhetorical Criticism: Context, Method, and the Book of Jonah*; Guides to Biblical Scholarship; Old Testament Series (Minneapolis: Fortress, 1994), 25–48.

12. See Trible, *Rhetorical Criticism*, 36–40, and Part II of the book.

13. See Jack R. Lundbom, *Jeremiah: A Study in Ancient Hebrew Rhetoric*, SBL Dissertation Series, 18 (Missoula, Mont.: SBL and Scholars Press, 1975). Muilenburg himself was writing a commentary on Jeremiah when he died, and his manuscript has never been published.

14. See A. Berlin, *Poetics and the Interpretation of Biblical Narrative* (Sheffield: Almond, 1983).

15. Bibliography of Gitay's writings: *Prophecy and Persuasion: A Study of Isaiah 40–48* (Bonn: Linguistica Biblica, 1981); *Isaiah and His Audience: The Structure and Meaning of Isaiah*

strategies of classical rhetoric can be found in biblical prophecy. To obtain the size of unit that could plausibly be termed an argument, he must override the critical methods that break passages into small units and assign units to different authors, linked together by editors. This approach renders all of his work a hostage to fortune. The arguments he discovers may be the intentional, or accidental, design of editors assembling a book decades or even centuries after the prophetic speech event.

All rhetorical critics, in fact, have been inclined toward what is called "final form" analysis. In theory, one could analyze the textual units identified by source criticism for their rhetoric, but compositional rhetorical critics have opted instead to take the extant text as their point of departure. Most would accept (unlike Gitay) the composite authorship of their rhetorical units, but would argue that the final form actually exhibits an artful arrangement and meaningful communication in its own right. This view has the advantage of expounding a "public" text, rather than a scholarly construction, and of linking their readings to the readings of synagogue and church through the centuries.

Rhetorically Conscious Interpretation. When Allen Scult and I decided to write a book on the rhetoric of texts of the Hebrew Bible, we returned to Muilenburg's germinal address and meditated on its implications for interpreting texts. Rather than pursuing its program of stylistic analysis, we picked up on his "call to encounter texts in their concrete particularity."[16] We defined rhetoric *"as the means by which a text establishes and manages its relationship to its audience in order to achieve a particular effect."*[17] Rather than devise a method, it was our object to chart a way of reading that was sensitive to how the text under study exercises power, communicates its truth claims, and achieves an effect. With Muilenburg, we embrace the reconstruction of *Gattung* and then seek to supplement categorization with attention to its particular embodiment. Finally, because our perspective understands textual communication to be a transaction between text and audience, interpreters must place themselves in the position the text needs to communicate the truth it has to tell.

1–12 (Assen/Maastricht, The Netherlands: Van Gorcum, 1991); "A Study of Amos's Art of Speech: A Rhetorical Analysis of Amos 3:1-15," *CBQ* 42 (1980): 293–309; "Reflections on the Study of the Prophetic Discourse: The Question of Isaiah 1:2-20," *VT* 33 (1983): 207–21; "Rhetorical Criticism," in *To Each Its Own Meaning: An Introduction to Biblical Criticisms and their Application,* ed. S. L. McKenzie and S. R. Haynes (Louisville, Ky.: Westminster/John Knox Press, 1993), 135–49.
    16. *Rhetoric and Biblical Interpretation,* 12.
    17. Ibid.

Trible classified our book as belonging to the camp she termed the "art of persuasion."[18] While this characterization is true, we do not seek to apply classical rhetorical categories to biblical texts, nor are we wedded to the final form of the text. We are inclined to look to form criticism for the classification of speech conventions and situation, though we attend to the text for its implied audience as defining the audience and exigency. We employ the categories of the "new rhetoric" when they illuminate the appeal of the text,[19] and our consciousness of the transactional nature of textual communication allies us with Readers' Response criticism.[20] Thus, we are eclectic because we regard the study of rhetoric not to be a method but an art—the art of reading and reflecting on the way the text engages us.

In the pages that follow I will be proposing a model for conceptualizing a particular kind of revelatory transaction. The model provides an answer to how the authority of God is made effective in the transactions between selected texts and the readers of Scripture. The model applies to only certain types of texts. How this would fit into a comprehensive account of revelation in the Bible is beyond the scope of the argument. The texts are important enough, and sufficiently exemplary of many other passages, to condition a comprehensive synthesis, but I do not propose an answer regarding how it would do so.

Performative Utterances

Frequently, scholars schooled in classical Greek and Roman rhetoric are struck by biblical, Jewish, and Christian deviations from classical norms. While the species and structure, and even tropes and figures, can be associated, the foundations are different. All persuasion requires that the rhetor build on the knowledge, beliefs, and affections of the audience. The revelation of God—the knowledge of God ascribed to a communication of God—takes persuasion to its limits, because humans do not have the capacity to pass judgment on knowledge that cannot be supported by human reason and affections. The Greeks and Romans knew of divine

---

18. See Trible, *Rhetorical Criticism*, 25–48.

19. K. Burke, *A Grammar of Motives* (New York: George Braziller, 1955); idem, *A Rhetoric of Motives* (Englewood Cliffs, N.J.: Prentice-Hall, 1950); Ch. Perelman, *The Realm of Rhetoric* (Notre Dame, Ind.: University of Notre Dame Press, 1982); Ch. Perelman and L. Olbrechts-Tyteca, *The New Rhetoric: A Treatise on Argumentation* (Notre Dame, In.: University of Notre Dame Press, 1969).

20. The school of literary theorists known as Readers' Response has generated some similar concepts: see Wolfgang Iser, *The Act of Reading: A Theory of Aesthetic Response* (Baltimore: Johns Hopkins University Press, 1978); idem, *The Implied Reading: Patterns of Communication in Prose Fiction from Bunyan to Beckett* (Baltimore: Johns Hopkins University Press, 1974).

revelation, but they could not incorporate it into their rhetoric. The Bible, on the other hand, is permeated with revelation, and any account of biblical rhetoric would be seriously deficient without an account of revelatory discourse.

This point is precisely where J. L. Austin's analysis of performative utterances comes in. We are going to propose and test the hypothesis that God's utterances are—at least in significant cases—linguistic acts that put in force the knowledge they communicate.

Austin's Description of Performatives. J. L. Austin coined the term *performative*. His writings on the subject consist of the script of a BBC address, "Performative Utterances,"[21] and the text of his William James Lectures at Harvard University, published under the title of *How to Do Things with Words.*[22]

Austin plays off his theory against the dominant view of language within the philosophical tradition. Philosophers have rather unreflectively assumed "that to say something, at least in all cases worth considering . . . is always and simply to *state* something."[23] The overriding concern has been how language can in some sense capture reality, how it can refer to a world outside itself and how it can make meaningful or true statements about this world. Of any given statement, one can ask, is it true or false?

Austin sets out to undo this philosophical model of language by identifying a significant kind of utterance that does not *state* something about reality, but *does* something in the very act of saying it. The examples he offers are the words of a wedding ceremony, the christening of a ship, and the laying down of a bet. In each of these cases, the speaker or speakers bring about a new state of affairs. Conditions must be met to succeed. Conventions for the performance of these acts must be established, including who can say them and under what conditions. If one or more of the conditions are not met, if the performance is not done correctly and completely by the right persons under the right conditions, the performance "misfires," is "infelicitous." If the participants do not participate with a proper understanding and the right spirit, and do not conduct themselves appropriately as a result, the performative has been "abused."

Austin expends a good deal of effort trying to identify linguistic signs that would distinguish performatives from other types of utterances. The law contains some definite procedures for some types of performatives, for

21. J. L. Austin, "Performative Utterances," *Philosophical Papers 3* (New York: Oxford University Press., 1979): 220–39.

22. J. L. Austin, *How to Do Things with Words* (Cambridge: Harvard University Press., 1975).

23. Ibid., 12.

example, a court summons or the ratification of a sales contract. In oral ceremonies, a common indication of a performative is the use of a first person singular (or plural) subject and a present active indicative verb, such as "I take thee . . . ," "I promise that (or to) . . . ," "I christen it . . . ," "I bet. . . ." "Hereby" may underline the force of the utterance. The first person present active indicative cannot be converted into a past or a third person, or even into the progressive present, and still have this force.

Unfortunately, many, probably most, of the performative utterances used in everyday life do not have these formal markings to distinguish them from statements. "I will be here tomorrow" is a common form of promising, but it could be a prediction or a statement of intention. A command seldom begins, "I command you . . . ," but usually is expressed as an imperative or a second person future indicative (with "shall" in formal speech); indeed, commands and directives—especially in posted signs— are often impersonal, perhaps even passive: "Passengers are warned. . . ." Austin is left with the subtle and indeterminate conventions of living lan guage to signal the performative force of many statements.

As Austin explored the language of performative utterances further, he came to the conclusion that one could not simply draw a line between assertions about what is the case, about whose truth depends upon corre- spondence to how things are, and about utterances that put in force states of affairs within the discourse community. Assertions are true or false according to what they are used for, and performatives frequently include assertions that can be evaluated according to their correspondence to what is the case. He infers that the "doctrine of the performative/constative [statement] distinction stands . . . as the *special* theory to the *general* theo- ry."[24] His general theory concerns the dimensions, we might say, of a speech act. The *locutionary* dimension is what an utterance means and refers to; an *illocutionary* dimension is what the utterance accomplishes in the act of speaking (or writing or posting); and the *perlocutionary* dimen- sion is what the utterance's effect is on the addressee. The distinction between illocutionary and perlocutionary clarifies the force of illocution- ary acts and the effects those acts might have on the addressee. An apology expresses the speaker's regret and seeks to mend a relationship, but the recipient may rebuff the overture.

Having sought a list of verbs/actions that comprises the category of per- formative actions all through the book, Austin settles for a set of categories

24. Ibid. 148. There are differences among commentators as to whether assertions—con- stative utterances—are one kind of performative or to be distinguished from performatives. D. Evans, *The Logic of Self-Involvement* (London: SCM, 1963), 30–31, and elsewhere, classifies constatives as performatives.

of illocutionary acts we engage in in our speaking. (1) *Verdictives* are judgments—"verdicts"—on questions of fact, principles, and qualities. (2) *Exercitives* are exercises of authority or conviction as to a course of action. Commandments fall squarely within this category. (3) *Commissives* are commitments made by a speaker to a course of action. Most such commitments go by the name "promise." (4) *Behabitives* are expressions of attitudes or feelings of the speaker toward the addressee or about a third party. (5) *Expositives* are expositions, arguments, definitions, and the like.

How are we to employ these categories? Some of Austin's disciples began to elaborate them extensively, developing subcategories for every shade or nuance of each illocutionary act.[25] I propose to take them as paradigms of the way speakers can act within a "discourse community." When one studies an utterance, one needs not only to understand its propositional content but also the kind of act the speaker is performing in relationship to the addressee, how the speaker has designed the utterance to give it the intended force, and how the addressee should respond to receive the utterance in the way that it is intended.

Although the whole theory of illocutionary action in discourse is relevant to the textual exposition to follow, the special theory of performative utterances will provide the conceptual framework for the divine discourse to be examined.

Speech Acts and Rhetoric

Before we proceed to the application of speech act theory to biblical texts, however, we need to locate its rhetorical dimension. We need, that is, to move from viewing the illocutionary act as performance of a speaker to a transaction between speaker and addressee.

Austin distinguishes between the act of the speaker and the response of the addressee or audience. The latter he calls the perlocutionary effect. Speaking is not causing; the addressee or audience may refuse to respond appropriately.

The fact that the addressee of discourse is free to respond inappropriately produces the need of rhetoric. Most discourse is pragmatic: speakers seek to convince addressees to adopt particular views and/or pursue particular courses of action. The speaker desires efficacy. In the face of some question as to efficacy, a speaker will choose an illocutionary act and wording that promises to strike the addressee favorably.[26] One makes this

25. Cf. e.g., D. Evans, *The Logic of Self-Involvement*, 40–64, 88–110, 116–24.
26. Unless the speaker's desire is to offend, disturb, distract, or some object for which a favorable response would be self-defeating.

choice almost instinctively when one considers whether to request or command.

Not all discourse situations demand persuasion, though. Many situations are so taken for granted and ritualized that no persuasion beyond the act is necessary. When we order an item on a menu or purchase items at a grocery, customer and waiter or clerk perform their roles in the transaction automatically. Legal rights and duties govern the transaction, which support and enable it to proceed without persuasion.

When is rhetoric an important consideration? Certainly in delicate, intimate personal relationships where the wrong act or wording can set off an alarm about the relationship. Also acts that involve the exercise of authority that constrain addressees. We might call the latter *superintendence*. Cultivating the character of one's children and disciplining them for misbehavior is a paradigm case. Governing civil society is less personal and intensive, but invariably involves resistance from some portion of the body politic.

Performative utterances, properly executed, do bring about a state of affairs that did not exist before the utterance. When a ship is christened, the honoree bestows a name on the ship that is henceforth its public name. The actual audience and the broader public are now authorized and constrained to refer to this ship by this name. When a marriage ceremony is performed, the couple, the witnesses, the church, and the community at large have become duty-bound to regard the couple as constituting a particular kind of corporate entity under certain protections, rights, and obligations that did not exist before.

These ceremonies are not in themselves acts of persuasion, but they are modes of discourse that bring participants, audience, and community at large to adopt certain views and perform certain acts. Because the parties involved are free to act inappropriately, the ceremony not only puts the described state of affairs into force, it lends majesty and objectivity to it. The exhortation in the marriage ceremony, "What God has joined together let no man put asunder," articulates its rhetorical force nicely.

The ceremony itself may incorporate suasive discourse. The marriage ceremony incorporates a theological apologia for marriage: "Marriage is an honorable estate. . . ." This apologetic is largely laudatory, but it does advocate a policy.

Political authority has usually required both ceremonies and supplemental apologetics to establish and maintain its capacity to rule effectively. Ceremonies of state lend majesty and grace to officeholders. Public speeches justify the institutions and stir up patriotic feelings toward them. Under certain circumstances, shows of force add to state authority. When specific policies are announced, they are explained and justified in speeches. Despite the formal authority and coercive power of government, the populace can nullify laws by refusal to comply.

No single formula covers the interaction of performative acts and persuasion. In some cases, a speaker of a performative has no need to add persuasive force. In some cases ceremony bears the weight of persuasion as well as instituting, and in some cases, ceremony must be supplemented by suasive discourse. Knowing when to say what in order to be an effective speaker-actor is one of the chief criteria of social sophistication.

The rhetorical dimension of performative utterances has not been on the minds of the philosophers who have been developing this theory of discourse. It may in fact not be relevant to the "idea" in itself, but it is highly relevant to the practice of social intercourse. Speech acts are pragmatic, and that requires speakers to calculate strategies for achieving desired results. As interpreters of discourse, we are justified in regarding performative utterances, as well as other categories of discourse, as rhetorical phenomena.[27]

Revelation

To a reader with an attentive ear, combining the word *revelation* with rhetoric strikes a dissonant chord despite the alliteration. According to classical theory, rhetoric—as the art or craft of persuasion—appeals to the knowledge, attitudes, and convictions, and perhaps the prejudices and passions, of the audience to sway it toward the policy, verdict, or attitude advocated. In theological discourse, revelation is often reserved for a communication of knowledge that the recipient does not possess and cannot derive from human knowledge or intuition. This simple dichotomy breaks down on closer inspection—preaching would be impossible if persuasion could not be enlisted in support of revelation—but it does suggest the difficulty that inheres in the concept of revelation.

But we are getting ahead of ourselves. The word *revelation* is not the private reserve of theology; it has a broad range of usage in common speech. Because our focus is on Hebrew Scriptures, the place to begin is its usage in our texts. Only after coming to some understanding of this usage can we consider theological usage and whether it is justified.

---

27. Although this discussion has referred regularly to *speaker* and *addressee, audience,* and even *public at large* (when an illocutionary act has force for persons who do not actually hear it), I think that we can accord the same force to texts and readers. N. Wolterstorff elaborates on it extensively and sets forth a particular type of interpretation, which is guided by the illocutionary force of the author: see *Divine Discourse,* 37–57.

In the Hebrew Bible. My bearing for the concept of revelation comes from S. Talmon's essay "The Concept of Revelation in Biblical Times."[28] Three Hebrew verbs play a prominent role in identifying revelatory encounters: *glh* ("to uncover") in the reflexive and causative stems, *r'h* ("to see") in both active and passive/reflexive stems, and the causative and reflexive stems of *yd'* ("to know"). These all are a part of the normal Hebrew vocabulary for physical perception and contact. They occur in parallel frequently enough in theological contexts to indicate an overlapping meaning. Psalm 98:2-3 puts them all together:

> YHWH has made known *(hodia')* his salvation;
> he has revealed *(gillah)* his righteousness. . . .
> All the ends of the earth have seen *(ra'û)* the salvation of our God.

This proximity indicates a "semantic equivalence" of the three terms, and renders the effort to distinguish shades of different theological meanings suspect.[29]

From the evidence and a summary of rabbinic teaching, Talmon sets out the "essential features of man's experience of God" as recorded in the Bible:

> (1) The possibility that Divinity can be experienced in various con-cretizations is categorically denied. (This applies first of all to poly-theism, but it could apply to the scholarly search for different con-cepts of God in the Scriptures.) It is only God's ability to adapt his manifestations to men's differing situations which gives rise to a rich variety of forms by which he reveals himself in the life of the individ-ual and in the history of Israel.
>
> (2) The various names by which the Biblical God makes himself known are to be understood as verbalizations of his deeds in the world. . . .
>
> (3) God who reveals himself can be experienced in an almost bewildering profusion of anthropomorphic representations. At the same time, he is *inconceivable* and *beyond compare* with any created being. . . .[30]

Talmon goes on to stress that God is known in deeds—in both creation and natural process, and in history, particularly Israel's history. This inter-pretation is contrasted to what might be called a metaphysical knowledge: "God's essential nature, his identity, remained hidden even from Moses."[31]

---

28. S. Talmon, "The Concept of Revelation in Biblical Times," *Literary Studies in the Hebrew Bible* (Jerusalem: Magnes/Brill, 1993), 192–215.
29. Ibid., 199–204.
30. Ibid., 206–07.
31. Ibid., 209.

It also contradicts a more personalistic view of revelation in contemporary theology: "Divine revelation is thus not, as modern scholarship often describes it, a matter of 'self-disclosure' or 'self-revelation.' It is always an 'act of power.' . . ."[32] Particular events of revelation to individuals are not for the sake of the recipient, but for the sake of the people of God.[33]

For Talmon, God's revelation in deeds has a rhetorical import. By that I mean that "revelation . . . serves the purpose of promulgating enactments which impose obligations on mankind."[34] The conjunction of the exodus from Egypt and the making of the covenant between YHWH and Israel at Mount Sinai are paradigmatic for revelation. "The revelation transmitted by Moses to the people of Israel in Egypt and during the Exodus becomes at Sinai a first and unique revelation whereby YHWH makes himself known directly to all Israel."[35] "The revealed law is the basis of the Covenant proclaimed at Sinai, which YHWH contracted with this people, and which was hence forth to determine Israel's path in history and prove its value there."[36]

Readers may find aspects of Talmon's definition of revelation in the Bible so shaped by the positions he is disputing and the traditions he is defending as to render his conclusions too weak to build on. Whatever one may think of the slogan "history as revelation," with which he concludes his article, or his rearguard attack on source criticism, we should be able to agree that the vocabulary of revelation is used in accounts of events in human time and space in which the otherwise hidden God is manifested for humans to see and hear, even to converse with. These divine-human encounters are not depicted as ends in themselves, as though the fulfill-ment of life is to experience the divine presence, but as means of bringing about a change in the situation and/or behavior of the recipients. A knowl-edge of God is imparted in these revelatory events, but it is a "practical knowledge" for their partnership in the project initiated by the verbal exchanges in the encounter.

In the History of Interpretation. The concept of revelation has a way of migrating, so to speak, from *how* a message was communicated to *what* is communicated. The terms indicate visual and auditory experiences, and that is where Talmon begins; however, he moves by seeming inevitability to what is communicated in these events.

32. Ibid., 210.
33. Ibid., 210–11.
34. Ibid., 212.
35. Ibid., 214.
36. Ibid., 215.

Talmon restricts the content of revelation to "practical knowledge," "enactments which impose obligations on mankind." He has, however, already described divine revelation as "deeds of power." Obviously, the knowledge to be gleaned from God's utterances and action is expansive. A close reading of these texts will reveal the moral character and purpose of the divine speaker as well. As the theological mind meditates on them over time, even metaphysical knowledge will be detected.

When the Jewish religious community was absorbed into the Hellenistic cultural world, it encountered a tradition of philosophical thinking. Philosophy begins with the question: How do we know what we have been told? Tradition is not to be taken at face value; we must have reasons. Something of a contest between sacred tradition preserving memories of revelation and unaided human reason ensued. The term *revelation* came to mean, for Jews and Christians, knowledge of God and the creation that God had vouchsafed to God's people or to all who would receive it.

The contest between the knowledge of God communicated through the interpretation of Scripture and the knowledge attained by the efforts of unaided reason has certainly marked the term *revelation*. Thomas Aquinas's philosophical theology represents a classical articulation of this definition of revelation. He worked out a "division of labor" between revelation and reason parallel to grace and nature. Aquinas's axiom is that "grace does not abolish nature, but completes it."[37] In the fall, the power of reason was disturbed but not destroyed, so humans, using logic based upon self-evident first principles, could know a good deal about human nature and destiny. However, humans lost their "supernatural" endowment, so saving knowledge requires God's gracious intervention.[38]

Classical and medieval philosophy was suspicious of the imagination and emotions, and did not accord them any independence as sources of knowledge and wisdom. Since the Pietist and Romantic eras, many thinkers have accorded the power to gain spiritual knowledge to the emotions and poetic intuition.[39] Revelation could be allied with these "nonrational" modes of knowing in contrast to empirical experience and reason. The result was to virtually naturalize revelation, or to classify revelation as a mode of knowing that was natural to human beings. Probably Schleiermacher epitomizes this naturalization of revelation. He developed an

37. As quoted by J. Pelikan, *The Christian Tradition*, vol. 3 (Chicago & London: University of Chicago Press, 1978), 285.

38. See ibid., 284–93.

39. E.g., F. Schleiermacher, *On Religion: Speeches to Its Cultured Despisers* trans. J. Oman (New York: Harper & Bros., 1958).

apologetics that referred all religious language to the human experience of "the Absolute." The experience was an encounter with a reality that transcends the knower, but the knowledge gained from the experience was a human articulation of the impression left by the experience.[40]

Twentieth-century neoorthodox theology rose up in opposition to Schleiermacher, yet the movement was influenced significantly by his conception of revelation. The experience of the Absolute became an "encounter" involving divine "self-disclosure" or "self-revelation."[41] In other words, revelation was at God's initiative, but it had the quality of an "I-thou encounter" (Buber)[42] rather than the communication of doctrine; doctrine was a matter of human inference.[43] However, theologians did in fact assume that self-disclosure included lordship and love.[44]

Talmon rejects this model of revelation, though it was the Jewish philosopher Martin Buber who gave it classical expression. Perhaps, though, Talmon's position can be reconciled with self-disclosure. If we find God's utterances in theophanies to be performative utterances that forge a bond between speaker and addressee, obligating both to specific actions and attitudes, we could surmount Talmon's strictures. In other words, God enters into personal relationship with a people through speaking and acting. The knowledge of God divulged in revelations would be of the divine party to the relationship and of themselves as a party under God's authority.

The prospect of this study, then, is to tie together the different meanings of revelation that have emerged in response to the biblical text over history. Perhaps the transactions taking place in biblical narratives of revelation communicate a knowledge of God that cannot be known by philosophical reason because they "construct" what is to be known in the transaction of speaking and the commensurate response of human recipients.

40. Ibid.; and idem., *The Christian Faith* trans. John Oman (Edinburgh: T. & T. Clark, 1928). The term *ultimate reality* is Paul Tillich's.

41. See J. Baillie, *The Idea of Revelation in Recent Thought* (New York: Columbia University Press, 1956).

42. M. Buber, *I and Thou*, trans. R. G. Smith (New York: Scribner's, 1958).

43. So E. Brunner, *Truth as Meeting* trans. Olive Wyon (London: SCM Press, 1964).

44. See J. Moltmann's interesting discussion of W. Herrmann and K. Barth in *Theology of Hope* trans. J. W. Leitch (New York: Harper & Row, 1967), 50–58.

2.
THE CALL OF MOSES

W E ARE READY TO TEST THE FIT OF J. L. AUSTIN'S CATEGORY OF PER-
formative utterances on a classical example of communication
between the biblical God and a human character. Can YHWH's exchange
with Moses within Exodus 3 and 4 be subsumed under the types of illocutionary linguistic acts proposed by Austin? Does the overall conversation at the burning bush have performative force for Moses and the
Israelites? Does the passage elicit a performative transaction with the
readers of the text?

Why this particular text? It is undeniably one of the best-known
accounts of God's appearance and speaking in the Hebrew Bible. Moreover,
it has sufficient amplitude and complexity to test the applicability of
Austin's categories adequately. Finally, it is the text that originally led me to
recognize that God's utterances were performative acts.[1]

If we find that the utterances of God in this story fit Austin's description
of performatives, we have found that the knowledge of God communicated by God is not, within the world of this one text, of an assertive character and hence in competition with what can be known by reason and general experience, but a knowledge created by the exchange itself. For the
human recipient, Moses, God can be known only insofar as he responds
appropriately and risks his own life on the truth of what he has been told.

The reader of the narrative, of course, is not a part of the world of the
text. Does the text engender a performative transaction with readers or
does it present its account for readers to accept on a "locutionary" basis?
That is, are readers expected to judge the truth of this text on the basis of
its historicity or its typical truth (as fiction), or does it require the readers
to respond to what God says to Moses as though it was addressed to them
as well? If the latter, how are we to describe this level of transaction?

---

1. I had recognized that God's verbal revelations in Exodus 3–4 were performatives in a
previous work, D. Patrick, *The Rendering of God in the Old Testament*; OBT (Philadelphia:
Fortress, 1981), 94–96, but there I was concerned with how they entered into the depiction
of God.

How We Shall Proceed

The transactions within the narrative world itself will be analyzed to determine how they fit Austin's categories of illocutionary acts. We will also take up the question of the appeal of the text to the reader, a question that will lead to the consideration of whether texts can enter into performative transactions with audiences.

The text will be expounded in its extant form. That is to say, we will not break the account up into sources, though it shows many signs of being a composite text. Since it is not our purpose to reconstruct the historical event that may lie behind the text or the understanding of a particular era or cultural group, nothing would be gained by source criticism. The extant text has informed and still informs the communities that recognize the God of Scripture. The extant text is also recognized as a "classic" in the culture at large. Whether the interpreter invests canon with overriding theological weight or not, the text that has come into being as the result of the decisions of religious communities does have a public character and constitutes the benchmark for exegesis and theological reflection.

The Structure of the Text

While the analysis of that virtually indefinable phenomenon known as poetic or rhetorical structure is not as important to my exegesis as it is for those who developed a method from J. Muilenburg's proposal, it does make a good entrée into a passage in its extant form. It provides a sense of where the passage is leading, what its central point is, and how the point attracts and transforms other ideas, images, and words. I do not find a chiastic structure in the call of Moses, but rather a sequential structure with balances and transitions, repetitions with variations, recapitulations that carry the action forward, retardation to underscore a point, even a tangent or two.

The scene is marked by a narrative frame that records the arrival of Moses at the mountain of God (3:1), and his return to Jethro (4:19, and then departure for Egypt, 4:21). The mountain is only mentioned once within the dialog, at the conclusion of the initial promise and commission (3:12). The reference brings a certain closure.[2]

Exodus 3:2-6 sets the account off as revelation by employing several stems of r'h—a common verb for revelation as well as for regular perception[3]—five times in the first three verses. It is interwoven with 'mr, to say,

2. Moses could depart at this point with the "essentials" of his call.
3. S. Talmon, "The Concept of Revelation in Biblical Times," in *Literary Studies in the Hebrew Bible: Form and Content* (Jerusalem: Magnes Press, 1993), 199–204.

and by the end of the unit, rma predominates. The pattern of using *r'h* is broken in v. 6, when Moses hides his face to avoid looking *(mhbyt)* on God. The word *r'h* ceases to be used to describe what is transpiring in the narrative after the first unit, but a participial form, *nr'h,* "appearance," is used at the beginning of two subsequent units, 3:16 and 4:1 (repeated in v. 5) in discourse about what Moses will say to the people.

R'h does begin the next unit (3:7-12), but not in reference to revelation: YHWH has seen the plight of the people, and this, along with hearing and knowing their condition, has prompted him to leave his "observation post," so to speak, in order to act. The same motive recurs in v. 10, in reverse order. In v. 8, the divine intervention will remove the people both from the "grip" (hand) of the Egyptians and from their geographical location; the geographic move must have a goal, so the land to which they are going is described according to its natural and ethnic identity. The same message, with a few variations in wording and order, is repeated at the beginning of another unit, 3:16-20 (21-22). Following 3:9, which reiterates 3:7, Moses is told to go to the Egyptian pharaoh and procure the release of the Israelite slaves (v. 10). There is, we might say, a dialectical symmetry between vv. 8 and 10. Verse 10 does not mention the people's destination, however; that revelation comes out in v. 12—the mountain (of God). Between exodus and return, Moses demurs from God's choice of deliverers: he repeats the commission *verbatim* with the preface, *mi 'ehyeh* ("who am I . . . ?"). It gives God the opportunity to assure his presence and designate a sign. The assurance of presence *('ehyeh 'imak)* foreshadows his revelation of his name (v. 14) and returns in 4:12, where the object is Moses' mouth, and in 4:15, where it is both Moses' and Aaron's mouths.

Moses' expressions of resistance to his call become a structuring device after 3:11. He seeks God's name in v. 13, doubts the people's receptivity in 4:1, and denies his competence in 4:10. Having had all his reasons for not going stripped away, in 4:13 he tries simply to beg off. That reluctance leads to a confrontation; God gives up on persuasion and asserts his authority. Each question or problem posed by Moses leads to further communication.

Moses' question about the name of the deity with whom he has been speaking reaches back to 3:5, 6 and forward to 3:15. What is the name of the God of the fathers? The answer, which is delayed by mysterious hints as to its meaning, is prefaced by a prophetic commission, and concludes with the institution of its use from generation to generation. For a brief moment, the narrative horizon expands to include the reader. Moreover, the reader's curiosity about the meaning of the name, and hence the nature or essence of the one named, is aroused by the mysterious *'ehyeh 'ašer 'ehyeh.* Readers have throughout history been attracted to this revelation like moths to a lightbulb. Rightly so, I think, because it is the high point of the passage and the one place where what is revealed reaches into the reader's horizon.

But the revelation of the name is in many ways secondary to the action of the exodus. That is, the meaning of the name plays only a minor part in the narrative that follows.[4] It is the act of the deity who goes by this name that matters, so that God can later say, "I am YHWH who brought you out of the land of Egypt, out of the house of slaves" (Exod. 20:2).

Exodus 3:16-20 implements the announced deliverance. It begins with a reference back to the present and a repeat of the announcement of deliverance, now under YHWH's name. In a sense, 3:16-20 is a match or counterpart to 3:7-12. It starts with the promise and then describes its effect on the elders and on the Egyptian monarch. One twist is the difference between the promise to Israel and the request Moses makes to the king. Indeed, at this juncture the linguistic patterns change and the focus moves from the end or telos to the means of attaining it.[5]

When Moses speaks again (4:1), he returns to that initial meeting with the Israelite elders (3:16).[6] He doubts God's scenario, which gives YHWH occasion to equip him with signs to confirm his claims. 4:1-9 has an unusual structural feature: after the first sign is demonstrated, there follows an unattached "final" or purpose clause.[7] This passage steps out of the narrative genre to instruction.

Moses' next demurral concerns his own talent as a speaker—using the verb "speak" *(dbr)* rather than "say" *('mr)*. The word he uses to describe his problem, *kbd,* may have a double entendre here, both "heavy" and "glorious." After God disposes of this objection, Moses simply tries to beg off, so to speak. After expressing his anger, God proceeds to finish his plans for the conflict: Aaron will be brought in as the mouthpiece for Moses. This final unit, thus, fits with its two predecessors (3:16-20, 4:1-9) in setting forth plans for the oncoming struggle.

Now we can take a closer look at the text with a specific objective in mind: to classify the types of divine statements within Austin's scheme of performative utterances. I shall remain within the narrative world in the section, reserving the question of the relationship between text and audience for the following one.

---

4. Exod. 5:2; 6:2-3; 13:3. But only 5:2 raises questions about who he is, and of course the rest of the narrative answers pharaoh emphatically.

5. 3:21-22 strike me as a tangent.

6. It also recalls his question in 3:13, which concerns the reaction of the people to his message.

7. It occurs in prophetic speech. Micah 6:5 appends it asyntactically to a recitation of YHWH's deeds.

Revelation within the Narrative World

The introduction to the narrative (Exod. 3:1-6) sets the scene of the exchange between God and Moses. It must carry the weight of convincing the reader that Moses really was in contact with a deity. Even the location evokes mystery: Moses is herding his flock on the "far side of the wilderness," which cannot be a geographical location—one would have to ask, from where?—but an ontological one, a faraway place where one finds a "mountain of God," a sacred mountain, a meeting place between heaven and earth. This mountain was, at the same time, a well-known place to the Israelite community, for the mountain of God is Horeb, the location of the Lord's subsequent theophany before all Israel.

It is here—presumably at its base or sides, not at the top—that the Lord invades the human world of Moses. The medium is a natural wonder, a fire that does not consume its fuel. Fire is, of the four classical elements of nature, the most alive and fearful. Religion the world over testifies to the symbolic power of this element. The narrative does not describe the miracle, it dramatizes Moses' discovery: "and he looked, and lo, the bush was burning, yet it was not consumed" (3:2). Moses responds by describing what he has just perceived in words, and proposes to investigate boldly. Note that Moses does not sense the supernatural presence until God speaks. God warns him that he is in a danger zone, a sacred space, which requires a "desecularization" (so to speak) to reside in it. Removing the shoes is a sign of respect, hiding his face is for protection—for to see God is to die.

In the remainder of the account, the evocation of holiness recedes in the face of what God seeks to communicate to Moses. Only at the end, when the Lord becomes angry with Moses for resisting the call (Exod. 4:14), does the very presence of God provoke response.[8]

A Phenomenological Observation. Revelation is not only a theological concept, it is also a concept belonging to the phenomenology of religion. There it designates a distinctive type of experience, an experience of the supernatural or, to use Rudolf Otto's terminology, the "numinous." Indeed, one can identify virtually all of Rudolf Otto's characteristics of the "numinous experience" in this passage.[9] Moses encounters a mysterious presence that inspires fear and awe and the sense of creatureliness, which overpowers his resistance and sends him forth to confront the greatest human power on earth.

8. God does, of course, continually speak and act in his divine character, but Moses can interact with him as a virtual equal.

9. SeeR. Otto, *Idea of the Holy,* trans. J. W. Harvey (New York: Oxford Univ. Press, 1958) 12–40, 75.

If one were to take the experience of holiness itself as the essential feature of revelation, one would have no basis for speaking of revelation in the theological sense—privileged knowledge of God. Though Otto calls the experience "supernatural," antithetical in every way to "natural experience,"[10] its universality shows it not to be privileged or "special." It would appear to fall under the traditional theological category of "general revelation" despite the features that set the experience off from everyday experience.[11]

Could the phenomenological concept of revelation be adapted to theology? Samuel Terrien locates the center of Old Testament—indeed, biblical—theology in the "elusive presence," a concept that resembles Otto's numinous rather markedly.[12] Fortunately for us, he devotes a good part of one chapter to the revelation to Moses. He summarizes it as follows: the account stresses "the immediacy of the presence, the abruptness of the way in which the presence manifests itself or vanishes, the subordination of each scene to a dialogical speech, and the specific relatedness of such speech to the decision for man to act in history."[13]

In his exposition, Terrien focuses attention on the mode of God's presence and how the experience nevertheless "compelled [Moses] to elevate both the numinous aspect of the fire and the sacredness of a cultic structure ... to the level of a personal, a-topograpic 'holiness.'"[14] In the account of the call proper, Terrien emphasizes the divine promise to "be with you" (3:12), which he associates with the divine explanation of the name, YHWH (3:13-15). The "name indeed carries the connotations of divine presence, but it also confers upon this presence a quality of elusiveness."[15]

10. Ibid., 25–30, 35.

11. The phenomenology of religion illuminates our text by identifying how it makes its appeal to an audience. The author has not merely described a scene, he or she has evoked a particular domain of feeling familiar to the audience, or at least to the religious individuals in the audience. One might say that the audience can "authenticate" the account of the text introspectively. It is an immediacy characteristic of the mystical.

Classical rhetoric considered appeals to emotions to be a weapon in the rhetor's arsenal. However, it was in late antiquity when religious emotions were made the object of rhetorical art. I have in mind the rhetoric of the "sublime" (Longinus), which would fall well enough under Otto's sense of majesty; see G. A. Kennedy, *Classical Rhetoric in Christian and Secular Tradition from Ancient to Modern Times* (Chapel Hill: Univ. of North Carolina Press, 1980), on the sublime.

12. S. Terrien, *The Elusive Presence: Toward a New Biblical Theology* (Religious Perspectives; San Francisco: Harper & Row, 1978).

13. Ibid., 107.

14. Ibid., 112.

15. Ibid., 119.

Terrien's quest for a unifying phenomenon to bind all biblical witnesses together has forced him to concentrate on that aspect of the account of Moses' call that belongs to the experience of the numinous, and to distinguish the biblical representation of God from other religious traditions in terms of presence. He does illuminate one pattern in the text, but he has had to subordinate the dialogical speech to the manifestation of the holy.

Within the narrative, the dramatization of the encounter with holiness sets the scene for the exchange that follows. It is a necessary ingredient of the transaction, but not the substance of it. Moses sees a miraculously burning bush, and approaches out of curiosity, only to be warned that he has entered sacred space. By analogy, the account establishes the sacred "space" of the narrative. The narrative of their conversation is itself sacred space, to be approached with awe and humility.

Identification and Naming. Already in the segment of the narrative devoted chiefly to evoking the holy, seeds are planted of the issues to be hashed out in the dialog. Moses is addressed by name (3:4), and the speaker identifies himself (3:6). Moses and the speaker are set in tradition: "I am the God of your father—the God of Abraham, the God of Isaac, and the God of Jacob." Moses encounters a God who is already known.[16] The *numen* has an identity in the memory of the people, giving Moses a basis for assessing the truth of this revelation from outside the experience. Any new message must be appropriate to one who had established his identity in promises to and actions for Moses' ancestors.

But the identification was insufficient for Moses. "If I come to the people of Israel and say to them, 'The God of your fathers has sent me to you,' and they ask me, 'What is his name?' what shall I say to them?" (3:13). The tradition was probably ambiguous. More than one name may have circulated; indeed, more than one deity may have been honored. A person must have a name, it is essential to a centered, cohesive, continuous identity. Moreover, it is privileged access, for address is essential to prayer. If Moses spoke in the name of an anonymous deity, the people would hardly consider him to have had an authentic call.

There ensues the revelation of the name. One might expect a theophanic self-introduction, "I am . . . ," as we frequently meet in biblical accounts of divine communications of this kind (Gen. 15:1, 7; 17:1; Exod. 6:2).[17] The exchange here retards the meeting of this expectation to build up the

---

16. See J. Barr, *Old and New in Interpretation* (New York: Harper & Row, 1966), 89–90.

17. See J. K. Kuntz, *The Self-Revelation of God* (Philadelphia: Westminster, 1967), 52–55, 62–65, 120, 125–27.

weight of the revelation of the name. The name is finally divulged (in 3:15), but not until God has aroused our curiosity as to what it means. The mysterious declaration, *'ehyeh 'asher 'ehyeh*, which can be translated in at least four different ways and construed in even more,[18] invites the reader to search in it for the meaning of the divine name, YHWH, though it could very well be a denial of such knowledge.[19] Perhaps the name is to be found in the verb, "to be," or its meaning has to do with the idea of being, but the declaration could just as well be an assertion of the freedom of God to be what or who he chooses to be.[20]

Can this exchange be classified as a performative act? Giving a name to someone or something is performative. Assuming that the speaker has the authority to name this person or thing, it creates a reality that did not exist before the act. What is the force of this new situation, that is, of someone or something having a name? It incorporates the person or thing into the world of public discourse and shapes thought about what is named. In the case of humans, the name is incorporated into the bearer's identity and affords access to personal relationship.

When YHWH divulges his name to Moses, it sounds as though he is naming himself for the first time.[21] However, the name has been revealed and used before in the narrative (as early as Genesis 2). Perhaps Exodus 3:13-15 is meant to answer a question for the whole tradition. It carries the weight of naming, but of a persona whose name is from eternity.[22]

In the context of the narrative as it stands, YHWH is providing Moses with an answer to the people's question (v. 13). The "God of the ancestors" was not sufficient to establish God's or Moses' credibility. The self-introduction by name is a gracious act toward Moses and the people, for it grants accessibility to God in prayer.

There is one further performative act in the exchange. After commissioning Moses to use "YHWH" and identifying himself with the God of the ancestors once again—perhaps to avoid any suggestion that he is a new deity—he "institutes" its use: "this is my name forever, and thus I am to be

18. I am who I am; I am what I am; I will be who I will be; I will be what I will be.

19. Terrien is quite right that it is an *elusive* presence.

20. See B. S. Childs, *Exodus*; OTL (Philadelphia: Westminster, 1974), 60–71, 74–77, 83, 85. What is the rhetorical force of a cryptic utterance of this sort? It heightens the gravity associated with the name: the name itself has revelatory power. At the same time, it invites the audience to complete the revelation by construing the declaration in a particular way and constructing a theology around it. It is a classic example of a text that invites the audience to contribute the meaning of the text.

21. In Genesis and elsewhere, bestowing a name upon a child is accompanied by an explanation or pun on the name.

22. If God has always borne this name, it makes no difference when it is formally divulged to Israel; that is, it can be used before it is formally instituted.

remembered from generation (to) generation" (v. 15). This utterance has the force of a command, establishing the framework for all future commerce between God and people. Not that other names and titles are forbidden, but no other is authorized by exercitive force. This commandment is addressed as much to the audience—"from generation to generation"— as it is to Moses himself.

Promising. God's revelation of his name comes after the delivery of a promise. Within the dialog, the act of naming is designed to answer doubts about the veracity of the promise. To trust the promise, the recipient must know who gave it. It is not the name's linguistic meaning, though, that makes the promise more believable, but the fact that he offers with his name accessibility and trustworthiness.

The promise of deliverance from Egyptian bondage is the driving force of God's exchange with Moses at the burning bush. It is the utterance to which everything else is subordinate. The words that precede the promise in 3:8 give reason for the announcement of divine intention, and the words that follow implement it.

Promising is one of the illocutionary acts identified by Austin. When a person makes a promise, the act of speaking binds the speaker to fulfilling it, and the recipient to trusting the speaker and acting accordingly. We can say that a new relationship is created between speaker and addressee. The relationship involves risks and uncertainties for both parties, but without venturing trust neither the speaker nor the recipient can know whether the promise is true.

The promise of deliverance from Egyptian bondage needs support because its veracity cannot be confirmed by reason or experience. Moses— and Israel—must trust the speaker's will and power to fulfill what he says he will do. Nothing that is known about the Holy One, the God of the fathers, can guarantee that he in fact intends to follow through now and is capable of accomplishing it. To discover the truth of the knowledge of God, the recipients must venture their existence on it.

The initial promise goes beyond deliverance to the grant of a homeland (3:8). While that aspect is not the answer to an immediate concern, it does assure the people that their destiny is one of blessing and security. The paradox that the land is already inhabited is presented, but not resolved. For the present, it is sufficient to know that liberation is the beginning of a story with a happy ending.

Motivation as Rhetorical Backing. Before YHWH delivers his promise, he expresses his own state of mind: "I have seen the affliction of my people who are in Egypt, and have heard their cry because of their taskmasters so that I know their sufferings . . ." (3:7). The wording objectifies God's state of mind by depicting the condition of the people and connecting it with verbs of perception. Obviously this depiction is not meant to inform the audience that God knows what happens on earth; that is expected of a deity. Rather, he is saying, your suffering is on my mind, it dominates my concern. The last of the three parallel clauses, "I know their sufferings," underscores the implied emotions, suggesting that God actually enters empathetically into their condition.[23]

The expression of feeling is another type of performative. A subject has privileged access to her own state of mind. One's testimony to one's feelings has a certain irrefutable character.[24] It is different from a descriptive report, for it implicates the speaker in the truth of what is said. Moreover, an expression of feeling has a rhetorical import; it is often uttered to elicit a certain response, and the speaker may feel betrayed if the response is wrong. Sometimes, in fact, such expressions are substitutes for more formal performative acts, just as "I love you and want to marry you" carries the weight of "I propose that we enter into the state of holy matrimony."

Rhetorically, YHWH's statement of motive for deciding to liberate Israel from slavery gives a basis for trusting in the promise. There is a dramatic logic between what God sees, hears, and knows and his decision to act. While YHWH does not have to deliver Israel, he is virtually compelled to do so. Moses and the Israelites are given reason for relying upon the seriousness of YHWH's promise.

God's personal relationship with Israel converges with the needs of justice. As sovereign and judge, God virtually "owes it" to the victims of oppression to intervene in their behalf. The law actually promises that he will do so within Israel (Exod. 22:23-24, 27, 23:7, etc.). You might say, then, that God shows a "moral logic" in siding with Israel against the Egyptians.[25]

Israelite theological literature gives a distinctively personalistic twist to deliberative rhetoric. In classical rhetorical tradition, debate over policy centered on desirability and capacity. The will of the gods was considered only as a kind of ratification, in the auspices.[26] In the case before us, God "proposes" the policy, and the human decision concerns whether the

23. The Hebrew connective is somewhat puzzling; perhaps *ki* can be translated "so that," making seeing and hearing a basis for this final perception.

24. Psychologists and psychiatrists would probably object, and we would have an interesting face-off between humanities and the so-called sciences.

25. Note an article I once wrote: "Moral Logic of Election," *Encounter* 37 (1976): 198–210.

26. 1 Kings 22 depicts a biblical scene in which God was consulted after a policy was decided upon.

human party can trust God's promise. The uncertainty involved in all policy decisions is transferred to the character of God. If Israel were to consider the policy rationally, it would have to conclude that, though liberation is desirable, they had little chance to succeed. When God, for whom "all things are possible" (cf. Gen. 18:14), proposes a policy, calculations of human power have to be set aside, or subordinated to the status of planning.

Depiction of God's state of mind simultaneously builds up an impression of YHWH's character. The characters within the textual world, and the audience, learn to know YHWH in another sense. That is, they not only learn about what he says and does, they learn what is characteristic, what moves him. Indeed, learning that someone cares about one's suffering creates a bond between people—and the same sort of relationship operates between God and people. Already God has hinted at this intimacy in addressing Moses by name and calling Israel "my people."

Biblical God language is primarily the language of characterization rather than abstract description. The way one learns to recognize a dramatic persona is to gain an image of "what is in character."[27] YHWH's expression of feeling for Israel's suffering fits with the depictions of God in the patriarchal narrative, thereby reinforcing the trustworthiness of the promises for the characters in the story and the audience's knowledge of God's identity.

The sense of God's character, however, is never beyond doubt. In a moment of crisis, one may feel that God is hostile or indifferent. Once the people are delivered from Egypt and begin to suffer the deprivations of the desert, they begin to suspect a malicious purpose.[28]

Commission and Resistance. Exodus 3:9-10 recapitulates the expression of feeling and promise, but this time the promise is couched under a commission of Moses as agent: "Come, I will send you to pharaoh that you may bring forth my people, the sons of Israel, out of Egypt." Moses is made the subject of the verb, which only YHWH in fact can accomplish. The reader must fill in the logical gap by inserting the idea that Moses is an agent of YHWH, with the task of representing him before both the Pharaoh and the people.

Commissioning is a performative act, an exercise of authority related to the power to command. As in the case of promise, the addressee cannot reason from the nature of God or past history or the injustice of the situation

27. D. Patrick, *Rendering of God*, 28–45, 46–60.

28. Exodus 14:10-18; 15:24; 16:1-3; and others, dubbed the *murmuring motif,* were expounded some years ago by G. W. Coats, *Rebellion in the Wilderness: The Murmuring Motif in the Wilderness of the Old Testament* (Nashville: Abingdon, 1968).

to the commission. When the utterance is heard, Moses can confirm it by such reasoning, but the illocutionary act of God must "precede" reason. Moses must accept God's authority in the utterance and respond by taking responsibility for the role assigned him. Moses must obey, confident in the commission, to discover in the course of events whether it is true.[29]

It is characteristic of biblical literature to require the recipients of a divine promise to take part in its fulfillment. Virtually never are divine promises given "without strings," to speak colloquially. Even where God promises to give victory without his people fighting, as in this case, Israel must participate in some way; indeed, resisting the urge to fight requires great willpower in some situations. In the exodus, Moses must act as YHWH's ambassador and Israel's leader, and Israel must wait patiently until it is told to move, and then it must move confidently.

Moses does not directly deny God's authority at the outset, but he does raise all the objections he can think of. Each objection elicits a reply from God that provides additional support for his promise and commission.[30] While performatives of the sort we are examining finally depend on authority and acceptance of that authority despite uncertainties, they can be backed up with good reasons.

a. To Moses' initial objection that he is not the right person for the job (3:11), God answers that he will be with Moses (3:12), which should make up any deficiency Moses might have. This promise is linked to a "sign." Prophetic signs were demonstrations of God's power in support of a message by a prophet.[31] The sign referred to here lacks such a concretely demonstrative character. The acts of power Moses is later taught (4:1-9) fit the prophetic concept much better. If the presence of God with Moses is the sign, the concept of sign is highly unusual because the reference lacks concreteness and demonstrative power. If Moses' return to the scene of revelation with the people in tow is the sign, the sign has been identified with the fulfillment of the message. Although the latter is highly unusual, it would offer an interesting perspective on the action: Moses will find confirmation of the truth of God's promises and his own mediating activity in the outcome.

b. To the question regarding the name and identity of the deity speaking to him, God reveals his name in the powerful exchange already discussed.

29. Strictly speaking, the event of fulfillment does not demonstrate the truth of a promise because other factors may explain the outcome. Normally, though, we take fulfillment as "confirming" its trustworthiness.

30. This dialog resembles the rhetorical form known as *diatribe*.

31. B. S. Childs, *Exodus*, 56–60, divides prophetic signs into two categories, one for the benefit of the prophet, the other for the audience. He takes the reference here to be to the burning bush itself.

He follows it up with a prophetic commission: "Go and gather the elders of Israel together and say to them . . ." (3:16a). Instead of a messenger formula, Moses is to report his revelation and the message to the enslaved people (vv. 16b-17).

From this point on we shift into another mode of discourse. It is the language of prediction: "They will hearken . . . you and the elders shall go . . . I know that the king of Egypt will . . . so I will stretch out my hand . . . and he will let you go . . ." (3:18-20). These predictions are not performative in character, but rather assertions about what will happen. Their truth has nothing to do with the act of speaking and reception of the recipients, but on whether events conform to what is said. What is their rhetorical function within an account of a performative transaction? Because they are contingent on Moses' compliance with God's commission, we could take them as assurances that God has planned it all out, or that he has such a perfect knowledge of the future as to leave no uncertainty about the outcomes.[32]

c. To Moses' objection that he will not be able to establish his authority with the Israelites, YHWH offers three prophetic signs (4:1-9). These foreshadow coming events with the Egyptians rather than the Israelites [33]

d. Even the signs are not sufficient to bolster Moses' confidence. His final objection is his own capacity to speak. It is described as a physical condition, but it may be intended metaphorically. Does he have a speech impediment or does he lack linguistic eloquence? The text leaves the reader to speculate. The objection provides God with the opportunity to appeal to his power as Creator. It is the only reference in the whole exchange to his "metaphysical" status. It is a startling, even shocking assertion: God makes humans "dumb," "deaf," "seeing," "blind"—hence, God is able to instruct Moses in the art of powerful speech.

e. Rather ironically, this assertion of divine power does not succeed in persuading Moses. Is this point the limit of God's power? The answer to this question is not as simple as it might seem. Moses has exhausted objections, and his final refusal is an irrational assertion of will.[34] Without an

32. For the audience of the narrative, the predictions have the function of foreshadowing the outcome. Since the audience can be assumed to know what that is, this foreshadowing assures it that the whole course of events was under the control of the Deliverer. Precisely because the predictions can be construed either as a plan or as foreknowledge, the reader is involved in completing the meaning of the text. The final detail—about "despoiling" the Egyptians—may satisfy the yearning of the audience for justice as well as explain the source of the material that went into the construction of the "golden calf" (Exod. 32:1ff).

33. 4:30 reports Moses' performance of the signs before the Israelites, but only in the most general way. By contrast, compare Exod. 7:8-13, 17-20.

34. It actually sounds like a plaintive plea more than an assertion; yet it is sufficient to arouse God's anger.

objection, God has nothing to answer, no reasons to give. Persuasion has arrived at an impasse, not because Moses has another argument, but because he does not accept the logical conclusion of God's successful one. Here he has asserted a radical freedom, the freedom to reject the inferences of reason.[35]

The proper response of authority to irrational resistance to persuasion is the exercise of coercive power. If God had said, "Okay, Moses, I will try others until I find someone who is persuaded," he would be granting reason, or at least rhetoric, authority over his decisions. This scenario would contradict the biblical understanding of the relation of power to reason. God as Creator has the authority to define what is true and good.[36]

Divine anger is the expression of the force of authority applied to recalcitrance.[37] It takes the language of personal emotion, characteristic of the depictional logic of biblical God language; its transactional force is somewhat indefinite when no threat is articulated. Since Moses has not raised an objection, but simply refused to accept the conclusion to which the discourse has led, God's anger has the force of disposing of Moses' demur and putting the commission into effect unilaterally.

The introduction of God's power as Creator in the immediately preceding exchange (4:10-12) makes a subtle point: Because Moses has not accepted YHWH's promise to deliver Israel and command to Moses to act as his agent, Moses is not within the relationship created by these performatives. The only authority God can exercise over Moses derives from creation until Moses acts (under coercion)[38] and Israel receives the promises (4:28-31).

YHWH's overruling of Moses foreshadows his exchanges with the Egyptian pharaoh. God cannot argue to the pharaoh that the release of the slaves is to the advantage of Egypt, and he does not attempt to persuade the pharaoh that it is the morally right thing to do.[39] Rather, he issues a request,

35. When Moses does not raise a further objection, he cedes the argument to God. However, one could imagine further objections. Indeed, debate is frequently interminable in principle: K. Pasewark, *A Theology of Power: Being beyond Domination* (Minneapolis: Fortress, 1993), 266–68. God would be within his rights to terminate debate before it comes to a conclusion in order to act.

36. I am trying to apply K. Pasewark's argument for grounding reason in power, ibid., 260–70, to our text. It should be noted that Pasewark defines power as the "communication of efficacy," ibid., 4–6 and elsewhere. Hence, the exercise of power does not diminish the recipients and subjects of its exercise, but "empowers" them.

37. This may be a key to the concept of divine anger/wrath throughout the Old Testament, but I will not make such global claims here.

38. The performatives are not nullified, though, but suspended until Moses is coerced into obedience; once he is "on board," he is under the sway of the promise and commission. Likewise, when Israel later balks about proceeding (Exod. 14:10-11), God goes forward anyway.

39. I think such appeals are understood to be behind the address to Moses, and to the audience of the text.

then a demand, for their release under the threat of sanctions. When no common interest or moral principles are present between speaker and addressee, coercion becomes the basis of persuasion.

Exodus 6:2-13. Overshadowed by the revelation at the burning bush is another narrative, which in itself constitutes a call of Moses or at least a commission of Moses to deliver to the people of Israel. It is God's promise of deliverance from bondage (vv. 6-9) and Moses' appointment, along with Aaron, to act as God's agent (v. 13). In the extant text, this transaction renews or reassures Moses and the people that YHWH intends to proceed with his plan after the initial setback (5:1—6:1). Like the original call, it has performative utterances that create a relationship between speaker and addressees and inaugurate the fulfillment of the material and political implications of that relationship.[40] The difference is that the performatives now "re-create" a relationship and promise already in force.

The newly formulated message to Moses and Israel reflects in itself an understanding corresponding to its present position. In it, patriarchal tradition is represented in terms of performative transactions with them: "I appeared to . . . as El Shaddai . . ."; "I established my covenant with them"; "I swore to give them the land of Canaan . . ."; "I have heard the groaning . . . and have remembered my covenant." The force of these reflexive references to God's interactions with the patriarchs is to ground his response to the cries of his people in the relationship he had already established with them. His decision to deliver them is virtually predetermined by the past.

This realization stands in contrast to Exodus 3, which renders YHWH's decision to act solely as a response to his people's troubles. To be sure, they are assumed to be his people, and he identifies himself as the God that Moses and Israel already know, but YHWH is portrayed as acting in freedom and Moses and the people must freely venture their lives on God's word.

These two accounts call for a kind of dialectical reading. The initial promise and commission require a leap of faith, the renewal reassures the recipients that what God is doing now is in continuity with what he has done in their history, and God will bring it off whatever the subjective condition of the people (6:12-13).

---

40. We find a revelation of the divine name, YHWH, in vv. 2-3; God's motive for acting (vv. 4-5) and promise to deliver (v. 6); to establish an ongoing relationship between them (v. 7); and to settle them in a land of their own (v. 8). One might say that we have an "abstract" of the message of Exodus 3–4.

Between Text and Audience

Exegetes have usually ignored the question of the transaction the text seeks to engender with its audience.[41] It is not on the surface of the text. How are we to know how readers respond to the text? Is that not a subjective matter—a matter depending on the disposition of the reader? Does not a story simply offer the reader an account of how things are, or what happened, for the reader to accept or reject?

The rhetorical approach to communication takes it as axiomatic that communication is not one-way; that is, the audience or reader is not passive over against an active speaker or author. Rather, the audience must construe and apply the communication. The speaker or author designs the text to lead or constrain the audience to take the communication in a particular way and, depending on the rhetor's objective, arrive at a particular conclusion. It requires both clarity and persuasion, so that the audience will know what the communication is about and adopt the decision or judgment or attitude the author seeks to instill.[42]

Ultimately, I want to show that the call of Moses communicates revelation by engendering a performative transaction with readers. If it does not, the "revelation" changes from a performative transaction within the text to descriptive discourse whose truth depends on its correspondence to nonlinguistic facts or to experiences known by introspection. If the text does seek to enter into a performative transaction with its audience, we need to bring out how it does. Beyond that, we must address J. L. Austin's exclusion of performatives uttered on the stage—or in a book— from his category.

We cannot proceed directly to these questions, though. I want to meditate first on some qualities of our text that may provide insight into how the text is shaping our perception of the story in order to shape our conception of who we are. The word *meditate* is deliberate. To understand how the text transacts with readers we need the knowledge gained by introspection. We cannot adopt the stance of impartial observers. We must meditate on how the text is affecting us, guiding us to a certain view of life and mode of living.

How Is Suspense Created? Literature must be interesting, it must entertain, even if it aspires to do a lot more. To accomplish its goals, a story must create some kind of suspense. If the narrator is inventing the plot as he writes,

---

41. Or they have "historicized" its rhetoric as a question of what the text sought to persuade the original audience and how it employed the available types of discourse to do so.

42. See the book by A. Scult and D. Patrick, *Rhetoric and Biblical Interpretation*, 12–13, 15.

the challenge is to arouse the reader's curiosity and anxiety early in a story and not resolve it too predictably. If the narrator is telling a story familiar to the audience, the task of creating suspense is more difficult. If the narrative simply reviews what the audience knows, only the interest in the story itself can sustain interest in the author's telling. As time goes on, the story will, usually, lose its fascination and the author's telling will die with it. Indeed, the author's telling may be the reason that the story ceases to attract. Serious literature is marked off by its capacity to create suspense when the audience knows the outcome. I can see *Hamlet* or *King Lear* time and time again without losing interest; my memory may in fact generate anticipation of scenes to come. Members of my son's generation have the same experience with *Star Wars*.

The exodus was certainly known to the Israelite audiences. When the narrators of the written text penned their versions, their audiences would have been celebrating it annually throughout their lives. Are the authors' tellings of the story—now forming the composite text of Exodus 1–15— simply a review of the cult legend? Some parts are a requirement, such as the fixed elements: a series of plagues and the deliverance at the sea. What about the call of Moses? The existence of Exod. 6:2-13 alongside 3:1—4:21 indicates how much freedom narrators had with the event. It may not even have been a part of the original cult legend, but an invention of the first author. In any case, the authors had freedom to shape their versions of the call to supply what they thought the story needed to achieve the effect they desired.

We cannot ignore the fact that call narratives do have generic features. The very choice of a call narrative seems to be set by the cultural tradition. A person who was to speak and act in the name of YHWH was presumed to have had an encounter that bestowed that power. Even if the Passover ritual did not dramatize the call, the narrator of the cultic legend would assume that such an event stands behind Moses' actions.

Common to call narratives is a theophany and words commissioning the addressee to speak and/or act with the authority of God. Frequently the accounts record resistance or objection on the part of the recipient.[43] It is quite possible, then, that the author(s) of Exodus 3–4 drew upon a tradition in their depiction of Mosaic resistance. The motif of resistance may have served the function of authenticating the divine origin of the recipient's words and action by demonstrating that it was not the recipient's desire to say or do these things (cf. Amos 7:14-15). It would also serve the function for readers of "humanizing" the recipient, allowing for identification between the persona of the narrative and the reading audience.

43. Judges 6:11-19; Jer. 1:4-10. Perhaps one would categorize Isaiah 6:5 and Amos 7:3, 6 as equivalent, but neither is really an objection.

The scholarly era that generated these theses tended, to my mind, to exaggerate how rigid and "programmed" ancient speech forms were. If one compares the parallels closely, it will be clear that we do not have stereo-typical language; in each passage, the objection arises from the character of the addressee and the situation, and God's strategy for overcoming it fits the exigency and reinforces the message to the reading audience.

The narrative of Moses' call did not have the same function as the calls of the prophets: to the reading audience, his authority would have been unquestioned, whereas the authority of the classical prophets was in dispute until the canon was settled on. One might think that the author(s) would respect Moses' status to such a degree that he would be rendered as a model of faith and obedience. Precedents for such treatment can be found among call narratives.[44] The narrative actually starts out that way: when the angel calls out to Moses from the burning bush, "Moses, Moses!" he answers just as Abraham did in Genesis 22, namely, "Behold me." This statement says, in effect, I am ready to do your bidding. When, a few verses later, he responds to the commission with "Who, me?" (3:11), we are taken by surprise; now we must think more deeply about this call.

Perhaps Moses' stubbornness was a solution to the problem of the audience knowing the outcome of the story. It would be virtually impossible to reproduce the suspense that the participants in the story would have felt. They could not be sure that YHWH could and would bring it off. The author needs to create another kind of suspense for the audience that cannot be resolved by the knowledge of the outcome. He refocuses the suspense from YHWH's power and resolve to Moses' willingness to comply. Moses responds to the promise inappropriately by refusing to play his part. While the audience knows that he finally obeyed, his resistance gives them pause. If God's chosen instrument is not a model of pious obedience, it must be difficult indeed. The external suspense has been transformed largely into an introspective one.

The "fickleness" of the Israelites seems to play an analogous role in the subsequent narrative. The people initially accept the promise joyfully (4:9-31), but the minute the struggle gets tough they begin to waver (5:21, 6:9). Throughout the plague narratives and departure, they play a rather passive role; they are essentially there as witnesses to YHWH's deed for later generations. However, when they find themselves trapped between the sea and the pursuing Egyptian host, they begin their "murmuring" (Exod. 14:10-15). This distrust continues in the wilderness; indeed, the exodus generation proved so lacking in trust and obedience that they were forced to live out

---

44. Isaiah 6 and Ezekiel 1–2 fit such a definition. Isaiah 6:5 is really parallel to Exod. 3:3-6.

their lives in the wilderness (Numbers 13–14). Again, the audience must examine its own staying power.

Why would the narrator be seeking to provoke the readers' introspection? It makes the narrative "more real," students will say. Exactly, it fuses the "horizons" between the characters in the story and the readers. The story is dealing with the readers' own lack of courage, their own uncertainties about trusting and obeying God, their fears about the dangers that confront them as Jews in their generation.[45] The story communicates both the ideal—how one should respond to God's call—and how difficult it is.

Other elements of the call of Moses build suspense, but the resistance of Moses is, to my mind, the most risky and most effective. It does not constitute a performative transaction with the audience, but it does bring the horizons of narrative and audience together so that such a transaction might take place.

The Expanding Horizon of the Promise. The narrator must spell out the promise within the narrative horizon simply to make the story work, but for rhetorical purposes the readers must identify with it and even see it as applying to them. A promise of the sort that we have in Exodus 3–4 and 6 must be specific enough to be relevant to the situation. There must be a specific object in view, a change the participants can regard as fulfillment. In this case, the enslaved Israelites need to be able to say, we are free from servitude. When this point is reached, the speaker has met the obligations he assumed. Note that the promise to Moses moves rather smoothly toward a plan of implementation, including the recruitment of agents of the speaker. The readers are outsiders observing the plot unfold in the imaginary world of the text. They do not apply the promise to themselves. Yet, in subtle and unobtrusive ways, the narrative is eliciting identification with the people of the textual world in such a way that readers will say, we were in Egypt and YHWH brought us out with a mighty hand and an outstretched arm. Let us attend to the various components of the exchange that elicit this identification.

The revelation of the divine name reached out beyond the narrative horizon to include the audience. When the name is divulged, its use is immediately instituted: "This is my name for ever, and thus I am to be remembered from generation to generation" (3:15). This utterance is both command and promise, for it instructs the audience in how it can gain access to YHWH; obviously it applies to the reading audience just as much as to the personages of the narrative world.

45. Disciples play the same role in the Synoptic Gospels.

It is not surprising that interpreters have been drawn to this revelation of the name. It concerns them directly. Moreover, the passage provides mysterious hints as to the meaning of the name, and therefore the nature of its bearer. Names, particularly names of deity, were thought to participate in the power of the one named. Even when the cultural presuppositions of the audience have changed, the sense that the meaning of the divine name is revelatory of his being or character has persisted.

There is a bit of irony about the revelation of the name for the contemporary reader. In the postexilic period, the divine name became too sacred for Jews to utter. By the time of the translation of the Hebrew into Greek, the tradition customarily substituted "Lord" (Adonai, Kurios) for the name. The result was to "mediate" the institution of the name; the title spoken became an allusion to a "silent" name. Exodus 3:14-15 would now have a doubly "hidden" revelation: it evokes a completion of the meaning by the reader, and the name itself "hides" behind another noun.

The behabitive statements that provide the rationale for YHWH's decision to intervene (3:7, 9, 16) also provide an identity to go along with the name. These expressions of the divine state of mind are indirect, but they imprint the divine "character" on the audience's minds. This character will endure along with the name, so all who call upon this name will appeal to his traits of mercy, justice, and faithfulness (cf. Exod. 34:6-7).

When YHWH promises to deliver Israel from Egyptian slavery, he continues on to include the provision of a land: I will "bring you . . . to a good and broad land . . . to the place of the Canaanites, the Hittites . . ." (3:8, also 3:17). Before the exiles of 722 and 587 B.C.E., the audience could regard itself as living within the fulfillment of the promise; it would imply an assurance of continued enjoyment. Later, Jews have taken this passage as entitlement to the land of Canaan, and it is a manifesto of the Israeli "religious right." However, 3:8 is not an entitlement, but an assurance that once the people are out of Egypt, they will be given a place of their own. The "recapitulation" of the call of Moses in Exod. 6:2-13 does base the promise of Canaan as a homeland for the slaves on a promise to the patriarchs, which does have the force of an entitlement: "And I will bring you into the land which I swore to give to Abraham, to Isaac and to Jacob; I will give it to you for a possession—I am YHWH" (6:8). Those Orthodox Jews who claim all of Palestine today do in fact appropriate the call of Moses as a performative applicable to them.[46]

---

46. Christians have never accepted the continuing validity of this claim. Some fundamentalist Protestants do claim to accept it, but their acceptance is mediated through an apocalyptic scenario that sees the return of the Jews as a day among the last days. Perforce Christians

How about the very heart of the promise given to Israel at the burning bush—the deliverance from Egyptian slavery? To bring the readers within the horizon of this promise, the narrator must collapse the distance, so to speak, between the event being recounted and the readers. The readers are not in Egypt under conditions of slavery, but living in the wake of deliverance. The author must persuade the readers to identify with their ancestors so that Jews in every generation can say, we were in Egypt. Nothing is said about doing so in the call of Moses; the readers need a command, analogous to the command to Moses (Exod. 3:9-10), to receive the promise and its fulfillment.

The Commandment of Ritual Reenactment. If the reading audience is to be addressed in performative utterances, it must occur outside the call of Moses. The reading audience is addressed in the legislation for Passover, Unleavened Bread, and the redemption of the firstborn (12:1-20, 43-49, 13:1-2, 3-16).[47] Does this legislation transfer the promise of deliverance from Egyptian slavery to the reading audience?

The narrative world of the exodus is "broken" by this legislation; what is commanded applies to the reading audience as well as the Israelites of the narrative world. Some material is first person YHWH (12:1-20, 43-49, 13:1-2), some first person Moses (12:21-27, 13:3-16). Only the material with YHWH as speaker has the full transactive force of commandment, but the final form of the text lends this force to Mosaic instructions as well. The audience—assumed to be Israelites—is put by these utterances under obligation to perform Passover.

Does this legislation transfer the promise of deliverance to the reading audience? Several objections could be raised to any claim that it does. It is not connected textually to the call of Moses and it prescribes no reenactment of that call. Moreover, how can a command be substituted for a promise? And how can a promise that concerns the people of the narrative world apply to those outside?

It is rather easy to see how the performance of the commands for Passover situates the addressee in the exodus drama:

> It is YHWH's Passover. For I will pass through the land of Egypt that night, and I will smite all the firstborn in the land of Egypt, both

cannot accept the promise in unmediated terms, namely, that the Jews are entitled to this land as long as the sun rises and sets. Many Jews, religious as well as secular, would also be uncomfortable introducing such religious claims into politics. Such claims are incorrigible. The state of Israel must be justified on principles of international justice and prudence, and the nation must be flexible in coming to an accommodation with the inhabitants of the land.

47. Henceforth, we will simply refer to this as Passover legislation.

> human and beast; (and on all the gods of Egypt I will execute judg-
> ment: I am YHWH). The blood will be a sign for you, upon the house
> where you are; and when I see the blood, I will pass over you, and no
> plague shall fall upon you to destroy you, when I smite the land of
> Egypt. (Exod. 12:11c-13)

The act performed at a later time (note the demonstrative adjective "that")
is located in the original event. By obeying the command, the addressee
becomes the recipient of the promise of deliverance the command
implements.[48]

The command entails more than a commemoration of the archetypal
deliverance of God: it requires the addressee—the head of the family—to
adopt a role in the ceremony:

> And Moses said to the people, "Remember this day . . . unleavened
> bread shall be eaten. . . . And you shall tell your son on that day, 'It is
> because of what YHWH did for me when I came out of Egypt.' And it
> shall be to you as a sign on your hand and a memorial between your
> eyes, that the Torah of YHWH will be in your mouth; for with a
> strong hand YHWH has brought you out of Egypt. (13:3, 8-9)

While this particular unit does not mention a child's question, v. 8 puts
words into the father's mouth, which would fit "what does this mean?"
(13:14, cf. Deut. 6:20). The rite enjoined is not so much explained (see 12:39
for that) as made emblematic of the deliverance—"a sign on your hand and
a memorial between your eyes" (v. 9). The father's answer is formulated in
very personal language, "It is because of what YHWH did for me when I
came out of Egypt." As the commandment itself says, this statement is to be
made by a member of a generation that was not literally in Egypt. The
father "fuses" (or grafts) his identity into the textual world for the sake of
the son. The son now relates to his father as a representative of the found-
ing event of their people, and when he becomes a father he will represent
it to his child. The horizons of textual world and the people of Israel are
thereby "collapsed" so that all generations can say "YHWH brought *us* out
of the land of Egypt."

One odd turn of phrasing calls for further reflection: one performs the
ceremony as a sign with the purpose "that the Torah of YHWH may be in
your mouth." The addressee is to perform the commandment in order that
he may pass on the Torah. If this word is taken in its full measure, it is all of

48. If the rite is an apotrophic practice of agrarian origins, as many scholars suppose, it
may have continued for a long time to have that meaning for the celebrants; as that meaning
faded, perhaps the fact of being commanded became more important, and the performance
of the command became a conscious decision to identify with and pass on national identity.

God's commandments and laws. In the act of confessing YHWH's deliver-ance, the addressee becomes a communicator or teacher of obedience. Praise and obedience, promise and commandment have been woven together as woof and warp of a single fabric.

The catechetical passages are an essential component for the Passover Seder, perhaps even its living heart. In that setting, the first persons—I, we, me, us—are given concreteness by the family around the table. The Seder text itself, the Haggadah, is a compendium of midrashic glosses on the basic story as well as accounts of significant Seder celebrations throughout history. Thus the family sitting together around the table can expand the range of its communal identification by connecting itself to the historical stream of retellings of the story commanded by the biblical passage and recorded in the Haggadah. As the same text is repeated year after year in the family setting, the look and sound of the exodus become even more intensely familiar—as if they were an image in a family album. It would seem that the text has successfully reinforced its objective of forging the community's identity by the prescription it makes for the continued repe-tition of its story.[49]

How can the promise of deliverance and its fulfillment be more than "make-believe" for the celebrants—later generations of Israelites? The par-ticipants in the Passover are not in fact in Egypt, so how does it concern their own situation? Perhaps the answer is that the performance of the commandment does the same thing for each generation: it passes on the people's identity from generation to generation. Through it the people of the Lord continue to exist among the peoples of the world as a witness to "what YHWH has done for me." In quiet times, this witness may not seem to be of great moment, but in times of persecution, and in times of assim-ilation, it requires courage and perseverance. It is a decision by Jews to be Jews, and to pass on that identity to the coming generation.

The preservation of Israel as witness to YHWH's deed is not a human achievement. The Jewish interpretive community does have to play its role, but implicit in the commandment is a promise of God to give efficacy to the act among the children and to preserve the people from their enemies. The preservation of the witness to YHWH's mighty deed of deliverance is itself a witness to YHWH's continuing empowerment of his people.

The promise of deliverance from slavery becomes the inauguration of a continuing relationship between YHWH and Israel, a relationship that continues into the Passover present. The people become the recipients of this promise by identifying themselves with Israel in the performance of

---

49. The last paragraph was originally written by A. Scult for our coauthored book, *Rhetoric and Biblical Interpretation*, 51–52.

God's commandment. Thus, in summary, the text enters into a performative transaction with the audience not by promises that apply to the audience, but by commandments that incorporate individuals into the people whose Lord is a God of promise.

How Can a Speaker within an Imaginary World Enter into a Performative Transaction with Readers?

Although I have satisfied my own criteria for identifying God's utterances in the call of Moses as performative, and have found a way, though circuitous, for the revelation to Moses to be communicated as a performative to the audience, it is doubtful that I have satisfied J. L. Austin's criteria. He takes it as self-evident that "a performative utterance will . . . be *in a peculiar way* hollow or void if said by an actor on stage, or if introduced in a poem, or spoken in soliloquy."[50] He can only mean by this statement that the performative does not have force for the audience; within the narrated world, a performative would have force for the personae in that world, otherwise it would not mirror the world of the audience.

When Austin proposed to describe how we "do things with words," he totally ignored the literary artist, who creates an imaginary world with words. In fact, striking similarities can be found between a play or narrative and the ritual by which some performatives are enacted. Each creates a "world" through language. But alas, we must grant Austin's point that imaginary characters do not actually have the ontological capacity to breech the proscenium arch, though it is not uncommon to pretend to do so.[51]

But what if the imaginary world is the history of one's family and nation? That past history can be rendered as an imaginary world may present philosophical conundrums, but in fact it is a common mode of presenting history. The exodus narrative does present itself as Israel's story. Here the recognition factor is not, or not primarily, the reader's humanity, but the reader's own identity as a member of this people. Now we are in the realm of performatives that impinge on the audience, for the identity of this people is constituted by specific performative acts. The audience's ancestors participated in some identity-creating performative transactions that continue to bind the people together when the reading audience obeys.

---

50. *How to Do*, 22. It is safe to say that this observation would apply to the call of Moses, though the specific genre of prose narrative is not named.

51. Cf. Scult and Patrick, "A Rhetorical View of Historical Narrative," in *Rhetoric and Biblical Interpretation*, 45–56.

The critical scholar of biblical literature will object that the story told in Exodus falls short of history as the historian would reconstruct it. The account of the call of Moses would be a case in point. Would not a reader be deceived if she took the transaction between God, Moses, and Israel depicted in it as having binding force for a Jew or Christian?

The answer I would give is that the biblical narrative "represents" the people's history so as to persuade generation after generation to recognize who they are and what commitments they are obligated to. The story of the call of Moses is an imaginative reconstruction of the transaction that motivated Moses to lead the people in their struggle for freedom and motivated the people to follow his leadership. According to this scenario, an actual event called forth the story. The narrative gives rhetorical power to the event, makes it an event that imparts a particular identity to a people. The narrative itself is empowered by the commandment to reenact the event annually. The telling generates and reflects the force of Israel's transactions with YHWH in the exodus and the history under its sign.

Perhaps Austin would admit that a narrative of this sort has performative force. However, he might well question the reality of the divine party to the transaction. Can "God" be regarded as a speaker of genuine performative utterances? That the original participants believed that they were encountering this being is granted. That "Israel" is constituted by sole recognition of YHWH as its God and sovereign is granted. It does not mean that there was/is a "real being" with whom to transact; Jewish identity may well be based on a fiction.

The exodus narrative is in fact designed to answer this type of objection, though more for an ancient audience whose doubts were different. A refrain runs through the exodus narrative indicating that the story demonstrates YHWH's power. In one message to Pharaoh, YHWH explains why he hasn't simply wiped him and his people out: "for this purpose have I let you live, to show you my power, so that my name may be declared throughout all the earth" (9:16). With power goes renown and majesty. Just before YHWH unleashes his destructive power against the Egyptian host, he explains to Moses: "I will harden the hearts of the Egyptians so that they will go in after them, and *I will get glory over Pharaoh* and his host, his chariots, and his horsemen. And the Egyptians *shall know that I am YHWH...*" (14:17). The praise of YHWH for his overthrow of the Egyptians (15:1-18) is devoted primarily to his demonstration of power. The theme is sounded in 15:3: "YHWH is a man of war; YHWH is his name." In vv. 4-10, the poem piles up one image after another to describe the decisive blow: the enemy is cast into the sea like a great stone (vv. 4-5); shattered by a blow of God's hand (vv. 6-7a); set on fire like a field of stubble (v. 7b); drowned by the primeval sea stirred up by the puffing of an angry God (vv. 8, 10). Verse 9 dramatizes the self-destructive will to power of the enemy. This poetic depiction of the deliverance concludes with an assertion of YHWH's incomparability (v. 11) and one more image of his destructive power (v. 12).

The demonstrations of divine power so impressed the community that when the exodus was recalled in other texts, we constantly meet the stereotyped formula, "with a mighty hand and an outstretched arm."

Why this focus on God's power? Ancient Israel was a part of a polytheistic world. A god in a polytheistic system had power superior to humans, even nations, but other gods and supernatural forces limited the power of even the highest gods. Within this perspective the issue for an early Israelite audience would have been whether YHWH's power surpassed that of the Egyptian deities. One Exodus text actually affirms as much (12:12). Further, when Moses' father-in-law, Jethro, hears the report of Israel's deliverance, he infers "that YHWH is greater than all gods because he delivered the people from under the hand of the Egyptians . . ." (Exod. 18:11). The same line of reasoning is involved in the declaration of YHWH's incomparability in the Song of Moses (15:11).

This reasoning has to be reconstructed because the narrative makes virtually no concessions to it. The reference in Exodus 12:12 to the "gods of Egypt" is completely isolated; nowhere else in the account is there the suggestion of a conflict between YHWH and another deity. No other deity is depicted as active in the conflict, and the Egyptians themselves do not call upon any or exhibit any religious behavior. The only opposition figure with power is the pharaoh, and he is no more than a human tyrant. He requires God's power—"hardening of his heart"—to stand up to God.[52]

We can regard this "monotheistic" rendering of the exodus as itself the most potent persuasive argument for the power of YHWH. Israel's God has no rival. By so telling the story, the power manifested in particular signs and wonders becomes an objective manifestation of the divine monopoly of power. Even the pharaoh's resistance is a manifestation of YHWH's power.

Within the polytheistic world of the ancient Near East, *the issue of power was the issue of reality*. It continues to be the message to an audience for which monotheism is taken for granted. Now the power of God must be affirmed against the finite world, which frequently gives the appearance of being an autonomous system.[53] The repeated intervention of God in the

52. See my "The First Commandment in the Structure of the Pentatuech," *VT*, 45 (1995), 113–16.

53. Individual laments frequently describe the plots of the supplicants' enemies (or the sicked) as though they would succeed if God does not intervene, e.g., Ps. 5, 12, 17, 35.

course of this deliverance is a challenge to that appearance of autonomy, though these interventions can have the reverse effect on those who are impressed by finite principalities and powers.

The Rhetoric of the Interventions. One might expect that the narrative would be designed to persuade the readers that the great signs and wonders took place. Even though the ancient audience would not be familiar with critical history and a conception of nature as a closed system of law, it would bring its own experiences of life and history to its reading. However, nothing in the plague narrative suggests a need or desire to answer doubt. The narrative pattern is the most repetitious and stylized in the Hebrew Bible. Moses and Aaron approach the pharaoh with God's demand, the pharaoh refuses, a plague is announced and comes about; sometimes the pharaoh promises to comply if the plague is halted (8:4-11 [Eng. 8 15]), sometimes he simply waits it out (e.g., 9:1-7). Very little progress is made from plague to plague until the last. The Egyptian magicians imitate the first few plagues (7:11-12, 22, 8:3 [Eng. 7]), but meet their match with the gnats (8:14-15 [Eng. 18 19]) and themselves suffer from the boils (9:11). This failure to match feats does not, however, bring the pharaoh any closer to releasing the Israelites.[54]

An odd discrepancy occurs between the weight given the plagues as revelations of divine glory and the mood of their representation. YHWH is essentially "playing" with the pharaoh. He gives the human ruler the power to resist—"hardens his heart"—in order to show off divine power. The plagues themselves are not portrayed in such a way that one might feel sympathy for the suffering they caused; they are simply demonstrations of power that force the pharaoh to take notice.

The clue to the rhetorical aim of the narrative may be found in 10:1-2:

> Then YHWH said to Moses: ". . . I have hardened (the Pharaoh's) heart and the heart of his servants, that I may show these signs of mine among them, and that you tell in the hearing of your son and your son's son how I have made sport of the Egyptians and what signs I have done among them; that you may know I am YHWH."

The plagues are performed for the exchange around the table at Passover. The addressee is not really Moses, but the patriarch of each household who tells the story to the young—as a witness. The mood is not particularly serious, for YHWH "made sport" (*'ll* in the Hithpael) of the Egyptians. Father and children are, one might say, engaged in a kind of play.

---

54. The magicians do not even try to stop the plagues, which is an indication that no power struggle occurs here, but competitive exhibitions of power.

The deliverance at the sea is treated somewhat differently. Some motifs continue. The pharaoh reverses himself (14:5-9) as he has repeatedly done in the plague narratives. God again will enhance divine honor at the pharaoh's expense (14:17-18). Moses uses his "rod" to divide the sea (14:16, cp. vv. 21, 26). Thus, we can say that drowning the pharaoh and his army is the "showdown" of the plague narrative. They hold significant differences, though. God's act is not only to demonstrate divine power but to bring about the deliverance of God's people from mortal danger and leave them free of Egyptian bondage. The people succumb to fear and murmur against Moses (14:10-12),[55] eliciting a call to believe (14:13-14). The reader must take this account in a different way; it is a "saving fact." The conclusion of the narrative has a quasi-forensic character:

> Thus YHWH saved Israel that day from the hand of the Egyptians; and Israel saw the Egyptians dead upon the seashore. And Israel saw the great work YHWH did against the Egyptians, and the people feared YHWH; and they believed in YHWH and his servant Moses. (14:30-31)

The people now become witnesses to the saving fact: they "saw," "feared," and "believed." Even a critical bit of physical evidence is cited, namely., the dead bodies on the shore.[56]

The Song of the Sea (Exod. 15:1-18) is designed for the readers of the narrative to respond along with the Israel of the narrative world. It is another case of the breaching of the proscenium arch, but this time for the people to cross over into the narrative world to praise the God known in the story. A confession of trust (v. 2) designed for all generations of Israel is spliced in between the rephrased Song of Miriam (v. 1) and the depiction of YHWH's mighty deed. The Song extends the story beyond the deliverance into the "conquest" of Canaan (portrayed as a holy pilgrimage) and concludes with an affirmation of YHWH's everlasting sovereignty over his

---

55. Foreshadowing the wilderness period; see G. W. Coats, "The Traditio-Historical Character of the Reed Sea Motif," *VT* 17 (1967), 253ff.

56. Two accounts are given in 14:19-29 of how YHWH accomplished his deliverance. These take virtually antithetical strategies in their presentation of God's miracle. My intuition is that the differences are shaped by rhetorical aims. The natural explanation seeks to persuade sophisticated readers who require a reasonable explanation, while the miraculous account would satisfy readers who desire confirmation of supernatural reality. The synthesis of the two accounts aims at persuading both kinds of readers. The analogy has been offered of a political candidate who is trying to hold together a coalition by "sending signals" to one constituency and then another; each is expected to interpret what it doesn't want to hear in the light of what it does: see J. W. Watts *Reading Law: The Rhetorical Shaping of the Pentateuch* (Biblical Seminar 59; Sheffield: Sheffield Academic Press, 1999), 73–84.

people. If it were a part of the narrative world, it would incongruous; its purpose is to encompass all of Israel's history with YHWH, up to the Passover feast.

To summarize, the "fact" of YHWH's liberation of Israel from bondage is a demonstration of the reality of God who promised deliverance to Israel through Moses. It is not the sort of "fact" that stills the doubts of the critical mind. The narrative is its own argument for its truth, designed to persuade successive generations of Israel that they are called to be witnesses to YHWH's deed. The audience—the people of Israel—can continue to demonstrate its truth by obeying the commandment to celebrate YHWH's powerful deed, concluding with praise of their everlasting King.

The Theology of Promise

If the narrative of the exodus is told to impart an identity to Israel, if the celebration of the Passover is the means by which this narrative is to have its effect, and if the promise attendant on the performance of the Passover commandment is that God will preserve a witness to his saving deed for Israel, how can Christians lay claim to the exodus as a saving event and receive its promise? Christians have not historically heard the command to perform the Passover as addressed to them. It is a Jewish holy day to impart a "national" identity, and the church is called to transcend the division between Jew and Gentile (Gal. 4:27, etc.).

In the New Testament and through much of church history, Passover was identified typologically with the Eucharist, Christ was identified as the Passover lamb, and the deliverance from Egyptian slavery was spiritualized into redemption from sin and death. This radical refiguration of the exodus did not preclude drawing analogies between the exodus and the interpretive community's struggles,[57] but this type of application was not much closer to the rhetorical force of the literature than was the typological reading.

Christian typology progressively lost is cogency with the growth of historical consciousness. The critical study of Scripture enshrined the original meaning of texts and tended to dismiss their reapplication in subsequent eras. Typology was reduced to "poetic license." The biblical theology movement tried to revive it on a new basis; one of the most influential contributions was an article by W. Zimmerli, which replaced "prediction" with promise, and abstracted an ongoing promise from the individual promises of the biblical text.

---

57. See M. Walzer, *Exodus and Revolution* (New York: Basic Books, 1985), for historical examples.

> When we survey the entire Old Testament, we find ourselves involved in a great history of movement from promise toward fulfillment. It flows like a large brook—here rushing swiftly, there apparently coming to rest in a quiet backwater, and yet moving forward as a whole toward a distant goal which lies beyond itself.[58]

It is the movement forward that leads to the Christian Gospel, not any particular set of "predictions" or "figures." The latter are the surface, and have become problematic for the historically conscious interpreter of Scripture. It is the underlying, comprehensive movement or action of God toward fulfillment of the promises that constitute the "real" connection of the Testaments.[59] Moreover, the coming of Christ does not stop the stream, it is a fulfillment that expands and intensifies the promise, the movement forward toward the revelation of God's glory to the whole world.[60]

J. Moltmann began his theological sojourn building on this concept of promise and attempting to correlate it with the neo-Marxist E. Bloch's phenomenology of hope. The latter is outside the purview of this chapter, but his exposition of biblical theology of promise falls within it. Molt-mann has Zimmerli in mind when he writes that

> the more recent theology of the Old Testament has indeed shown that the words and statements about the "revealing of God" in the Old Testament are combined throughout with statements about the "promise of God." God reveals himself in the form of promise and in the history that is marked by promise.[61]

To underline its significance, he goes on to identify "promise" as the idea that distinguishes Israelite religion from other religions:

> The examination in the field of comparative religion of the special peculiarity of Israelite faith is today bringing out ever more strongly the difference between its "religion of promise" and the epiphany religions of the revealed gods of the world around Israel.[62]

This characterization of Old Testament religion is on a much more abstract plane of generalization than our passage, but the case that YHWH is "a God of promise" has passages like Exodus 3–4 as its exegetical base. The

58. "Promise and Fulfillment," in *Essays on Old Testament Hermeneutics,* C. Westermann, ed., J. L. Mays, trans. (Richmond: John Knox, 1965).

59. "Promise and Fulfillment," 113–22.

60. Ibid., 114–15.

61. J. Moltman, *Theology of Hope,* trans. J. W. Leitch (New York and Evanston: Harper & Row, 1965), 42.

62. *Theology of Hope,* 43.

combining of revelation with promise occurs right here, indeed, it is a pre-eminent case. The problem with Moltmann's development of this concept is that he moves toward a generalization about the nature of God rather than a phenomenological analysis of the performative act of promising.[63] Promises are specific; they can be expanded but not generalized. It may be characteristic of YHWH to promise, but each promise is an act whose force does not depend on it being characteristic.

The problem for Moltmann is that the promise to ancient Israel during its enslavement cannot be made universal; it doesn't apply to all humans under all conditions, but only to this one community. It is expanded to include all generations of Israel but is not universal in the sense of a religion of promise that gathers up all human hopes and sets us all on the road toward fulfillment.[64]

This universalizing of the exodus promise and corresponding general-ization about God's character is found in many strands of liberation theol-ogy. The essence of the event is YHWH's liberation of the enslaved, not his liberation of the Israelites from slavery. In this way the exodus can be trans-ferred to every enslaved or oppressed people and God be defined as the one who intervenes in every event as the "savior of the oppressed and punish-er of oppressors."[65] A promise so construed is no longer a particular per-formative act by a speaker who enters freely into relationship with those whom he chooses.[66]

Moltmann might justify his universalizing the scope of divine promises to Israel by reference to the new exodus in the prophets. B. W. Anderson's characterization of this typological use of the exodus would seem to fit Moltmann's thesis nicely.

> A faith which takes history with radical seriousness is expressed in a typology that juxtaposes "first things" and the "new things," the begin-ning and the end. Second Isaiah's eschatological hope is shaped by images drawn from Israel's *Heilsgeschichte*, particularly the crucial event of the Exodus, from which flow consequences reaching into the present and on into the future. The Exodus, then, is a "type" of the new Exodus which will fill in a more wonderful fashion, with a deeper

---

63. C. Morse, *The Logic of Promise in Moltmann's Theology* (Philadelphia: Fortress, 1979), 54–56, has shown that Moltmann adopts Picht's description of time as a description of promise.

64. See J. Moltmann, *Theology of Hope*, 15–36.

65. J. P. Miranda, *Marx and the Bible* (Maryknoll, N.Y.: Orbis, 1974), 81.

66. This does not preclude an interpretation of biblical teaching that stresses God's just character; but the interpreter must take responsibility—as a prophet—for representing God in any promise with performative force to a specific group of poor and oppressed.

soteriological meaning, and with world-wide implications, Yahweh's purpose revealed by word and deed in the beginning.[67]

In more recent scholarship, typology has been transferred from the framework of history and eschatology to the literary process of "intertextuality." M. Fishbane has led the way in this approach. His analysis attends to the verbal repetitions and echoes, a disciplined method of establishing the presence of analogy, and a system of classification. It is Fishbane's overall thesis that intertextual biblical interpretation reflects the same general practices as classical Jewish exegesis, so he employs the categories known in rabbinical tradition. The "new exodus" is classified as one of several kinds of "haggadic" interpretation, which is distinguished from legal or halakic by its object and method. The range of styles, topics, and hermeneutical techniques of haggadic exegesis is broad. The application of a received tradition to a new situation involves a shift in historical and literary contexts. Haggadic exegesis addresses three types of exigency: a crisis concerning the whole covenantal tradition, of specific teachings within it, and of the survival of the tradition from one historical era to another. The new exodus typology is a response to the third.[68]

We cannot, of course, expect Moltmann to have foreseen this turn of biblical scholarship, nor does Fishbane's analysis necessarily undercut Moltmann's position that the old promises have been expanded to project an eschatological horizon. Fishbane is working at the level of exegetical operations, not theological substance. However, what Fishbane does require is attention to the linguistic level and how discourse is generated in a particular tradition. The new exodus is an event with eschatological dimensions, but it is still concerned with Israel's survival and its role within the future denouement of history. In the very same units that announce a new exodus in Isaiah 40–55, for example, we meet the theme of witness:

"Do not remember the former things
nor consider the things of old.
Behold, I am doing a new thing;
now it springs forth, do you not perceive it?
I make a way in the wilderness,
and streams in the barren waste . . .
to give drink to my chosen people,

67. B. W. Anderson, "Exodus Typology in Second Isaiah," in *Israel's Prophetic Heritage* (New York: Harper & Brothers, 1962), 194–95. Cf. also G. von Rad, *Old Testament Theology* II (Edinburgh and London: Oliver & Boyd, 1965), 244–48.

68. This and the following two paragraphs are drawn from Scult and Patrick, *Rhetoric and Biblical Interpretation in Ancient Israel* (Oxford: Clarendon Press, 1985), 408–30.

the people whom I formed for myself
that they may recount my praise. (43:18-21)

The new exodus, like the original, is for the sake of the people who are God's witness among the nations. The nations of the world are invited to join with Israel in acknowledging YHWH (45:22-23), but they must become "offspring of Israel" (45:25) to participate in the new order.

Christians can share in the promise of the exodus only by recognizing that it was a saving event for Israel, and it is mediated through the people who observe the Passover. Paul says of the Jews: "They are Israelites, and to them belong the sonship, the glory, the covenants, the giving of the law, the worship and the promises . . ." (Rom. 9:4). These gifts of revelation are uniquely bestowed on this people, and they are maintained through the practice of Jewish people. The exodus lives as a witness and promise through the Passover. Christians are called to witness to the saving work of God in the Jewish witness to God's deliverance from Egypt.

It is indeed the calling of Christians to witness to the universal in the particular. It is our task to elucidate how the reign of God is manifested in the just and merciful demonstration of power in the deliverance of Israel. It is our task to engage in apologetics, but not by effacing the performative force of the call of Moses and the command to perform the Passover. A message of liberation from oppression, persecution, and degradation is present in the exodus, but it first of all concerns the practice of those who have been liberated: "You shall not oppress a sojourner (outsider) for you were sojourners in the land of Egypt" (Exod. 23:9, cf. 22:21).[69]

---

69. See R. K. Saelin, *The God of Israel and Christian Theology* (Minneapolis: Fortress, 1996).

3.
COMMANDING FROM
MOUNT SINAI

C AN J. L. AUSTIN'S CONCEPTION OF THE ILLOCUTIONARY FORCE OF DIS-
course be applied as fruitfully to other texts of the Hebrew Bible in
which God speaks to humans? Can the identification of divine discourse as
a particular kind of performative utterance yield any insight into what this
utterance intends to accomplish with its audience? Does it afford insight
into how it is designed to have this effect? What is the force of the utterance
for the reading audience?

Our trial text is the Ten Commandments. It is equal to any text in the
Hebrew Bible for rhetorical effectiveness, if such effectiveness is gauged by
how well it is known and how paradigmatic it is for understanding the
identity of the biblical God. If the conception of performative utterance
can comprehend the rhetorical transaction engendered by this text, its paradigmatic power allows the interpreter to impute analogous dynamics to
an unlimited number of other texts. Within the law, it has the capacity to
subsume the legal corpora under its provisions.[1]

The Ten Commandments are depicted as revelation. God speaks these
words to all Israel in the midst of a theophany. They are proclaimed in the
midst of a spectacular visual display indicating the presence of the divine
majesty. Within the Hebrew Bible, the terms for revelation refer to phenomena of this sort.[2] The text also fits a more theological definition of revelation: God communicates knowledge of his identity in setting out what
is expected of his people.[3]

---

1. The whole of the Sinaitic revelation is summed up in the Ten Commandments in
Deuteronomy 5. John Calvin works this out rather systematically—rather forced, but a sound
sense of the paradigmatic status of the Decalogue in the final form of the Pentateuch.
2. S. Talmon, "The Concept of Revelation in Biblical Times," in *Literary Studies in the
Hebrew Bible: Form and Content* (Jerusalem: Magnes, 1993), 199–204.
3. See my discussion of Wolterstorff's proposal to distinguish between divine discourse
and revelation, c. 7.

The Ten Commandments are certainly pertinent to my thesis that God's verbal communication with Israel is characteristically not of an assertatory nature, but discourse that creates in the act of speaking the knowledge to be known. They are like the call of Moses in this fundamental respect. The speaking itself is an indispensable dimension of what is revealed. On the other hand, the commandments belong to a different illocutionary category than the promise of deliverance. Promises belong to the category of "commissive," for their primary force is to commit the speaker to a particular act; commandments belong to the category of "exercitive" because they exercise authority over the addressee.

The promise of deliverance to Israel did entail a command to Moses. Indeed, God's promises invariably do entail some command, or implied obligation, on the addressee's part. The command to Moses is subordinate to the promise; one might call it instrumental in that obedience to the command contributes essentially to the fulfillment of the promise. The proclamation of the Ten Commandments is not subordinate to another action: its object is to put the obligations specified in force within the community addressed. The obligations are intended to serve a purpose: obedience that results in good for the people and its members. The illocutionary act is intended to elicit actions that are the good.

How do the Ten Commandments compare to the command to perform the Passover? Both belong to the law obligatory on all Israel; the textual audience is commanded along with the addressees within the textual world. Both acts of commanding are the object of the discourse; that is, they do not serve another performative (as the command to Moses does). The fundamental difference is that the command to perform the Passover is a scene within the exodus narrative whose object is to give the exodus narrative a performative force for the reader, whereas the transactions on Mount Sinai construct the authority of the Law-giver so that the commandments have obligatory force for the reader.[4] The Ten Commandments impose responsibilities on members of the community for the good of the community.

Prospectus. A commandment depends for its efficacy on the relationship between speaker and addressee. The speaker must have authority to govern

---

4. Perhaps this distinction seems too "fine." Let me explain: it is my judgment that the command to celebrate Passover in Exodus 12–13 is to give efficacy to the exodus rather than the story of the exodus being to give reason for the Passover. The theophany and covenant-making at Mount Horeb, on the other hand, are to construct the authority for issuing the commandments; the commandments are the "point" of the account. Passover is also commanded at Sinai (Exod. 23:15, 34:18; Lev. 23:5-8), and in this context it has a different character, namely, community construction, analogous to the Sabbath commandment.

the actions of the addressee for the utterance to be "felicitous," as the speech-act philosophers put it. On many occasions, social equals both command and obey, but only a hierarchical relationship allows for the issuance of commandments, such as prohibitions and prescriptions that are binding in perpetuity and under all conditions. The first order of business for this chapter will be to examine the Sinaitic texts, which "construct" the authority of YHWH to issue commandments to Israel and the duty of all Israelites to obey them.

The agreement of the people to do all that YHWH says (19:8) constitutes the bridge between divine discourse designed to elicit Israel's acceptance of YHWH's authority to command and the promulgation of the commandments. The pledge to obey concludes the offer of relationship (19:3-6)— meeting the condition set forth in v. 5a—and in principle puts the following commandments in force. However, the same pledge is repeated several more times and sealed with a sacrificial rite (24:3-8) after the people have heard the commandments and the code of laws mediated through Moses. In this way, the people are bound to obey YHWH not as a matter of abstract principle, but also in concrete detail.

Between the pledge to obey and the promulgation of the commandments, the people are prepared for the theophany of their sovereign, culminating in the appearance in which the commandments are spoken by God directly to the people. The depiction of theophany can also be regarded as designed to augment the authority of YHWH; it evokes the power and majesty of the Law-giver.

A complication arises after the covenant has been ratified, and Moses has returned to the mountain to receive instructions for the construction of the wilderness shrine. The people grow impatient in Moses' absence and make an image to worship (Exodus 32). The commandments have been seriously violated, breaking the "covenant" and requiring a purge of the people. Now the covenant is reinstated on a unilateral basis with different commandments (Exodus 34). This event raises some question about the status of the Ten Commandments and the terms of the original covenant.

After exploring the texts constructing the authority of YHWH, we can turn to the act of commanding. The issuance of the Ten Commandments enacts the relationship put in force by commissives, but it is a performative action with distinctive force, requiring a different type of response on the part of addressees. In other words, it creates a new dimension in the relationship between God and Israel. The force of the act is reflected in the ordering of the commandments and their augmentation by motive clauses. It requires an interpretive practice to shape the everyday life and judicial decisions of the society under YHWH's authority.

It will be obvious to the scholarly reader that I am expounding the final form of the Sinaitic narrative. This text has shaped the consciousness and interpretive practice of Jews and Christians for millennia, and nothing important to the argument would be gained by reconstructing sources. The unevenness and incoherence of the extant text clearly indicate that it is a composite text, but source critics have been singularly incapable of coming to agreement as to their delineation—one more reason to go with the final form.

The Obligation to Obey

How did Israel incur the obligation to obey YHWH? Perhaps divine authority is "by nature," which is to say, by YHWH's position in the hierarchy of being. If so, he could be compared to a parent whose authority derives from being a procreator of a child. Perhaps a hereditary monarch can also claim the authority to rule his or her kingdom by some principle of natural order.[5] On the other hand, political authority can be ascribed to some sort of contract or consent of the governed, historical or implied. In this case, authority derives from an actual or putative performative transaction.

Although the biblical narrative derives the authority of the Creator over the human race from the order of being (Genesis 1–11), it records performative transactions establishing YHWH's authority to command Israel. The premier example is the act of covenant making on Mount Sinai (in Exodus 19–20, 24, 34).

According to Exod. 19:3b-8, the people were offered a choice to accept a relationship with YHWH in which they would be set apart for him if they would acknowledge the binding authority of his will; they accept it by pledging "to do all that YHWH says" (Exod. 19:8, cf. also 24:3, 7-8). The divine offer or proposal contains two arguments with a family resemblance to the classical types of *ëthos* and advantage. The argument from *ëthos* is to demonstrate the trustworthiness and righteousness of the speaker. I think that we can regard Exod. 19:4 as an argument to the effect that YHWH is deserving of the status he is asking that Israel give him:

> You have seen what I did to the Egyptians,
> and how I bore you on eagles' wings
> and brought you to myself.

5. Cf. James Stuart (King James VI of Scotland, James I of England), "The State of the Monarchy and the Divine Right of Kings," speech at Whitehall, March 21, 1609, in *British Oration from Ethelbert to Churchill* (London: J. M. Dent, 1960), 18.

This statement is not in itself a performative utterance, but an appeal to what the addressees have experienced. They are called to witness to themselves, so to speak, as to YHWH's power and benevolence as evidenced in recent events. The recitation is an appeal to the people to regard their experiences in a certain way. A subtle coloring has been added to the recitation of his deeds: The metaphorical, "bore you on eagles' wings and brought you to myself," intimates YHWH's attitude toward this people. This type of language falls under Austin's illocutionary category of "behabitive." The audience is expected to hear an overture of affection and respond accordingly.

This approach is not the only way to view the course of events told in Exodus 14–18. The people's experience has been sufficiently ambiguous to arouse their suspicion—their murmuring—periodically and they will soon break out in overt rebellion. To accept the story as an overture to a permanent relationship, the people must resolve the ambiguity in favor of YHWH. Indeed, the acceptance of the story as an overture coincides with the acceptance of the offer and obligation of permanent relationship.

There follows a conditional promise, an offer of a relationship in which Israel will be united with YHWH in a unique relationship if it will submit to YHWH's authority:

> And now, if you will obey my voice
> and keep my covenant,
> you shall be for me, out of all peoples, a peculiar treasure,
> for the whole earth is mine.
> And you yourselves will be for me
> a kingdom of priests and a holy nation.[6]

This argument appeals to advantage. Israel will be set apart from all other peoples, honored and prized by the sovereign of the whole earth. Implicit is a promise of exclusiveness. The owner of all the earth is, by implication, free to dispose of each people as it so pleases him; it is within the prerogatives of sovereignty to set Israel apart as a *segullah*, a private royal treasure.[7] Another set of metaphors describes what that relationship will be in political terms: Israel will be a people ruled by the God of all the earth, and partake of their ruler's divine attribute of holiness. It seems clear to me that "obey[ing] my voice and keep[ing] my covenant" is simply the subjects' duty within a "holy nation": the condition and the promise converge, fit together as complementary descriptions of the same relationship.

6. I owe some of my phrasing to S. Terrien, *The Elusive Presence*, 122–23.

7. See R. B. Y. Scott, "A Kingdom of Priests, Ex. xix, 6," *OTS* 8 (1950): 213–19; J. Muilenburg, "The Form and Structure of the Covenantal Formulations," *VT* 9 (1959): 347–65.

When the people respond to the offer by pledging to obey everything YHWH says, the transaction is complete. Each party has committed itself to "do" something vis-à-vis the other. While this relationship belongs to the same category, commissive, as the promise of deliverance, it is in fact quite different. The promise of deliverance is unilateral: YHWH commits himself, Israel receives. In the covenant, each party commits itself. In the promise of deliverance, the fulfillment is a specific event that will liberate the people from their oppressive condition. It fits relatively well into Moltmann's description of divine promises that negate the negative and inaugurate a new reality.[8] The promises made in the covenant are of continuity, constancy, and begin in the present and continue on forever, or until it breaks down.[9]

Although the relationship exists in principle from this moment on, before any law has been promulgated, it is ratified after the issuance of the commandments and Covenant Code. The ratification ceremony in 24:3-8 repeats the pledge of obedience after the will of God is known, hence includes it. Rather strikingly, the concluding ritual of sprinkling sacrificial blood on the people is accompanied by words indicating that the people are claimed by God by means of the commandments and laws:

> Behold the blood of the covenant which YHWH has struck with you in accordance with all these words. (24:8)

Text and Audience. Before we proceed to an exposition of other relevant accounts, it may be worthwhile to consider how the text engages the textual audience. It is my contention that the audience is expected to recognize its obligation to obey the Ten Commandments, and that the account of covenant making is meant to persuade it of this obligation.

Jews and Christians through the centuries have taken the Decalogue to be directly addressed to them as well as to the people of the narrative world. The ten have been proclaimed in liturgies and taught in catechisms as words addressed to all people who recognize the God of Israel as their God. The fact that they were promulgated at one time and place has not been a barrier to their continuing authority, for, as the Jewish midrash says, "we all stand at the foot of Sinai."[10]

---

8. For this expression, see Moltmann's *Theology of Hope*, p. 131 below, though Moltmann is specifically characterizing prophetic eschatology.

9. One can find both in prophetic literature: Hosea names his third child "not my people" (1:8-9); Isaiah 54:4-8 assures Israel the relationship endures despite the breakdown.

10. Cf. the title of J. Plaskow's *Standing Again at Sinai: Judaism from a Feminist Perspective* (San Francisco: Harper, 1991).

The account of covenant making is designed to persuade the audience to identify with its ancestors and to affirm the ancestral decision to obligate all Israel, for all time to come, to obey YHWH. When the audience reads, "You have seen what I did to the Egyptians, and how I bore you on eagles' wings," it can confirm the allusion by recalling the narrative of Exodus 1–18; it also has its own memory of Passover celebrations to build on.

It was common during my teachers' generation of scholars to hypothesize a covenant renewal ceremony behind the account in Exodus 19–24. While that interpretation is a distinct possibility, no provision for it is made in the festival calendars of the extant text. Deuteronomy 31:9-13 commands the reading of the Deuteronomic law every seven years, but that text assumes that the covenant between YHWH and Israel, including the law, was transacted by the exodus generation once and for all.[11] Each new generation enters for itself (cf. Deut. 29:10-15), but the covenant between YHWH and Israel antedates the audience. The account of the "original" event does not require a reenactment—as the exodus does—to have its rhetorical effect.

The scholar may doubt that Exodus 19–24 reports the actual historical origin of the Ten Commandments or the covenant relationship that grounds them. Rhetorically speaking, it is not of great importance: the account itself has effected the relationship for Jewish readers for millennia. The narrative creates a community based upon promises and obligations that are chosen by it, or at least accepted by generation after generation as their own choice. Whatever the historical process that brought the narrative into being, those who participated in the process understood what they did as a free choice in response to an offer of God, and produced a narrative that involves later generations in the same choice.

Theophany

Theophany, the "appearance of God," permeates the narrative and leaves a most memorable impression of the event. One might judge theophany to be the original core tradition, and covenant and law to be later grafts; it is certainly too important to ignore.

The task of this study is the *rhetoric* of revelation, so we are not concerned with theophany per se, but with the suasive function of the descriptions of God's appearance to Israel, its representatives, and Moses. How do the depictions of God's appearance to these parties work to persuade the readers, and of what? It is one thing to witness the appearance of God in

---

11. See my *Old Testament Law* (Atlanta: John Knox Press, 1985) 235–40.

person, another to be told about one. It requires a distinctive act of imagination for readers to see God for themselves, and powerful narrative to
facilitate it.

One might expect the challenge of the authors of these descriptions to
resemble the mystic's. Mystics will tell their audience that the experience
was ineffable, and then try to describe it anyway.[12] The Exodus account,
however, does not suggest the experience of a mystic; everything is depicted in "objective" terms. The people witness a natural spectacle, their representatives and Moses also have nonvisionary visual experiences. None of
the accounts mention the ineffability of the event, but in fact describe what
was seen quite effortlessly. There is, on the other hand, much room left for
the reader to fill in.

What is the purpose the descriptions serve? How is that purpose—or
those purposes—communicated to the reader? What is the relationship of
theophanic description to the performative acts of covenant making and
promulgating commandments and law?

Finally, we must consider the rhetorical appeal of these descriptions.
What is their role in the communication of the performative transactions
to the textual audience? How does the audience know that what is reported really happened? Is that a relevant question?

The Presentation of the Theophanies. The public spectacle precedes all other
appearances of God, which seems to establish its credibility. To dramatize
the momentousness of the event, an extensive preparation is made for it.
Holy space is marked off for God to "enter," as it were, and the people must
be in a state of "purity" (Exod. 19:10-15).[13] The visual spectacle itself is of
eruptions in nature. The imagery of thunderstorm is juxtaposed to imagery
of a volcanic eruption. These displays are two of nature's most awe-inspir-
ing and overwhelming to the human witness. The text simply throws the
imagery at the reader, reproducing the unassimilated perceptions that
overload the mind in such charged situations.

Note that the theophany was granted as a result of the successful initial
negotiation of the covenant (19:3-8). Once Israel has agreed to obey
YHWH, he begins issuing directions for his appearance. Thus, the order is
not: theophany, then covenant making. The interpreter cannot say that the
people of Israel were so impressed by the theophany that they entered into
relationship with the deity who appeared to them. Rather, theophany is

---

12. This is actually an effective way of communicating evocatively: it was like this but so
much more.

13. Similar prescriptions are reiterated after (vv. 20b-25) the depiction of the public spectacle (vv. 16-20a); it is hard to say what their purpose is.

granted to the people as a result of their initial agreement, and it adds force to a relationship already in force in principle.[14]

The proclamation of law takes place within the public spectacle. According to the extant text, God speaks from heaven, the content of which was the Ten Commandments (read 19:16-20a, 20:1-17, 22). Admittedly, the sequence is rather clumsy, and the people's response to hearing the commandments would be more appropriate to incoherent sound and visual display (20:18-20). The extant text is certainly not easy to read in a straightforward sequential manner. Nonetheless, the purpose statement delivered by Moses—"in order that fear of him will be upon your faces so that you will not sin" (20:20)—does subordinate the theophany to the relationship created by the issuance of commandments.

After the promulgation of the Book of the Covenant (20:22—23:33), several actions show the force of ratifying the covenant. One of these depicts a theophany witnessed by representatives of the people—Moses, Aaron, Nadab and Abihu, and seventy elders. The scene is different from the public spectacle, it is up on the mountain (24:1-2). They will be close to God, so to speak, and what is seen is of a different order. The select party is said to have "seen/beheld the God of Israel," and they "ate and drank" (vv. 10, 11). Presumably the representatives were granted an "audience" with God in which he was visible in some bodily form. The description is careful, however, not to describe the divine visage, but only the mysterious brilliant crystalline pavement under his feet. The wording suggests, first of all, that the humans lowered their eyes in humility. By averting a look at the divine bodily shape, the reader feels his presence all the more. Unlike the public spectacle, no words are exchanged; the experience is of silent presence, the "ineffable" in dramatic form.

The Purposes of the Theophanies. The narrative provides interpretations of why God appeared to his people and its representatives in purpose clauses scattered throughout the text. The first of these is found in 19:9. YHWH tells Moses beforehand that "I am coming to you in thick cloud, that the people may hear when I speak to you, and may believe you forever." This rationale is striking. The theophany itself dwarfs all that is human, but it is to have the paradoxical effect of enhancing the authority of Moses. The theophany itself demonstrates the reality of the one who is hidden, and yet it is to bestow majesty on the visible agent.

---

14. The text disconfirms Terrien's observations, *Elusive Presence*, 121, 130, that theophany is prior to covenant. Of course, one can argue that this is true in a more fundamental sense.

While the theophany enhances Moses' authority, it is not for his benefit. In the public spectacle and the sacred meal of the elders, nothing is said of Moses' experience. He becomes a part of the spectacle in 19:19: "Moses spoke and God answered him in thunder." When Moses ascends the mountain to receive further revelation, he enters into a mysterious cloud glowing with the glory of God (24:15-18); the depiction is from the point of view of onlookers. When Moses spoke with YHWH in the Tent of Meeting, the people saw a "pillar of cloud" descend to the tent and they prostrated themselves (33:9-10). In all these cases, the theophany is viewed by the people, and the force of it is to enhance Moses' authority as YHWH's spokesman.

Numerous critical commentators have argued that the enhancement of Moses' authority was an apologetic for the political or religious hierarchy: the question is, who or what does Moses "stand for"? If one looks at the offices in Israel, he is most often linked with the prophet, and most resembles one. He is not regarded as a priest, though he is said to be from the tribe of Levi (Exod. 6:20).[15] Though he plays the political role of a ruler, he is clearly distinguished from kings.[16] He is, on the other hand, called a prophet and speaks as a prophet to the pharaoh (Exod. 5:1, 7:7, etc.).[17] In the conflict with Miriam (and Aaron), he is distinguished from prophets (Numbers 12) by the directness of his access to God; in Deut. 18:15-22, he is considered to be the prototype of the prophets. One might say that Moses is a prophet to the ultimate degree. The force of the enhancement of Mosaic authority in the narratives may be designed to support the authority of prophets, or to set apart the Mosaic tradition as superior to the (later) prophets. The latter seems to be the point of Numbers 12, the former of Deut. 18:15-22.

In Exod. 20:18-20, we have an account of the people "electing" Moses to the office of mediator. This event follows the theophanic proclamation of the Ten Commandments. The people cannot bear direct communication from God; they are willing, even eager, to hear it through a human messenger. Moses responds by interpreting the theophanic display as a "teaching" to the people: "God has come in order to test you," and "in order that fear of him will be upon your faces so that you will not sin" (20:20). What exactly is meant by "testing" (nsh) is hard to say; nothing in the situation suggests a moral trial, and they "fail" the test of courage. Perhaps it is a matter of "toughening" their wills, empowering them to do what they know they are supposed to do. In any case, God is stamping an impression on

15. B. S. Childs, *Exodus*, 351–60, finds both priestly and prophetic characteristics in the Mosaic "office." One maverick tradition in Judges, 18:30, traces a priestly line to Moses.

16. Above all, in Deut. 17:14-20.

17. For some reason, he does not use the messenger formula in messages to his own people.

Israelite consciousness: his power is fear-inspiring, probably in the sense that Rudolf Otto uses the term, namely, a numinous dread or awe in the face of majesty.[18]

Another purpose clause is added, "that you will not sin." It would suggest that one learns to fear divine punishment. However, one should not narrow the majesty of the Law-giver to his power to punish; the law itself must be taken as good and right, and holy, and its sanctions only act as the earnest defense of its honor.

The purpose of the theophany to the representatives of the people is of a different order. There is no purpose clause in the pericope, but there is the statement that God "did not lay his hand on the chief men of the people of Israel" (24:11a). In the background is the danger that "to see God is to die." Thus, it was an act of grace to these humans to see God and come to no harm. It is God's accessibility that is depicted. One is reminded of the declaration God makes to Moses regarding his request for a private theophany: "I will make all my goodness pass before you, and will proclaim before you my name YHWH; I will be gracious to whom I will be gracious, and will show mercy on whom I will show mercy." However, Moses does not get to see what these representatives see (33:20-23).

The Appeal of Theophany. It is not accidental that Samuel Terrien treats the revelation to the people of Israel at Mount Sinai in the same chapter as he treats the call of Moses. Aside from the common venue, the two events offer a convergence in the representation of God's presence. Both represent paradigmatic instances of the encounter with the holy as described by Rudolf Otto.[19] As such, it appeals to a universal kind of human experience to persuade its audience. As Terrien says, "Few pages in the literature of mankind compare to this awesome description of an encounter between God and man. Yet, mountains have played a significant part in most religions."[20] He could have gone on to say that the appearance of deities to humans on mountains has played a significant part.

When I speak of the "universal," I am not saying that all humans experience the phenomenon or that the narrative presentation is simply a conglomeration of typical motifs. Regarding the first, Otto insists that the experience of the holy is an extraordinary state of consciousness, and that some people are more attuned to it, so to speak, than others: it is universal in the sense that the same phenomenological features are found in religions all over the world, and even secular individuals have some sense of the

18. R. Otto, *Idea of the Holy*, 13–23.
19. Ibid., 75–76.
20. Terrien, *Elusive Presence*, 120.

experience evoked by the words.[21] A narrative of such an experience can have distinctive features, indeed, it can have the specificity of a unique, unrepeatable historical event. It attains universality by its power to evoke in the audience its numinous feeling.

The text evokes the holy in the reading audience to give the illocutionary actions of covenant making and command affective power. While the divine imperative itself is encounter with the transcendent, it needs an "objective correlative," so to speak, an image that confirms the divine origin of the imperative. The readers "know" that this really happened because we ourselves experience it in the reading.

Rebellion and Restoration

The story of Sinai does not end in Exodus 24, and a final-form exposition would be remiss to stop there. In particular, Exodus 32 records a violation of the first and/or second commandments, resulting in a dissolution of the covenant. The relationship is restored on a new basis, with another Decalogue, in Exodus 33–34. Perhaps everything that has been said is nullified. To avoid this conclusion, it will be necessary to devise a reading strategy that incorporates the breaking and remaking of the covenant in a framework that preserves the teaching of the earlier portions of the text.

Until recently, critical scholarship would take recourse to source divisions and redaction to solve the confusion produced by Exodus 32–34. If one desires narrative coherence and consistent ideological viewpoints, one must deconstruct the composite account of the received text and reconstruct the works from which it was assembled. There was virtual consensus that Exodus 19–24 and 32–34 could be distinguished from the revelation and construction of the portable sanctuary (Exodus 25–31, 35–40); the latter could easily be identified by vocabulary, style, narrative sequence, and ideology as Priestly (P).[22] The non-Priestly material was more of a challenge, and critical scholars have never arrived at a broad consensus on the reconstruction of sources and how they were edited.[23]

The same phenomena that invite and undo source analysis of Exodus 19–24, 32–34 confront the effort to interpret the extant form of the narra-

---

21. R. Otto, *Idea of the Holy*, 112–16.

22. There are a few verses in Exodus 19–24, 32–34 that belong to P, for example,19:1-2, 24:15-18; the last verse of Exodus 31 belongs to the following chapter, probably associated with 24:12-14.

23. Childs, *Exodus*, 344–51, surveys the attempts to break chapter 19 into sources; 499–502, chapter 24; 584–86, chapter 33; 604–61, chapter 34. My own proposal, published under the title, "The Covenant Code Source," in *VT* 27 (1976): 145–57, receives no mention.

tive, only the kind of explanation must be different. How do we find coherence in a narrative sequence that is frequently interrupted, tells several different versions of what appears to be the same act, and turns back on itself to undercut what has been said? The "wedge issue," I believe, is how to construe the replacement of one Decalogue with another. The tablets of the first Decalogue (20:2-17, 24:12-14, 31:18) were destroyed to void the covenant implemented (32:19-20),[24] and a second Decalogue (34:1) was proclaimed (34:10-26) and written down (34:27-28).[25] Is the second Decalogue the one in force, and the first voided? This conclusion might seem the obvious one, but in fact it is highly improbable. The first is quoted in prime position (despite the fact that its written form was purportedly destroyed). Deuteronomy 5 reproduces the first (with relatively slight differences) when it recalls the revelation at Horeb; Deut. 10:2-5 indicates that the new set of tablets has the same words as the first. Jews and Christians have uniformly taken the first Decalogue as the summary of God's will for believers. The narrative cannot be and has not been read sequentially in the case of the Decalogue.

Does the same ambiguity present itself in the case of the performative transaction of covenant making? Rolf Rendtorff, who attempts to rethink Old Testament interpretation and theology within a canonical context, takes the position that the reestablished covenant replaces the original. In the course of an argument calling attention to a certain parallelism between the primeval history and Sinai, he states:

> Just as humanity no longer lives within the original creation, but in a restored one whose existence is guaranteed by God's grace, so also Israel no longer lives within the first covenant, but in a reestablished one guaranteed by God's grace. . . . In this (second) covenant the sinfulness of humanity or Israel is, so to speak, taken for granted. In other words, humanity's or Israel's sin no longer can endanger the very existence of the creation or the covenant because God himself guarantees its continuation, despite human sin, because of his grace.[26]

Rendtorff only qualifies this position by the laconic, "Of course, a number of diachronic problems remain."[27]

24. So R. Rendtorff, *Canon and Theology: Overtures to an Old Testament Theology*, OBT (Minneapolis: Fortress, 1993), 130; also G. W. Coats, *Rebellion in the Wilderness* (Nashville: Abingdon, 1968), 188–89.
25. In contradiction to 34:1, where YHWH says he will do the writing, as does 31:18.
26. Rendtorff, *Canon and Theology*, 131.
27. Ibid., 130.

Is there another way to read Exodus 19–34? My solution is to read the narrative as constructing a picture and then *superimposing* other pictures on it. It is, of course, a metaphor. What I mean by it is that the text sets out its primary story—Exod. 19:1—20:21 (20:22—23:19 is incorporated), 24:1-11—and then supplements it with other narratives, some of which simply add to the agenda, as Exodus 25–31, 35–40 do,[28] or "qualify" the primary story, as Exodus 32, 33:12—34:35 do. In the case of the Ten Commandments, the qualification is minimal. The second Decalogue—the so-called cultic Decalogue—really doesn't replace the first, it acts as a stand-in for the narrative of restoration. The text of the first remained fixed in the memory and imagination of the interpretive communities, reinforced by Deuteronomy. The actual text of the "second Decalogue" fades into the tradition of Sinaitic law, aided perhaps by the parallel at the end of the Book of the Covenant (23:10-19, 20-33).

The account of covenant making in Exodus 34 could be said to qualify the rituals of Exodus 19 and 24. In the primary story, the people are offered a relationship, supported by the recitation of YHWH's deed of deliverance, and they accept the offer by pledging to obey YHWH (19:3-8). After the proclamation of the Ten Commandments and promulgation of the Book of the Covenant, the people reaffirm their pledge in a ratification ceremony. The covenant is *given* its *performative force* by a thorough-going *transaction* (Exod. 19:3-8, 24:3-8). The covenant is *restored* by a *unilateral act* of YHWH (34:10) in response to the pleas of his servant and mediator, Moses (32:11-15, 33:12-16, 34:8-9). The narrative ends not with a ratification ritual, but with a story whose force is to enhance Moses' authority (34:29-35).

Is the audience expected to forget the original transaction, in which its ancestors played an active part, and accept the covenant on the basis of YHWH's unilateral act? Is it expected to acquiesce in the demands because YHWH promises to perform marvels in their its (34:10)? A straightforward sequential reading would suggest that, but that is not the way it has been read because it is not the way the text is designed to impact the audience. Exodus 32–34 is not intended to replace the initial account, but to supplement it. When the people broke the covenant, the punishment would "logically" be destruction (32:11ff.). When they are spared, the implication is that the initial relationship would be restored by an act of divine grace. The restoration could not be mutual because Israel had lost its rights, so to speak; the aggrieved party had to restore the covenant unilaterally. It was,

---

28. These chapters do not depict either covenant making or the proclamation of a Decalogue; consequently, they pose no serious contradictions to the primary story. They can be left out of the study of the rhetoric of the Ten Commandments.

however, the original covenant that was restored, now with the qualification that God "guarantees" it through his forgiveness.

Commanding

The people's pledge to do what the Lord says completes the "commissive" transaction and "invites," let us say, its implementation in an "exercitive." The relationship now in force could not function without YHWH's
commanding; it is incomplete in itself. However, there are several different
ways YHWH could exercise his authority over Israel. He could still give
commands on an ad hoc basis, as he has—with the exception of Passover
and related prescriptions in Exodus 12–13—up till now.[29] He might adopt
the legal traditions of the cultural environment and amend them to suit his
particular conception of justice and right.[30] The act of issuing a set of commandments encompassing the life of the people involves a decision as to
what sort of exercitive would implement the relationship most effectively.

The focus of this monograph is not on the content of the "revelation,"
but on the transaction between divine speaker and human addressees within the textual word and between text and reading audience. We will examine the text of the Ten Commandments for its rhetoric, that is, what sort of
illocutionary force it has, how it is designed to accomplish this object, and
what sort of response it seeks to elicit. Before that, however, it will be worth
our while to explore the dynamics of transactions involving commanding.

Why distinguish between the act of commanding and the commandments promulgated in the act? Speech-act philosophers distinguish
between the propositional content of an utterance, called its "locutionary"
force by Austin, and the act of commanding it. The propositional content
can be the subject of different illocutionary acts; indeed, sometimes the
wording of an utterance leaves it unclear as to its illocutionary force. Is a
sign reading "no smoking" a command, request, warning, or descriptive
statement? Is it different from "smoking is not permitted"? From "thank
you for not smoking"?

One still might wonder whether much can be learned from thinking
about the action apart from the content. Perhaps certain features of the
transaction of commanding belong to the transaction per se, without considering the content. Perhaps there is a correlation between what is to be
communicated and how it is communicated. We could call such analysis a
"phenomenology" of commanding.

29. Actually, there is an odd discrepancy in Exod. 15:25: "There he made for them a statute
and an ordinance and there he proved them."
30. In fact, that is probably the origin of the Book of the Covenant.

The next section will reflect on the range of exercitive actions of a commanding sort. The object is to locate the kind of action performed in the issuance of the Ten Commandments in relation to actions of a similar type. What I am offering does not amount to a phenomenology of commanding, but a phenomenological description of promulgating commandments by comparison with other acts of commanding. A full-scale phenomenology would examine each subtype in its own right, and cover the whole range systematically.

The phenomenological description of issuing commandments will be followed up with a consideration of how ascribing commandments to God affects the transaction.

Different Kinds of Exercitives. We are concerned with actions performed by speakers (or writers), that intend to obligate the addressee to do or refrain from doing something. We have already distinguished the propositional content of a command from its illocutionary force. We should now remind ourselves that illocutionary force is not to be identified with the effect the utterance has on the addressee. The speaker seeks to "cause" the addressee to do something, to act in a certain way. However, the speaker does not have causal power over the addressee. The object of discourse is, thus, to put the addressee under obligation and count on his moral commitment to fulfill obligations to elicit compliance.

While a command imposes obligations—assuming the authority of the speaker over the addressee—the speaker is well advised to formulate it as persuasively as possible or at least proportionate to the degree of expected resistance. This presentation begins with etiquette, may include reasons and appeals to the relationship, and might promise or warn of sanctions. Under certain circumstances, evocations of authority itself are the most effective, depending upon the relationship between speaker and addressee.

Commanding is extremely sensitive to the relationship of speaker and addressee.[31] Equals do not command each other. The proper mode of approaching an equal (or superior) is to request, often with a reason for not doing the act oneself. One of the signs of the pervasiveness of modern egalitarian thinking is that husbands do not command their wives, as once was the practice.[32] It would be counterproductive in most marriages now. This generalization is not to say that equals can never legitimately com-

---

31. I am describing the normal practices of a discourse community, not violations. It may be that my descriptions are not as generally applicable as I think they are; I offer them only to elicit the reader's reflection and modification.

32. Traditional liturgies quoted Col. 3:18, "Wives, be in subjection to your husbands. . . ."

mand each other. An emergency grants one temporary authority to demand help. One has the right to give certain stipulations about the use of a gift. In an interpersonal crisis, one party may issue an "ultimatum." And so forth.

But, in general, commands belong to relationships of a hierarchical character. The most obvious, and most common, is that of ownership or proprietorship: owners of property govern use. Society does recognize many other forms of temporary or limited authority in order that society members can pursue legitimate and productive activities. Drivers doing some operations are granted "right of way," and others are required to yield. Public officials have the authority to regulate traffic flow on public thoroughfares. Whenever someone has authority over some institution, practice, or property, others are duty-bound to observe rules and, on occasion, commands.

Authority is generally restricted in its authorization. The phone company can require users to follow certain procedures and pay for services, but it cannot govern what is said over its lines.[33] A public school can govern the behavior and activities of students, including restricting admission, but it cannot prohibit nondisruptive expression of opinion. Authority, thus, is related to the mission an institution serves and its efficient operation. It does not extend, especially in our individualistic culture, to forming and reforming the character of those who come under its authority.

Institutions with restricted authority do not, except under special circumstances, have the authority to issue commandments, because commandments are meant to form character. Commandments should be distinguished from commands, rules, laws, and requests, petitions, and the like. A commandment can be defined as a directly addressed injunction concerning matters of moral gravity, binding under all relevant conditions and for an unlimited duration. To avoid getting bogged down in definitions, let us simply note that a commandment is a statement with the word *ought* or *ought not* or some comparable expression, which the addressee should recognize as having the force of declaring an action right or wrong, good or evil. To violate the injunction is not just inexpedient, but to commit an evil, to betray, to dishonor, to harm, and so on. A commandment may, of course, be ill-advised, prejudiced, or malicious from the point of view of a sound judge, but the speaker intends to prescribe intrinsically good actions and prohibit intrinsically evil, harmful ones.

A commandment can also be described as unconditional. I am distinguishing it from a command, which strictly speaking is for a particular

---

33. Except when law prohibits certain activities, such as soliciting for illegal activities. Then the phone company is acting as an agency of government.

action by a specified addressee for one time only.[34] The term *rule* is used for a more general stipulation of what to do or refrain from doing, and commandments are often dubbed *rules of conduct*. In a sense, that label is accurate, but a rule does not imply any moral obligation to the one who issued it, whereas a personally addressed commandment certainly does. A commandment is, we might say, a rule of conduct that imposes an obligation on the addressee to the speaker.

A commandment not only defines the status of the addressee vis-à-vis the speaker, namely, responsibility to the speaker for the specified conduct, but the status of the speaker vis-à-vis the addressee. The speaker takes responsibility for the addressee's conduct. In doing so, the speaker is expressing explicit concern for the addressee's welfare. Whatever the private motives the speaker may have, officially and publicly the speaker expresses the desire that the addressee act in the specified way.[35] Finally, assuming that a commandment concerns a matter of moral gravity, the speaker obligates herself to the same conduct, allowing for the differences in position.[36]

Because the issuance of commandments seeks not only to obligate the addressees to specified conduct, but to motivate them to act accordingly, the illocutionary act has a rhetorical dimension. The speaker seeks to persuade. The apodictic style of the biblical commandments, and numerous imitations through the centuries, is itself a potent form of persuasion. This style does not preclude supporting reasons. Some "motive clauses" explain why the action is right or wrong, perhaps to elicit imaginative identification with the one protected; others promise rewards or threaten punishment. The transaction between speaker and addressees in commanding assumes that the speaker intends the good for the addressee, and therefore reasons do not erode but enhance the authority of the speaker.[37]

---

34. Admittedly, it is often used more loosely, but seldom with the weight that I am giving a commandment.

35. This is tricky area, but I would maintain that one takes a commandment as a prima facie revelation of the speaker's subjectivity.

36. Some commandments enjoin deference to authority—to the speaker—which could not be commanded of the speaker; cf. Wolterstorff, *Divine Discourse*, 82–85, 108–9, 110–13. In societies that recognize caste duties, members of one caste might command a member of another to abide by caste-specific duties. The self-involvement would be the implied "and I will abide by mine."

37. One would have to qualify this in several ways. The commandment itself must retain its forceful formulation, and reasons would have to retain the same authoritative "voice." An essay on the subject would not do: the obedience of the addressee then would depend on the rational force of the argument. Proverbs represent an instructive comparison to commandments: they are not forceful statements that put the addressee under obligation to a speaker; they offer reasons for an action or virtue.

The philosophical tradition has not been kind to commandments in ethics. Leaving aside the divine command tradition, philosophers have sought to "ground" the rightness of an act in rational principles or values. The propositional content of a command is to be assessed apart from the authority of the speaker; rightness is in some sense an inherent property of the act.[38] The illocutionary force of a commandment does not alter the rightness or wrongness of what is commanded, though it might have a functional or motivational role to play.[39]

If a commandment is going to have the force of creating obligation, autonomous philosophical reason must be significantly qualified. The addressee of a commandment must acknowledge the obligation apart from his rational (or emotional) judgment as to its rightness and wisdom. The addressee must agree that he owes it to the speaker whether or not it matches the addressee's own convictions. The addressee's task is to understand the rationale of the commandment and how it should be applied. If these reasons still do not appear to be justified, the addressee must admit that there is a conflict of obligations: one's "conscience" does not nullify the obligation to the speaker, but creates a conflict of obligations.

More often than not, the wisdom and rightness of the commandment depend upon how it is to be applied. As the proverb goes, "the devil is in the details." The speaker may be consulted, but an answer would be something on the order of a new commandment, or perhaps a command regarding a particular case. Then the addressee has to reason about the congruence. Commandments do not interpret themselves, but authorize the addressee to apply them; the addressee is not only responsible to the speaker for obeying, but also for applying them wisely and justly. This double responsibility nurtures the formation of strong moral character.

Only a few hierarchical relationships have the authority to form character, hence, to issue commandments. In classical theological tradition, parents were given primary responsibility for their children's character, the state the citizen's, and the church the prospective citizens of the city of God. Parents, for example, had primary responsibility for forming character in the formative years. The baptismal vow still imposes that responsibility on parents.[40] Schoolteachers and other members of the society,

---

38. That is what I take to be the direction of Socrates' argument in the dialog *Euthyphro.* Kant makes autonomy of moral judgment a criterion of ethics: see his *Fundamental Principles of the Metaphysics of Morals,* 3. Of course, by no means do all philosophers fit this description.

39. By functional, I mean that an authority can allocate responsibilities to different persons in a corporate setting. As for motivation, a command may lend to what is commanded a sense of personal obligation to the speaker.

40. The Lutheran baptismal liturgy asks parents to vow to teach their child "the Lord's Prayer, the Creed, and the Ten Commandments" (*LBW* [1978], 121).

particularly those in the church, were to reinforce parental nurturing. As parental authority declined, civil authorities and the church assumed primary responsibility. This whole network of hierarchies has so broken down under the pressure of democratic conceptions of equality and individual rights that it is hard to say whether anyone has the authority to issue commandments that bind one for life to a particular quality of character.

God's Commanding. Commandments seem to be irresistibly drawn toward God as speaker. It is as though God were exercising gravitational pull. Parents are the source of a person's first encounter with unconditional claims, and responsibility to one's parents is inscribed deeply on one's conscience for life. In societies where extended families are alive and well, responsibility to grandparents and, to a lesser degree, aunts and uncles reinforces parental authority and at the same time represents the obligations of citizenship. There are, nonetheless, limits on parental authority and it declines as children reach adulthood. It is not, thus, accidental that biblical law has ascribed parental authority to God's "deputation," so to speak, and thereby anchored personal obligation for obedience in a enduring relationship.[41] Even during a child's formative years, parents need authority for their character-forming commandments stronger than their relationship can sustain, one which can resist outside influences and compensate for their own shortcomings. Once children reach adulthood, wisdom dictates releasing them to their own judgments. Ideally, their sense of obligation to God comes to bear their sense of obligation to parents.

The skeptic is bound to ask, how can God speak? Are we alleging some unheard of miracle? Well, Exod. 20:1 does say that God spoke these words directly to Israel. Of course, the reader of the narrative might raise a question as to whether the commandments really came from God. A critical reader of our era is likely to ascribe them to human authors. God is a character of the biblical narrative, just as Moses and the Israelites were; what he says and does are the product of literary art.

In a sense, this objection is beside the point. The author depicts God so that the "character" makes claims on the reader. The text is designed to persuade readers that in this "character" they meet the living God. The readers who are so persuaded would as a matter of course accept God's exercise of authority.

---

41. Since E. S. Gerstenberger's *Wesen und Herkunft des "apodiktishen Rechts"*: WMANT 20 (Neukirchen-Vluyn: Neukirchener., 1965), many scholars have derived at least the "second table" of the Decalogue from clan ethos. Could well be. That would recapitulate the "logical" development I am describing.

In another sense, the objection does have force. How can humans presume to render God as a character to be believed and obeyed? By their very nature, performatives have to have YHWH's authority behind them. Yet at some point in the formation of the tradition, someone placed these words in YHWH's mouth.

I suggest the following schematic scenario. The author would have been deeply steeped in Yahwistic tradition and would "know" YHWH's identity by intimate acquaintance in study and worship. This knowledge of YHWH's identity would give the author an intuitive sense of what is fitting for YHWH to say and do in any given situation. It would set the parameters of what could be said. Yet, something more must prompt the formulation of a performative utterance, especially one with the import of the Ten Commandments. Here we must speak of the "leap," when the author felt addressed and communicated that encounter to the audience.[42]

In a sense, I am suggesting that what lies before the text—the performative transaction depicted in it and engendered in the audience, stands behind it. The performatives require a response of trust and obedience on the part of the audience; the author of the performative account must have experienced something similar.

The Force of God's Commandments. The dynamic of issuing commandments described in the last section applies to God and the Israelite addressees. Obviously the divine commandment is intended to obligate the addressee to the divine Law-giver. Indeed, one of the "functions" of the Ten Commandments is to bring every Israelite into an immediate relationship with the community's focus of loyalty and locus of authority. When the people pledge to obey everything the Lord commands, they make a collective decision; it does not engender a personal relationship between God and the individual Israelite. The Ten Commandments address the people distributively, imposing personal responsibility to the Law-giver for obedience to each injunction.

---

42. I have been treating the "authors" as though they were apolitical oracles of tradition. The rhetorical urgency of the literature, however, suggests the opposite. Whatever the exact public positions—and in this respect they were quite successful in concealment—they were political actors, seeking to unite and maintain a people. Yahwistic religion as embodied in its literature was political, legal, and social as well as cultic and agricultural. Undoubtedly the formulation of many performative transactions originated in public acts, then entered the literature. And the publication of the literature would have been a political act—most notoriously in the case of Deuteronomy. So when we speak of a performative act, we are first of all speaking of one in the public—national, regional, or city—arena. There was no substantial dichotomy between narrative world and the "real world" of the audience until the text moved toward canonization.

The commandments clearly are intended to define right and wrong, good and evil, for the addressee. They are formulated for the whole of life, to be obeyed under all conditions from the beginning until the end. They express God's concern for the welfare of the people, both individually and collectively, and imply the ethical norms God exemplifies as well as requires.[43]

The Commandments

Two slightly variant versions of the Ten Commandments can be found in Exod. 20:1-17 and Deut. 5:6-21. The latter is said to be the same as the former, which would suggest that the editors did not consider the different wording to be of any substance, and for a final form reading of Scripture that should encourage us not to be too "literalistic." That is, by communicating two slightly variant versions, the Scripture gives the reader "space" for interpretation.

A text of this magnitude confronts the exegete with the question, what can I say about this text that has not already been said? One must avoid not only the clichés but the impulse to say something new. Sound exegesis synthesizes what an attentive reader already knows in a configuration that elicits insight into what the text is getting at and why its meaning is important. It *is* worthwhile to read against the grain of expectations, not because such expectations are misleading but because readers often miss other levels, so to speak, of the text's communication. The natural tendency of readers of the Ten Commandments is to think about the actions and practices the commandments cover and the reasoning that may lie behind them. What if we bracketed out this inquiry into content and meditated on the text as a communication in its own right? Let's take it as a summary of what it means to belong to YHWH, the God of Israel.

Our object is to decipher the way the text is shaping the consciousness of the reader, how it is imposing an identity on the community that recognizes the authority of this God. This way of stating it is, to be sure, a modern framing of what rhetoric is about. We are engaged in a kind of "meta-thinking," reflection on what is happening between text and audience as the audience engages in the interpretation of the text. Whether meta-thinking is a legitimate practice for scholarly interpreters to undertake will have to be judged by another level of meta-thinking.

---

43. See Wolterstorff's interesting discussion of a way to ascribe obligations to God: *Divine Discourse*, 110–13.

How should we go about our "meta-thinking"? We can begin by attending to the structuring of the text—the ordering of provisions, the distribution of motive clauses, the variation of stylistic features, and reference (to other texts and to the world outside textuality). One of the clues to the rhetoric of this text is the areas where religious communities differ; the fact that the commandments are counted differently indicates a "mixture" of textual signals, with different communities giving greater weight to different signals. Beyond the structuring of the text, our inquiry into its rhetoric will consider the transaction the text is designed to engender and the community it is designed to create or shape.[44]

I propose the following hypothesis: an analogy can be made between the act of commanding the Ten Commandments and what is commanded. The first prohibition has the force, within the text, of saying, "obey only me." That gives all the commandments that follow unconditional claims. This implication is made explicit in the motive clause that concludes the first unit: YHWH will stick by all those who love him *and keep his commandments*. All the other commandments have, thus, been made ways of fulfilling the "first" commandment, ways of loving God.

Numbering. While all religious traditions find *ten* commandments between Exod. 20:2 and 20:17, Jews and the different Christian traditions number the commandments differently. All the differences derive from how to number vv. 2-6: Does v. 2 belong to the commandments or form an introduction? Does v. 4 constitute a separate commandment or is it an explication of v. 3? Should v. 5a be counted another commandment? If it is an explication of vv. 3 and 4, does it regard these verses as one or two commandments? What commandment are the motive clauses in vv. 5b-6 supporting or explicating?

One's answer to these questions will not only decide how to number them, but involve the interpreter in a particular construal of their meaning. If one is going strictly by "grammar," so to speak, one faces three prohibitions in these verses. No tradition, however, counts v. 5a as a separate commandment; it has a pronoun ("them"), which subordinates it to a previous statement. If one is attending to the practices that are proscribed, v. 4 is logically different from v. 3: "recognizing" another God than YHWH is different from "making" images. One could honor a deity

---

44. *Create* and *shape* are two aspects of the same event: communities actually come into being by particular actions, and those actions may retain illocutionary force as long as the community exists. On the other hand, no community comes into existence ex nihilo; there was a nascent community before, or at least language and culture that must be shaped to make community.

without having an image of that deity; one could make an image of YHWH. It is v. 5a that introduces ambiguity: does the pronoun refer back to the *elohim* (gods) in v. 3 or the cosmological entities in v. 4? Although it is customary to think of "bowing down" as a gesture of worship before an image, it is used of other deities as well (see in Exod. 34:14 a parallel version of the "first commandment"). Moreover, the "jealousy" of YHWH (v. 5b) concerns his claim of exclusive recognition; only if images are implicitly identified with the *elohim* in v. 3 would they arouse divine jealousy.

The wording of this unit is in the process of fusing two commandments, and the interpreter must decide whether to follow through on the fusion or not. Jewish tradition adds another twist: it sets off the "theophanic formula"[45] or "self-introduction"[46] or "historical prolog"[47] in v. 2 as a commandment in its own right. Because that tradition uses the textual term, *debarim*, "words," rather than "commandments" for the Decalogue, one cannot object that v. 2 is an indicative statement. A case might be made on the basis of the pronoun in v. 3—"me"—which refers back to the speaker, that vv. 2 and 3 constitute one commandment.

If the interpreter construes vv. 2-6 (or 3-6) as one commandment, another one has to be found to add up to ten. The only feasible candidate is the last—v. 17. Coveting is prohibited twice in a kind of poetic parallelism: Do not covet your neighbor's x, do not covet your neighbor's y, z, or anything else.[48] Finding two commandments, or words, here is a bit forced, which is an additional reason to give the prohibition of images a number.[49]

The Chief Commandment. Exodus 20:2-6 constitutes a unit—whether one counts one or two commandments. Moreover, this unit is the hermeneutical key, so to speak, of the Decalogue. Let's examine its structure closely, recalling what we have already turned up and then considering its relationships with other parts of the text.

As the Jewish tradition recognizes, the prohibition in v. 3 refers back to v. 2. No other commandment has that internal reference to v. 2. Thus, while v. 2 clearly functions to introduce the speaker of all ten, it does "fuse" with

45. J. K. Kuntz, *The Self-Revelation of God* (Philadelphia: Westminster, 1967), 89–91.

46. W. Zimmerli, "Ich bin Jahwe," reprinted in *Gottes Offenbarung: Gesammelte Aufsätze*; Th. B. 19 (Munich: Chr. Kaiser, 1963), 11–40. [ET = I am Yahweh," in *I Am Yahweh* (Atlanta: John Knox, 1982).

47. G. E. Mendenhall, *Law and Covenant in Israel and the Ancient Near East* (Pittsburgh: Biblical Colloquium, 1955), 32, 35–38.

48. "X" is "house" in Exod. 20:17, "wife" in Deut. 5:21.

49. Although I recognize that there is no "right" numbering of the commandments, I find the following to be the most useful for thinking about the topics and their history: v. 2 a self-introduction of the speaker, v. 3 the first commandment, v. 4 the second, v. 7 the third, and so on, and v. 17 the tenth.

v. 3 in a special way. The God who has delivered Israel from Egyptian slavery claims exclusive recognition from the beneficiaries. Israel's identity is
"enfolded" in YHWH's, so to speak. It means, given the performative force
of the text for the reading audience, "our" identity is enfolded in YHWH's.
The "gift" of belonging to the people redeemed by YHWH entails recognizing him alone as our God.

Verse 3 as a prohibition covers any cultic or quasi-cultic action. Verse 5a
explicates that aspect; the same application is found in 34:14; sacrifice is
covered in 22:20; invoking deities in 23:13. And so forth. But note, v. 5a also
mentions "serve them." Obedience is the issue internal to the Ten Commandments. The wording of v. 3 is comprehensive, "there shall not be to
you any gods before me." It covers authority as well as honor. Within the
Ten Commandments, it eliminates competitors: YHWH is your only
authority; no other deity has any claim on you.[50]

Verse 4 is independent of v. 3, but has been brought together with it by
v. 5. There is one grammatical link as well: both v. 3 and 4 have a reflexive
following the verb. The prohibition itself has an interesting ambiguity: Is it
the "making of an image" that is condemned, or worshiping a creature (by
way of an image)? When v. 5a is thrown in—"bowing down to them"—we
have an additional ambiguity: Is it making an image or worshiping it that
is proscribed? While one might say that this is too fine a set of distinctions,
in fact the religious traditions have moved in quite different ways simply by
construing different reasons for the prohibition. Orthodox, Roman
Catholic, and Reformed Protestant Christians derive radically different
practices from this very text. Within the history of Judaism, applications
have varied widely, as an examination of the iconic richness of the Hellenistic synagogues demonstrates.

Verse 5ab changes the import of v. 4, making it a philosophical critique
of the gods. That is, with the fusion of vv. 3 and 4, the *elohim* are identified
as images made in the likeness of creatures. YHWH competes for Israel's
loyalty not with other deities, but with lesser powers that humans make
into deities by making images of them and worshiping the images.

Why does YHWH insist on the exclusive loyalty of his people? The
answer is a metaphor: YHWH is a "jealous" *(qnh)* God. A good deal of discussion has been centered on what this means, how it should be translated.[51]
I think the traditional translation, "jealous," is in fact what is meant: The
relationship is an exclusive one, analogous to marriage; any relationship of

---

50. How about humans? The text does not deal with that, but Israel resisted giving humans
independent authority. Kings were deputies of YHWH. Some traditions doubted that kings
had any right to rule Israel (cf. Judg. 8:22-23; 1 Samuel 8).

51. Cf. G. von Rad, *Old Testament Theology*, I, 203–12.

YHWH's people with other deities is on the order of unfaithfulness, betrayal, adultery. Hosea was the first author to offer this analogy, but it was so cogent that practically every subsequent prophet took it up.[52]

YHWH's jealousy is the "character trait" that corresponds to the command to "love YHWH your God with all your heart, with all your soul and with all your might" (Deut. 6:5). I would take this to mean, "with undivided loyalty." This implicit link between jealousy and love is made explicit in the following predication: YHWH shows "loyalty *(ḥsd)* to (. . .) those who love *('hb)* me . . ." (v. 6). This part of a larger unit describes YHWH's double role: judge of those "who hate me" and patron of those who "love me and keep my commandments." While this description functions as a sanction, the focus is on the roles God plays in the community corresponding to the relationship the members have to God, its focus of loyalty and locus of authority. Those who give themselves over to God and take responsibility for the good of others will reap the benefit of community, those who do not will be hounded out.[53]

Before and After. Now we can explore the relationship of this chief commandment to what has gone before and what comes afterward. How does the command to recognize YHWH alone relate to what the people have pledged? When the people agreed to "do all that YHWH speaks," they have not agreed to obey him alone. It is possible to grant this authority assuming that this god will preside over a specific area of life—perhaps the military and judicial matters of national life—and others will take care of crops and herds, crafts, and the dead. Something of this sort is the logic of polytheism.

Yet their unrestricted commitment did leave itself open to an all-encompassing claim. They obligated themselves to go all the way if that happened to be YHWH's will. They were not, however, trapped by their words, but were given a chance to reaffirm their commitment after YHWH had spoken.

It was YHWH's will to be all that is deity for Israel, which included all that is authority. For Israel, to acknowledge any other authority is to "make" the authority. Anyone who sets up the powers of the creaturely world as competitors with YHWH will become his enemies, rebels against the communal order he is establishing by commandment.

The commandments that follow the chief commandment are set apart by a stylistic device: from v. 7 on, YHWH is referred to in third person.[54]

---

52. Hosea 1, 2, 3; Jer. 2:1-3, 23, 33-35, 3:1-5, 6-11; Ezekiel 16, 23.

53. The multiple generational punishment may reflect the significant role of family in instilling character.

54. Deuteronomy 5:6-21 has the same switch despite some differences in wording.

This format has been taken by critical scholars as evidence that the Decalogue combines materials from different origins.[55] While that may be true, it is highly probable that the switch from first to third person is deliberate. It would take little revision to formulate third person utterances in first person, and the idea that the author or editor was too respectful of tradition to alter it simply justifies a particular scholarly method.

If the switch is deliberate, what is its purpose? It is certainly not to remove YHWH as the speaker of the rest; no reader gains that impression,[56] and there is no one to speak it if not YHWH. The change is, in fact, mysterious. Its effect is to distance the other commandments somewhat, to focus attention more on what is prohibited or prescribed and less on the speaker. One is still directly responsible to YHWH for obedience, but its "mediated" quality tends to locate that responsibility in the chief commandment.

The three commandments following the chief commandment share some features. Most obvious is the fact that these three, and only these, have motive clauses along with the commandments. Moreover, two of them are formulated positively. The prohibition of "taking YHWH's name in vain" is something of a transition from the commandments protecting YHWH's status and those concerning inter-Israelite actions. It protects the honor of YHWH, for the abuse of the name is an affront to the divine majesty. The motive clause is rather odd: it is a threat, but not a direct threat of punishment; rather, the offender is denied the forgiveness that is characteristic of God (Exod. 34:7).

The next two commandments are prescriptive, which suggests to me that they are designed to construct community, and the ones that follow to protect it. A mysterious linkage in the tradition connects observing the Sabbath and honoring parents (cf. Lev. 19:3). Each limits the addressee's authority, integrates the addressee into a larger network. One has six days to pursue one's enterprises, but the one day is claimed by God. One's authority over others is also curtailed; indeed, on the Sabbath Israel is a community of equals (even work animals included). Exod. 20:11 grounds the release of control over the day in creation, Deut. 5:15 grounds the release of control over those under one in the exodus. The honoring of parents encourages and reinforces the exercise of authority over character formation and intergenerational continuity. A people that holds each generation to the standard of those who nurtured them can maintain possession of its inheritance among the nations.

---

55. E. S. Gerstenberger, "Covenant and Commandment," *JBL* 84 (1965): 46–51.
56. In fact, most readers or hearers do not even notice the change.

The next four commandments have a completely different style. Their force is in their extreme brevity. If any style reflects unconditionality, this style does. The first three subjects covered are the chief topics of criminal and civil law, protecting life, property, and marriage. The fourth protects the judicial process meant to enforce the other three. Each calls for moral and legal elaboration: to be effective, the Ten Commandments require addressees to engage in a practice of interpretation and application.[57]

The double prohibition against coveting introduces a motivational obligation along with obligations regarding actions. In a sense, this last commandment supplies a "motive clause" for the four concerning a person and her neighbor.[58] Although human motivation is far too complex to be covered by one motive, if one takes "covet" in the broad sense of inordinate desire one would come close to the roots of motivation.

Summary

Let us wrap up the exposition of the Decalogue within its narrative setting before we take up its exchanges with interpretive communities. Identifying the Ten Commandments as "exercitive" utterances may seem only the application of a new, rather esoteric, nomenclature. The burden of this chapter has been to show that the classification does make a difference to our understanding of the rhetorical force of the Exodus texts.

First of all, it places the act of covenant-making, divine appearing, and reconstructing of the covenant after a breach, in a new light. These transactions construct the authority of YHWH to command Israel. Within the

---

57. The Ten Commandments engender interpretive practices reflected in the legal corpora of the Pentateuch and, post-canonically, Talmudic discussion. It would be a mistake to regard the codes as an extension of the Ten Commandments, as if the community consciously worked out the implications of each commandment. Rather, the Book of the Covenant, the oldest biblical code, begins with ANE law and modifies it to conform to the requirements of faith in YHWH. Its provisions show both how Yahwism reshaped ANE legal concepts and principles, and how cultural tradition resisted reformation. The codes, for example, continue to permit and regulate slavery, though the acts of YHWH for Israel would seem to call for its abolition: see P. D. Hanson, "The Theological Significance of Contradiction within the Book of the Covenant," in *Canon and Authority*, ed. G. W. Coats and B. O. Long (Philadelphia: Fortress, 1977), 110–31. The Sabbath and coveting commandments of the Decalogue also assume it. Slavery symbolizes the challenge and limits of rhetoric: the law-givers had to accommodate God's will to a practice too deeply ingrained and widespread to be eradicated; they did try to humanize it and devise utopian schemes for transforming it, but rhetoric can accomplish only so much.

58. One of its oddities is that it applies explicitly to a man; the others apply to men and women alike. The Sabbath commandment does not mention "wife" along with those under the addressee's authority.

narrative world, the promises and manifestations of YHWH elicit Israel's acceptance of the relationship in a pledge to obey all that YHWH says. Even after the people break this pledge and provoke YHWH's wrath, the relationship can be, and is, reconstructed, with the added provision for divine forbearance. The narrative seeks to persuade the textual audience to accept this transaction as binding on it.

The Ten Commandments are the exercise of the authority constructed in the commissives exchanged between YHWH and Israel. By placing the act of divine commanding within the context of commanding in general, we first of all see why a command—or request—cannot be reduced to its propositional content. The act obligates the addressee to perform even when the addressee may have misgivings. When the exercitive is formulated specifically as a command, this obligation is to the speaker. In the case of the commandments, the speaker takes responsibility for the good of the addressee in obligating the addressee to the speaker. Given the fact that commandments are character-forming and community-forming, they are reserved for a few quite distinctive hierarchical relationships.

When the Ten Commandments are regarded from this phenomenological perspective, it becomes clear why trust and obedience constitute the classical components of faith. Faith is not a disposition or attitude. When addressed by divine commandments, it is an act of entrusting one's good to God, trusting that God's commandments are for one's own and one's people's good, and of applying them to specific situations in responsibility to God.

What is commanded in the Ten Commandments can be regarded from several perspectives. For our purposes, the rhetorical shaping of the text was the relevant one. Within the Ten Commandments, the chief commandment—which may well contain two commandments—protects the speaker's unrivaled authority to issue commandments, rendering all the commandments "unconditional." The chief commandment also subordinates the others, rendering disobedience to any a breach of one's relationship to God. The structuring of the text, thus, is analogous to the illocutionary force of the act of commanding.

The Interpretive Tradition

The commandments of the Hebrew Bible call for interpretation. God's commandment imposes a responsibility on addressees to understand and apply what it requires. The addressees are addressed as members of a community—a community of interpreters by virtue of the responsibility imposed by the commandments. The community generates a tradition as it moves through time. In this section I will focus on the interpretive tradition of classical Judaism, in particular, the Talmudic tradition.

Talmudic Judaism has complied, I believe, with the rhetorical specifications of the revelation of the law at Mount Sinai. This interpretive tradition does not privilege the Decalogue in the way the church has; it regards the whole Pentateuch as containing embedded commandments—613 by traditional count—that deserve equal respect and discussion. The very number of commandments called forth systematization and supplementation. The system involved implied principles and concepts to explain and harmonize different teachings. The Talmud emerges an ordered presentation of divine law for Israel, a timeless law for an ideal Israel—with land, temple, priesthood, monarchy, scholars. In addition, Talmudic practice had to make provision for the application of the law to less than ideal conditions.

The Christian church's relationship to the commandments of the Hebrew Bible is more mediated than that of the synagogue. It has privileged the Ten Commandments and sifted through the rest of the commandments and laws to determine which remain in force, and how they are to be applied in the spirit of Jesus Christ. These all flow quite naturally from Jesus' utterances and actions, and his death and resurrection.

Nothing in the interpretive tradition of the Christian church is comparable to the halakic discussions of the Talmud. Christian theology has frequently been blind to the relationship-creating power of the commandments, as though requirements would drive believers away from God. Indeed, Christian theology has put emphasis on the role of commandment in instilling a consciousness of guilt; the nearest thing to Talmudic discussion to be found in church tradition is the categorization of sin for the practice of confession.

It is appropriate, thus, to limit our reflections on the exchange between Sinaitic text and community to the Talmudic interpretive tradition. Our interest is not in the content of its teachings nor a history of Talmudic discussion, but in its hermeneutics. For a guide I have chosen E. Levinas, who has applied his philosophical acumen to the practice of Talmudic discussion. Levinas's interpretation of Judaism may be skewered by his apologetic urge, but his narrow focus and philosophical depth give his analysis illuminating power on divine exercitive discourse.

Scripture and the Interpretive Tradition. According to Levinas, biblical commandments and law invite commentary, indeed more than commentary in the expository sense, a continual reconstruction of the rationale and application of what God demands of his people. The Talmud is an oral tradition, even after its inscription, because the tractates preserve and invite debate. The peculiar thing is that Torah is "frozen" in its rulings, and legislates for an ideal community with an institutional structure quite at variance with those of the Israel in whose life the scholars participated.[59] So Talmudic discussion can be said to hover between time and eternity, reconfiguring eternity for each time.

In an illuminating exchange with his fellow philosopher and Gentile friend, P. Ricoeur, Levinas insists that Judaism is "heteronomous." God creates community—with himself and among human members—through exercitive action. Levinas himself criticizes Christianity for cultivating an immature relationship with God. The commandment places responsibility on the people, responsibility for one's own character and for the good of the neighbor. It runs against the grain of modern individualism: our obligation to the other is as "primordial" as our rights (our claim on others), and our self-realization is not self-fulfillment without the self-realization of the other.[60]

The divine commandment both distances and draws together. To be commanded is to be drawn together with the sovereign in a hierarchical relationship. It is a false modern idea that the only "true" relationship is between equals. When authority concerns itself with the good of those governed, it is "grace." The commandments are for the good of each Israelite and for the people in its collective existence. The commandment does distance. It distinguishes between speaker and addressees, and places responsibility on the addressees for their fulfillment and to cultivate maturity, adulthood. However, God does not stand aloof and calculate whether the addressees are meeting the divine standards; rather, God promises to support the people in their effort to be a just and righteous and holy people. Prophetic judgment is necessitated by the breakdown, according to Amos, of the system of justice and welfare God has hitherto upheld and supplemented.

Levinas sees this relationship created by commandment as faithfully preserved and invigorated by the rabbinical tradition codified in the Mishna and discussed in the Talmud. It is the essential Judaism. The essay entitled "Revelation in the Jewish Tradition" converges so nicely with the subject of this book that I will simply review its argument.[61]

59. The oddity of debating a law that is already settled for a community, which is an ideal abstraction, actually freed Talmudic scholars to be at a "philosophic" remove that practical decisions on the issues brought to judges to decide do not have. Talmudic scholars did exercise judicial oversight within Jewish enclaves.

60. G. D. Mole, trans., *Beyond the Verse: Talmudic Readings and Lectures* (Bloomington and Indianapolis: Indiana Univ. Press, (1994) 142–43 and frequently. Levinas has not, in the literature I have read, developed a political conception of obligation beyond the personal. He has discussed the state of Israel.

61. Ibid., 129–50.

The Fact of Revelation. The philosophical question about revelation is how to understand a claim that within the world in which we live, that which is not of this world has . . . what? Manifested itself? Delivered timeless truths? Intervened to inaugurate a holy history? Fackenheim, followed by Ricoeur, located revelation in history-making events. But holy history does not end with the biblical story, it continues in the "passion" of Diaspora Judaism.

For many Jews, the sacred story told in the sacred book still informs their life. For them, a theology along the lines of a holy history may configure their identity sufficiently to negotiate between faith and modernity. However, the majority are informed by modern secular thought, so revelation demands new conceptions and requires both an in-depth examination of how the Talmudic tradition appropriated the texts of revelation and a correlation of the concerns of this tradition with modern concerns.

Despite the many and varied ways God is said to be revealed in Hebrew Scripture, for Judaism "prescriptive lessons" are privileged for the relationship they establish with God.[62] This concentration is complemented by a drive to go beyond the plain sense. The historical sense of the text, of course, restricts the text's relevance to different times, conditions, and moral sensibilities. One could abstract some concepts and principles for later times, but that would make the text into a means one could set aside once one had the result. For the sacred text to continue to communicate knowledge of God's will, "space" must be found in and between the words. The strategy was to discover ambiguities and contradictions in and between teachings.

The interpreter participates in revelation by bringing out new meanings. In this transaction, a word comes from elsewhere and dwells within the person who receives it. Within the receiver the word takes on a unique figure but still is a word from outside the reason or sensibility of the self. Revelation is enriched, actually "constituted" by entering into the unique in each person. The uniqueness of each act of listening carries the secret of the text in its unity, diversity, and plenitude. The word announces the same truth in different persons and times through the multitude of interpretations. As one rabbi observes, "The slightest question put by a novice pupil to his schoolmaster constitutes an ineluctable articulation of the Revelation which was heard at Sinai."[63] The practice that saves this notion from subjectivism is the requirement to be in dialog with commentaries.

The requirement that the interpreter be in dialog with commentary introduces the concept of dual revelation, written and oral. The oral tradi-

62. Ibid., 132.
63. Quoted in ibid., 134.

tion is not just a commentary, it is a second, correlative source of Sinaitic revelation. Yet the Talmud is not separable from Scripture, but a kind of supplement that goes behind, reworks, and fills in. It operates on the principle that every text of Scripture is relevant to every other one. This dialectical movement balances spiritual flights with down-to-earth problems, severe texts with generous ones. This "kerygma" does not forget the weight of the world or the inertia and dullness of human understanding.

The Talmud is said to be oral tradition, yet it is a voluminous text. The way it is written does make it an oral tradition. It is a record of rulings and debates over the rulings. The arguments of the losing position are recorded along with the winner, inspiring debates over the debates, recorded in the margins. "The religious act of listening to the revealed words is . . . identified with the discussion whose open-endedness is desired with all the audacity of its problematics."[64] "The Revelation is a constant hermeneutics of the Word. . . ."[65]

The Talmud is divided between halakah (prescriptive discourse) and Haggada (parables, stories, essays, epigrams). The prescriptive is primary, giving Judaism "its physiognomy" and maintaining by means of orthopraxis "the unity of the very body of the Jewish people throughout dispersion and History."[66] The "thought that issues from the prescriptive goes beyond the problem of the material gesture to be accomplished; although, right in the heart of the dialectic, it also enunciates what conduct is to be kept, what the Halakah is."[67] The Haggada is the more immediately accessible type of Talmudic discourse, and the type of text Levinas usually addresses in his own lectures on texts. Aggadic stories and essays converge in perspective with the more densely argued halakah.

The Content of the Revelation. Levinas summarizes the religious practice he finds in the Torah quite succinctly:

> This will undoubtedly be an invitation to follow at all times the highest path, to keep faith only with the Unique, and to distrust myth which dictates to us the *fait accompli,* the constraint of custom and land, and the Machiavellian State with its reasons of state. But to follow the Most High is also to know that nothing is greater than to approach one's neighbor, than the concern for the lot of the "widow and orphan, the stranger and poor."[68]

64. Ibid., 138.
65. Ibid., 138.
66. Ibid., 139.
67. Ibid., 140.
68. Ibid., 142.

He places primary stress on the responsibility of the devout for the other person. At times, he sounds as though all the other practices commanded in the Torah are to cultivate responsible character.[69] He defines humanity as "the rupture of being which produces the act of giving."[70] He is willing to speak of Israel as the elect because it "expresses the awareness of an indisputable summons which gives life to ethics and through which the indisputability of the summons isolates the person responsible."[71] Eschatology is the hope that humans can master history and establish the rule of the ethical. Yet this process involves a "waiting for the Most High which is a relation to Him—or, if one prefers, a deference . . . to the beyond which creates here the concept of the beyond or a towards-God."[72]

Revelation and Reason. The question raised by revelation is: Can an intelligibility be sought in some traumatic experience in which intelligence is broken? Only in the "thou shalt," which takes no account of "you can."[73] Intellect is not sacrificed with this understanding of revelation. The God who relates to humans as command, as a calling to responsibility for the other, is not vulnerable to the exposure of the God who grounds stability, the God of metaphysical thought. The God who commands calls one out of oneself to be one's self, imposes responsibility to love one's neighbor prior to any reason.

Levinas further expounds his understanding of the relation of revelation to reason in an essay entitled "The Temptation of Temptation"[74] It is a meditation on a Talmudic Haggadic text on how Israel accepted the offer of Torah. The pledge of the people to do all that the Lord tells them is central to the discussion. The people offer their pledge before they know what is demanded of them. A philosopher objects that they should have waited until they had learned what it says, and considered their own capacity to fulfill it, before they accepted it. The rabbis not only defend the acceptance of the Torah first, they glory in it. Is it a case of endorsing blind faith? Not at all, replies Levinas. The acceptance of the Torah sight unseen is a "reminder of (. . .) consent prior to freedom and nonfreedom."[75] "That which must be received in order to make freedom of choice possible (=Torah) cannot have been chosen, unless after the fact."[76] Revelation is prior to reason, the condition for responsible reason.

69. Cf. ibid., 143–45.
70. Ibid., 142.
71. Ibid., 142; he quotes Amos 3:2.
72. Ibid., 143.
73. Ibid., 146.
74. A. Aronowicz, trans., *Nine Talmudic Readings* (Bloomington and Indianapolis: Indiana Univ. Press, 1994), 30–50.
75. Ibid., 37.
76. Ibid.

He offers some analogies. Just as acceptance precedes examination, practice precedes adherence.[77] This sequence avoids the "temptation of temptation," which is the desire to know before doing, to be detached from everything and yet to experience everything. The Talmudic conception does not avoid temptation and sin, but it does not allow sin to question the certainty of good and evil. The devout place themselves beyond violence before they confront the choice of violence.[78]

Levinas coined the expression *obedient reason* to capture the interpretive practices of the Talmudic sages.[79] This description does not characterize the logical forms of Talmudic discourse, though the sages employed certain customary, rather labyrinthine exegetical strategies for deriving prescriptive teaching from texts. Rather, the essential factor is the a priori acceptance of the claim of the commandment of God and the employment of reasoning to apply it responsibly to life situations. The key term may be the word *responsibility*, yet we are not going to find a set of rules or principles for determining what is and isn't responsible application. It is a matter of sound, imaginative judgment as to the character of God and the good the commandment should promote. It includes accountability to God and to one's peers for the quality of one's judgment.

Obedient reason stands over and against autonomous reason, reason that refuses to submit to divine or any arbitrary authority, that reserves the right to pass judgment on the morality and desirability of every commandment. Autonomous reason does not take responsibility for discovering the moral truth of the commandment and answering to the Law-giver for interpretation.

Obedient reason makes a perfect match with the authoritative force of divine exercitives. It begins in trust that God takes responsibility for the welfare of the addressee in issuing commandments. It accepts responsibility for applying the commandment in conformity with the holiness, righteousness, justice, and mercy of God. It accepts the claims of the other on one's concern as equal to one's own, and seeks to instill comparable responsibility in the other. It is prepared to obey the commandment at whatever cost, and to respond to every situation as a call to responsibility. It expects to answer to God for the faithfulness of the exercise of responsibility.

Application to Difficult Texts. Levinas's exposition and defense of Talmudic tradition is an example of meta-level phenomenological reflection about an interpretive tradition. How does obedient reason fit in the trenches?

77. Ibid., 40.
78. Ibid., 43–44.
79. Levinas, *Beyond the Verse*, 145–50.

Does it provide, for example, any guidance for the interpretation of texts that portray God as commanding actions we find immoral or irrational? If we must approach the text having pledged, "All that the Lord says we will do and we will obey," are we required to assent to exercitives that offend our consciences? Can obedient reason find a way through the dilemma?

It is common, indeed inevitable, that an exegete encounters texts with theological, moral, and political standards and concerns, which strike him or her as wrong or unacceptable or even oppressive. This intellectual confrontation is not unique to the modern exegete. One can detect "cognitive dissonance" in patristic, medieval, and Reformation interpretation as well; in fact, an attentive interpreter can detect it within the biblical text itself.[80] Earlier eras were discreet about passing judgment on biblical texts. This caution undoubtedly had to do with the high esteem with which the text was held by members of the religious community. Perhaps, though, it was also a greater appreciation for how the text communicates revelation. If the scriptural texts communicate divine exercitives and commissives, they can be received only by obedience and trust. This practice too has its dangers—defending the indefensible or subverting a text allegorically—but it honors the text's claim to authority.

What is unique, or at least distinctive about contemporary exegesis, is how open exegetes are about their judgments. Even scriptural scholars within religious communities are counseling that it is the moral obligation of the exegete to criticize and even condemn passages of Scripture.[81] Even a scholar known for his judiciousness and prudence, James Barr, is calling for a forthright repudiation of passages with offensive moral teaching. He takes as his example the *herem* law of the holy war.

> The fact is that, on the face of it, the command of consecration to destruction is morally offensive and has to be faced as such. . . . Over questions of war and peace it is accepted that there is room for disagreement; . . . But over the deliberate destruction of entire populations by divine command there is no room for disagreement of this kind—not least when this century has seen horrifying examples of genocide at work. Moreover, the attitudes engendered by attempts to justify consecration to destruction spill over into wide areas of religion: . . . above all into belief that religious commands override morality and that it is good for us that this should be so.[82]

80. See the insightful article by R. Goetz, "Joshua, Calvin and Genocide," *Theology Today* 32 (1975), 263–75.

81. See R. J. Allen and J. C. Holbert, *Holy Root Holy Branches: Christian Preaching from the Old Testament* (Nashville: Abingdon, 1995), 107–31, *passim*.

82. J. Barr, *Biblical Faith and Natural Theology*, 218–19.

He quotes Steward Sutherland, for example, to the effect that "a religious belief which runs counter to our moral beliefs is to that extent unacceptable."[83] He then continues: "We cannot hope to make progress [on this problem] without willingness to accept that the whole tradition of the matter of the Canaanites involves a picture of God which is seriously defective in relation to the reality of his nature, and this on the grounds which Sutherland sets out, which are, in a way, grounds of natural theology."[84]

Sutherland's ethical requirement would pretty much nullify the performative force of exercitives. It would certainly remove the revelatory force of the commands of God recorded in Scripture, or at least reduce them to the status of "expressive utterances." Because most Jews and Christians do not allow for an expression of divine desire that is not ipso facto obligatory for addressees, Sutherland's and Barr's position implies that scriptural commandments are human inventions ascribed to God, requiring the reader to judge their fitness.

For the divine word to have exercitive force for the textual audience, the reader must be willing to join the Israelites at Mount Sinai in their pledge to obey "whatever YHWH says." This pledge is the initial commitment that is at the basis of what we have called "obedient reason." It is a response to God's offer of relationship, involving trust in God's benevolent intentions toward addressees. To receive the commandments rightly, readers must accede in the commitment of their ancestors.

Obedient reason is not a renunciation of reason, not a capitulation to the inscrutable and irrational, but the acceptance of responsibility for understanding and applying God's commandments according to the addressee's best moral and practical judgment, aware that one is accountable to God for one's reasoning and action. Moreover, no interpreter works alone; the whole people is under the authority of the same commandments, and the people's understanding and application involve discussion and persuasion. The conservatism of public and learned opinion is more of a problem for this discourse community than the demonic potential of charismatic prophets.

I do not have the space to explore how obedient reason might interpret the *herem* law in particular, or the conquest tradition in general. We should be quite forthright about the unacceptability of genocide; it is healthy for the religious communities to struggle with the face of evil. The task is to take responsibility for drawing from these offensive texts the will of God that has the power to offend. The next chapter offers occasion to do so on a problematic set of texts.

83. S. Sutherland, *God, Jesus and Belief*, 16, as cited by Barr, *Biblical Faith and Natural Theology*, 219.

84. Barr, *Biblical Faith and Natural Theology*, 219.

4.
THE FIRST COMMANDMENT

IF THE CHIEF COMMANDMENT (EXODUS 20:2-6) IS THE FOUNDATION OF the authority of all the commandments, it is appropriate to concentrate on its transaction with the audience to determine in what sense its truth claim is located in its exercitive force. My thesis is that the exercitive force of the commandments, and in particular the first commandment (Exod. 20:3), makes the divine communication something the addressees cannot know in any other way. What is known is an obligation to act according to a particular proposition. The proposition itself has to do with the relationship between speaker and addressees. The upshot is that the relationship created by performative utterance must be continually re-created by its "repetition" through time.

What is known in being addressed by the first commandment is not a body of knowledge, but it generates a body of knowledge, a *system of doctrine*, as it used to be called. How so? The construction of authority configures the knowledge the addressees possess in a particular way and the commandment itself gives responsibility to the addressees to apply it. Obedient application of the first commandment will, in the course of time, result in monotheism.

How do we "test" this thesis? We can begin by examining the wording of the first commandment. Yes, we will narrow our focus to the prohibition against recognizing any *elohim* but YHWH, though the prohibition of images will come into the picture before the end. Does the prohibition create an obligation that could not be derived from reason? Does it compel addressees to think and act differently than they would be inclined if they were not under obligation?

At several later junctures in the story of Israel, the people are led to renew their allegiance to YHWH. How can the people choose what they are already obligated under the first commandment to do? How is YHWH's claim upon Israel depicted? Is it an either/or, or is some accommodation negotiated? If an either/or is involved, what is the choice between? How is the choice of YHWH made appealing to the audience? Is the appeal consistent with a claim made by exercitive force?

A new rhetorical strategy begins to play a role in the confrontation between YHWH and competitors: the satirizing of the competitors, the gods. How does this fit, or contradict, the thesis that YHWH's claim to Israel's exclusive loyalty and obedience is by exercitive force? How does satire work? What is the rhetorical point of this satire?

This chapter surveys a historical sequence. Does it require an abandonment of the extant text in favor of critically reconstructed source? That would embroil the discussion in debates best avoided. The extant text does have its own chronology; whatever the dating of a passage, it offers to readers a rendering of a particular moment within the story of Israel. Our exegesis will follow the text's lead. The tribal convocation depicted in Joshua 24 and the contest provoked by Elijah (1 Kings 18) represent the challenges and responses of the people during the conquest and ninth-century Israel. Both portrayals reach beyond the particular moment to the long-range consequences of the events and explore the fundamental theological tensions of Yahwism, and both have apologetic import for the reading audience. This historical narration has a breadth and depth actual participants could not attain; it is the product of hindsight, a fusion of horizons designed to forge an Israelite identity through the interpretation of its history.[1]

These texts represent Israel as governed by the first commandment throughout its history, beginning at Mount Sinai. Many scholars would consider this extremely anachronistic.[2] If they are correct, our texts import the issue into the era represented rather than fuse horizons. This chapter is not the place to join debate on Israelite religious history. It would require not only a thorough going reconstruction of the tradition behind each text, but a much broader examination of the genres of biblical literature,[3] the structure of narrative complexes,[4] the symbolic significance of altars,[5] and the presuppositions of all Israelite consciousness.

---

1. All historiography involves a retrospection that surpasses the understanding of participants (see C. Morse, *The Logic of Promise in Moltmann's Theology*). Though the biblical modes of presenting the restrospection differ from critical historiography, they are of the same logical order.

2. E.g., R. Albertz, *A History of Israelite Religion in the Old Testament Period*, I (Louisville: Westminster John Knox, 1994); L. Handy, *Among the Host of Heaven* (Winona Lake, Ind.: Eisenbrauns, 1994); D. V. Edelman, ed., *The Triumph of Elohim: From Yahwisms to Judaisms* (Grand Rapids: Eerdmans, 1996).

3. I have written a paper with Ken Diable in this vein; it is entitled "The Impact of the First Commandment in the Form and Content of Psalmic Lamentation," read to Psalm Section at the 1994 Annual Meeting of the SBL.

4. See my "The First Commandment in the Structure of the Pentateuch," *VT* 45 (1995): 107–18.

5. I read a paper entitled "The Theo-Politics of Building Altars" to the Law Group at the 1993 Annual Meeting of the SBL.

The First Commandment

By "first commandment" I mean the Exodus verse conventionally trans-lated "You shall have no other gods before me" (20:3). The first command-ment is the only one of the ten that proscribes a relationship rather than an act. The reader commonly assimilates Exod. 20:3 to parallels that do have action verbs, for example, "bow down" (Exod. 34:14, also 20:5), "serve" (Josh. 24:14-24, also Exod. 20:5), "sacrifice to" (Exod. 22:19), and "mention" (Exod. 23:13). The wording of Exod. 20:3 is indeed too vague for positive law, but for that very reason it attains a greater breadth and depth than pro-scriptions of specific actions. Exodus 20:3 seems to proscribe *all* commerce with other deities.

I have been employing a political term, *recognition*, to describe the force of the commandment. Recognition is an act of one government toward another government, or of citizens to their own: it acknowledges that a government has the requisites of sovereignty, to make laws, levy taxes, enter into treaties, and the like. I am suggesting that YHWH claims the obedience of his people and excludes the claim of other deities, which is the obvious meaning of the prohibition against *serving* other deities. However, if a per-son cannot perform any act of worship toward a deity, it would exclude any acknowledgment of authority.

Perhaps a political model of divine power is operative in the rather com-mon practice in the Hebrew Bible of matching a people with a deity. When Jephthah negotiates with the Ammonites regarding who is the rightful owner of trans-Jordanian territory, he says: "So then YHWH, the God of Israel, dispossessed the Amorites from before his people Israel; and are you to take possession of them? Will you not possess what Chemosh your god gives you to possess?" (Judg. 11:23-24). Each deity exercises authority over a people and the territory the deity has procured for it. Micah 4:5 has a sim-ilar idea, though it has more to do with lifestyle than political order:

> For all the peoples walk,
> each in the name of its god,
> but [or and] we will walk in the name of YHWH our God
> forever and ever.

Whether other peoples would have recognized themselves in such a for-mula is hard to say. Cities or countries seem to have been under the patron-age of a particular deity, but ANE mythological texts would suggest that peoples recognized many other deities than the patron of their nation.

The prepositional phrase, *'l pny,* leaves a degree of ambiguity. "Before me" probably does not mean "superior or equal to me," allowing the addressee to acknowledge other deities as long as YHWH is recognized as supreme.[6] The phrase might, however, mean "in my presence," allowing for commerce with other gods in places other than YHWH's sanctuaries.[7] Perhaps at an early stage in the history of tradition it did mean that, but the extant text—with its address of all Israel, both in the wilderness and in possession of its land, and its function in relationship to the rest of the commandments—means "wherever Israelites are, and at all times." Hosea 13:4 renders the operative idea well when it uses two prepositions with the meaning of "except."

Finally, the word *elohim* requires interpretation. Its basic thrust is dictated by the wording: YHWH is (an) *elohim*, so it would mean "anyone in YHWH's class." Just how far this class extends will require interpretation by the community as it confronts new situations over time.[8]

The Addressees. Does the prohibition obligate addressees to think and act differently than they would be inclined if they were not under its authority? In accordance with the performative conception of commandments, the first commandment brings the addressees into a relationship of obligation to God for compliance with its propositional content. What is stipulated by God in this commandment is the kind of relationship he expects and demands of those who recognize him. Nothing is asserted about the reality or power of other deities, only that each and every member of the people of Israel not recognize them in any fashion. It is the responsibility of the addressees to apply the prohibition to particular questions as they arise.

Anyone who acknowledges the authority of YHWH will perforce acknowledge an obligation to the first commandment. However, those who are subject to it can and do exercise independence of judgment. They will assess its desirability according to a broad range of criteria, from its conformity with their interests, their conceptions of reality, and their sense of moral right.

Did the addressees of the first commandment agree or disagree with the policy it requires? The wording projects addressees who would resist its exclusivism. That is, it assumes the existence of "other gods," or at least the addressees' belief in and attraction to them. The Israelites were, after all, a part of ANE culture, and shared that culture's penchant to recognize a host of powers, divine and demonic, which impinge on human life; the object of religion was to manage these powers by honoring and obeying each in its place. The commandment requires those addressed to withhold any honor

6. See DBD for the linguistic evidence.
7. R. Knierim, "Das Erste Gebot," *ZAW* 77 (1965), 20–39.
8. Von Rad thinks it even covers ghosts and familiar spirits: *OT Theology,* 1, 208.

or allegiance to any supernatural being or power to which they might be attracted. The willingness of the people to comply with the commandment could not depend upon their natural inclinations, but had to rely on their sense of obligation to YHWH.

The biblical historians report that the people were not willing to comply. No sooner had they ratified the covenant than they made and worshiped the "golden calf," a paradigmatic story of the long struggle between YHWH and his people. Only as Israel lived with, and in contradiction to, the prohibition for centuries did the masses become persuaded that YHWH is sufficient.[9] It was the exile that putatively settled the issue, though even then at least some of the people drew the opposite lesson (cf. Jer. 44:15-18).

Despite Israel's continual relapses, though, the first commandment obviously had its effect. The people recognized their obligation even when they failed to live up to it. At various moments in their history, they reaffirmed their obligation to give YHWH their exclusive allegiance, and the classical prophets could appeal to the people's knowledge of their obligation in the prophetic accusations of unfaithfulness.[10]

From a Distance. The rhetoric of the first commandment and the preexilic history of Israel support a theological judgment that the knowledge communicated in it was not gained by reason or some other natural human capacity, but by divine revelation.[11] Even if the people, or some strong-minded, even fanatical element within the people, were monotheists,[12] the commandment was necessary to condemn the recognition of other gods as wrong. Intellectual monotheism would not be able to arrive at an obligation to God to recognize God alone. Greek philosophy arrived at a

9. One could regard many narratives of the Pentateuch and Former Prophets as arguments that YHWH was sufficient to all Israel's needs, and adamant that Israel honor its obligation.

10. Exodus 32 is paradigmatic in this regard as well: the "golden calf" is an imitation of YHWH, and Aaron seeks to assimilate it to YHWH. Israel could neither remain faithful to YHWH nor get away from him.

11. At least at a phenomenological level, that is, the persona, YHWH, had to command it.

12. J. Barr is of this opinion: "To me it seems possible, indeed plausible, that monotheism, in the sense of a situation where a people had only one god who really and essentially mattered, was 'natural' in Israel. It was a conviction already general and socially accepted, to begin with in a particular group no doubt, eventually throughout Israelite society. . . . A group, possibly quite a small group to begin with, was fanatically monotheistic, and its concentration on its one god succeeded in establishing itself as the national faith." "Biblical Law and the Question of Natural Theology," in *The Law in the Bible and Its Environment*, ed. T. Veijola (Göttingen: Vandenhoeck & Ruprecht, 1990), 18–19.

monotheistic theology, but blamed the polytheism and anthropomorphic myths of the masses on ignorance. Between ignorance and betrayal or rebellion there is a wide gulf (though we will discover a convergence in the biblical discourse known as "idol polemic").

What happens when the reading audience is not tempted to any sort of polytheism? After the exile, monotheism became a theology taken for granted among Jews. Did the commandment cease to have the performative force it had when the audience was inclined toward polytheism? Maybe its victory rendered it useless.

If the decision between YHWH and his competitors is as ultimate as the Hebrew Bible makes it out to be, that which draws people away from recognizing YHWH alone must be a perennial temptation. Once the literal application of the commandment no longer covers a temptation to addressees, the "other gods"—identified as "idols" humans make and worship—must be reidentified.[13]

Renewal for a New Generation

Joshua 24 is depicted as a renewal of the covenant after the initial phase of the conquest, by the conquest generation as it retires from the scene. It performs the function of reinforcing the obligation accepted at Sinai to recognize YHWH alone. The account belongs to what can be called the interpretive history of the first commandment. Indeed, it is one of the most salient renewals of allegiance to YHWH in the Former Prophets.[14] How this transaction is portrayed is an important test case for my thesis.

First we must ask why a renewal is called for. If the first commandment imposes an obligation on the people of Israel by exercitive force, is not its original issuance at Mount Sinai sufficient for all time to come? Does the renewal not indicate a degree of uncertainty, at least, regarding the efficacy of the commandment?

The first commandment is obviously of a different order from the rest, and it does seem to require renewal. It is hard to imagine a crisis requiring the renewal of the prohibition of killing, adultery, or theft; the promulgation of new legislation for the administration of the commandments, yes, but not a renewal of the commandment itself. The Sabbath commandment might be "renewed" in a communal convocation, but this would take the form of the promulgation of new policies for enforcing it (cf. Neh. 13:15-22). Only the first—or the combination of first and second—commandment invites a renewal of commitment to abide by it.

13. H. Richard Niebuhr, *Radical Monotheism and Western Culture* (New York: Harper & Row, 1970), is an instructive (though I think too idealistic) effort to do this.
14. Others: 1 Samuel 12, 1 Kings 18, 2 Kings 11, 23.

The first commandment happens to be a critical component in the recognition of YHWH, so the renewal of the first commandment is a renewal of the relationship between YHWH and Israel. It is YHWH's exclusive claim to recognition that makes recognition of him so momentous. It requires a renunciation of practices to which the Israelites, in common with their neighbors, were accustomed and loyalties to which they felt obligated. A decision was required. In a sense, each generation had to make or at least reaffirm that decision for itself.

Joshua 24 does not quote the first commandment; the commandment is embedded in a pledge of allegiance: to serve YHWH at all, he requires that one serve him alone. The decision to serve him is a decision *between* YHWH and other deities:

> Now therefore fear YHWH and serve him in sincerity and in faithfulness; put away the gods which your fathers served beyond the River, and in Egypt, and serve YHWH. And if you be unwilling to serve YHWH, choose this day whom you will serve. . . . (Josh. 24:14-15)

To bring the addressees to this point, Joshua has recited YHWH's gracious deeds on the people's behalf (vv. 2-13). This recitation is to identify the one about whom they are deciding (vv. 14-15). The people's role in YHWH's story is even more salient, for the issue is whether they will "own" this story by pledging their loyalty (vv. 16-18). They answer by reciting YHWH's deeds for them (vv. 16-18), framed by avowals to serve him "for he is our God" (v. 18, cf. v. 16a).

Their acceptance of YHWH is a renunciation of "serving other gods," but it is not entirely clear that this renunciation is fully exclusive. YHWH's acts for Israel do not demonstrate that he is the only deity to have acted benefi cially in Israel's behalf, only that he is the performer of this particular story of deliverance. From Israel's point of view, YHWH might be recognized as its national god, but other deities be recognized over other spheres of life.

Joshua 24:19-24 resolves that ambiguity decisively. YHWH demands such a degree of exclusiveness, he is so jealous of his status, that Israel is bound to fall short, and the consequences will be disastrous. Joshua sounds as though he is warning the Israelites against taking on this obligation. In fact it is a rhetorical strategy for underscoring the gravity of their decision.

The people reaffirm their decision despite the warning, and Joshua formalizes their commissive act by designating the people witnesses to their own pledge, and later setting up a stone as a witness to their witness. In the closest thing to a commandment in the chapter, Joshua exhorts the people to "put away foreign gods which are among you," perhaps an allusion to a ritual of burying images under the oak in Shechem (Gen. 35:2-4).[15] The people respond by making a formal pledge of obedience: "YHWH our God we will serve, and his voice we will obey."

The difference between Exodus 19–20 and Joshua 24 is that the former constructs the divine Law-giver's authority and then issues the first commandment (at the head of a comprehensive overview of what it means to serve YHWH), whereas Joshua 24 defines "serving YHWH" as itself excluding relationships with any other deity. Indeed, the focus of Joshua 24 is exclusively the issue of the first commandment. Joshua 24 also constructs YHWH's authority differently: there is no theophany, nothing is said about the benefit of the relationship for the addressees, and the recitation of YHWH's deeds is not designed so much to establish his worthiness for authority over them as to establish that he has had a long, beneficial relationship with them. Thus, the people must decide whether they will "own" the historic relationship or go back to serving the deities of their distant ancestors or of the peoples among whom they have been living.

This argument from the history of the relationship bestows on it a performative force, or the capacity to claim their loyalty. It is virtually an argument from friendship. It appeals to the people's sense of who they are and how deeply YHWH is implicated in their identity.

Joshua 24 does not have exercitive force for the reader: there is no commandment that addresses the textual audience. Rather, it is designed to elicit the readers' recognition of the historic relationship to which they belong. The warnings of judgment for betrayal of that relationship instill the gravity of YHWH's claim of exclusive recognition and thereby incorporate the "history of judgment"[16] into the history of the relationship. For the readers of the narrative of the Former Prophets, this warning has proven all too true. Their ancestors, as they were just settling in Canaan, had accepted the obligation to serve YHWH alone in full knowledge of the dire consequences for failure. The Assyrian and Babylonian exiles were the responsibility of the generations succeeding Joshua's. The warning sounds with even greater urgency for the reader—who must live with and overcome the consequences of this history.

---

15. A. Alt once argued that Genesis 35:1-5 was an etiology of a ritual: "Die Wallfahrt von Sichem nach Bethel," reprinted in *Kleine Schriften zur Geschichte des Volkes Israel* I (Munich: Ch. H. Beck, 1959), 79–88. Note that "foreign gods" are identified with images in Gen. 35:4.

16. Von Rad's term for the story beginning with the conquest and ending with exile: *O. T. Theology* I, 342–43.

Either/Or on Mount Carmel

Elijah confronts the people of Israel, assembled by Ahab on Mount Carmel, with a challenge to decide: "How long will you waver between two forks? If YHWH is God, follow him. If Baal, follow him" (1 Kings 18:21). The people are incapable of answering. They probably did not realize that they had to choose. King Ahab had erected a temple to Baal and a monument to Asherah in the capital city of Samaria (1 Kings 16:32-33), thereby legitimizing the peaceful coexistence of Yahwism and traditional Canaanite religion within the realm. Because Baal made no exclusive claim to the devotion of his adherents, the king and people probably saw no need to choose. Polytheism is tolerant, even moderately pluralistic.[17]

It is Elijah who disturbs this effort at religious compromise. His YHWH makes an exclusive claim. He confronts would be adherents with an either/or. Israel cannot be YHWH's people and still honor Baal, Asherah, or any other of Baal's companion deities.[18] YHWH has an identity different from Baal, and the world created by YHWH is incommensurable with the world in which Baal rejuvenated nature year by year. YHWH is known by his commerce with Israel's ancestors, by his covenant with the twelve tribes at Mount Sinai, by his confirmation of his prophets (see 1 Kings 18:31-37). The decision between two different deities is a decision about Israel's identity and destiny and moral character.

Reasons could be given for choosing YHWH, but these reasons themselves derive from Yahwistic tradition. The people had been formed and shaped by YHWH, which would certainly condition their decision. But Baal was no stranger to them either; they knew his powers from the sacred traditions of the indigenous peoples.[19] How were the people to decide a question of this sort?

Elijah proposed a contest. Each deity would be given the chance to demonstrate his reality by performing a miracle. By focusing the decision on a question of fact, Elijah was able to reestablish the boundaries between YHWH and Israel on the one side and other gods and peoples on the other. But it was also a dangerous move; "facts" do not always come out as one

---

17. Polytheism was not, to be sure, uniformly and intrinsically tolerant: According to L. B. Zaidman and P. S. Pantel, *Religion in the Ancient Greek City* (Cambridge: Cambridge Univ. Press, 1992), Greek cities suppressed unacceptable cults and executed communicants. On the other hand, there were ways of correlating deities between pantheons, importing them to fill niches, acknowledging regional and ethnic deities, and recognizing the patron deities of imperial states.

18. Only Asherah is mentioned (1 Kings. 18:19), and this sounds like an afterthought; the sacred tree or post named after her is mentioned in 16:33.

19. Many Israelites may themselves have been recruited from the "indigenous peoples," as G. E. Mendenhall and N. K. Gottwald have been arguing. See I. Finkelstein, *The Archaeology of the Isrelate Settlement* (Jerusalem: Israel Exploration Society, 1988).

hopes. Elijah placed his claim to be a prophet on the line, and YHWH's answer won his people back. The people could see that the God of their ancestors had demonstrated his sovereign power: "YHWH, he is God" (1 Kings 18:39). Their resolve would not last long, but for the moment they again belonged to YHWH.

The narrative depicts a revelation, a demonstration of divine power. This revelation forms the climax of the action and elicits the confession, "YHWH, he is God" (18:39). There is no divine discourse, so there can be no "revelation" in the sense of a performative utterance. On the other hand, Elijah's prayer portrays the lighting of the sacrificial fire in answer to his prayer as a confirmation: "that I am your servant and that I have done all these things at your word" (18:36). It is a case, to use Wolterstorff's terminology, of the "appropriation" of the discourse of a "deputized" speaker.[20] Elijah's either/or does, then, have the force of an illocutionary act of God, as does what he does to elicit Israel's answer. What is the illocutionary force of "all these things"?

First of all, there is Elijah's challenge to the Israelites to decide between YHWH and Baal. By what authority does he issue that challenge? What is its force? How does it shape what follows? What is the import of this challenge for the textual audience?

Next there is the proposal of a contest. Why does Elijah believe that the contest can decide the question? What, in fact, is the question to be decided? How does YHWH's demonstration of power "answer" it? What does it answer for the reader?

What is the significance of the depiction of the ritual performance of the representatives of Baal? By what authority, or for what purpose, does Elijah ridicule their efforts? What role does satire play in the argument of the narrative? How does this fit in with the challenge to decide? What response does the satire seek to elicit from the reader?

Finally, the relationship of the contest to the larger textual context deserves attention. In particular, how does 1 Kings 19 condition the interpretation of c. 18? How do the two texts contribute to the interpretive history of the first commandment? What is their illocutionary force for the textual audience?

Either/Or. Why did Elijah insist that Israel had to decide between YHWH and Baal? The short answer to that question is that YHWH commands it. The first commandment is indeed the text lurking in the background. Yet we should be aware that the prohibition is not cited, there is no appeal to

---

20. N. Wolterstorff, *Divine Discourse: Philosophical Reflections on the Claim that God Speaks* (Cambridge: Cambridge Univ. Press, 1995) 42–51.

an authoritative law. Elijah does not, in other words, take recourse to the rhetoric of authority.

So how do we know that the first commandment lurks in the background? Because the disjunctive either/or is foreign to polytheistic religion. The inner logic of polytheism is to touch all the bases—to honor every supernatural power in its place. The various powers were tolerant of the honor given others as long as they each received proper honor. It was YHWH who required that a decision be made between himself and any other deity, for he required his worshipers to recognize him exclusively; he was jealous of their devotion.

Why did Elijah not proclaim judgment on Israel when the people could not respond to his challenge to decide? The initial question could just as well function as an accusing question in a prophecy of judgment.[21] Israelites should know that they are under obligation to recognize YHWH alone, and when they cannot they are unfaithful to the relationship.

It was not that Elijah never announced YHWH's judgment. On other occasions he condemned King Ahab for killing Naboth and confiscating his estate (1 Kings 21) and Ahaziah for seeking healing from the Baal of Ekron (2 Kings 1). The latter prophecy concerns the same issue as 1 Kings 18:17-40, namely, loyalty to YHWH alone: "Is there no God in Israel, that you are going to inquire of Baal Zebub, God of Ekron?" (2 Kings 1:2). This rhetorical question assumes that Israelites owe exclusive loyalty to their national God. YHWH claims to be sufficient to all Israel's needs, including the power to heal, so an Israelite who seeks healing from another, "foreign" deity has YHWH's healing power withheld—a death sentence.

Perhaps the differences between Ahaziah's case and that of the Israelites are sufficient to explain why Elijah does not pronounce judgment on the people. Ahaziah's offense is rather blatant, and YHWH simply intervenes to give him the answer he did not ask for. Indeed, if Ahaziah had inquired of YHWH in the first place, as a loyal Israelite should, he might well have received a favorable answer. As for the people, they are not reported as having done anything.

Also, Ahaziah is an individual offender, and early prophecy of judgment was restricted to individuals.[22] The thinking behind this form of judgment was that the punishment of individual offenders against YHWH's law maintained the justice and holiness of the people; YHWH's judgments were saving deeds for the people. If Elijah were to convict the entire nation, the logic of judgment would change dramatically.

21. C. Westermann, *Basic Forms of Prophetic Speech*, H. C. White trans. (Philadelphia: Westminster, 1968), 142–44.

22. Ibid. See chapter 5.

On the other hand, one can argue that Elijah could very well have pronounced judgment on the entire people. The people's incapacity to respond to Elijah's either/or meant that they were already guilty of apostasy; they had adopted the polytheistic system that parceled out honor to each deity according to its sphere of influence. When Elijah appears before YHWH on Mount Horeb, he charges that "the people of Israel have forsaken your covenant, thrown down your altars and slain your prophets with the sword" (19:10, 14). This bill of indictment refers to actions recounted in 1 Kings 18. The slaughter of YHWH's prophets is reported in 18:13 (with Jezebel as the agent), and the condition of his altar is mentioned in 18:30. The incapacity of the people to confess YHWH is probably the basic evidence for Elijah's charge that they have "forsaken your covenant." Israel had entered into a binding relationship in the past by performative act, and the present generation inherited the obligation of complying with it. When it cannot, it is vulnerable to the penalty for covenant violation.

Nonetheless, on Mount Carmel Elijah does not prophesy judgment, but rather initiates a contest whose object it is to renew Israel's allegiance to YHWH. Elijah is offering the people one last chance before the prophets of national judgment make their appearance. He is able to turn the tide momentarily—the people do confess YHWH. This event is best understood as a new performative act, one that obligates the ninth-century generation of Israelites to a relationship entered centuries earlier.

In what sense does Elijah's "either/or" constitute a performative utterance? It is a restatement of the first commandment, formulated to draw out its significance for the ninth-century generation of Israelites. When the people do not respond, they have violated the commandment. Elijah could have announced judgment. Instead, he devised a contest to elicit obedience. YHWH, in his sovereign freedom, decides to be gracious to Israel. If, after his demonstration, the people had continued to be silent, judgment would have followed. First Kings 19 represents something like an alternative ending in which the people continued to rebel.

The Contest. How can Elijah reduce the question of truth to a contest of power? That is in substance what he does. Power is synonymous with reality for ancient Israel—indeed, throughout the ancient Near East.[23] Elijah proposed to resolve the question in a way everyone would have understood.

---

23. See G. van der Leeuw, *Religion in Essence and Manifestation*, 2 vols. (New York: Harper & Row, 1963); cf. vol. 1, 23–24.

When Elijah's turn comes to light the sacrificial fire, he makes the altar ready, and then he performs an act intended to convince the onlookers and readers that the ignition of the fire was not a trick:

> And he said, "Fill four jars with water, and pour it on the burnt offering, and on the wood." And he said, "Do it a second time"; and they did it a second time. And he said, "Do it a third time"; and they did it a third time. And the water ran round about the altar, and filled the trench also with water. (18:33-35)

No human could make it burn now.[24]

Elijah would have had to have been commissioned by YHWH to stage this contest. Humans do not have the authority to "put YHWH to the test," even if it is to vindicate his claim to deity. YHWH's power is such that it becomes available to humans only on YHWH's own initiative. Elijah acknowledges as much when he requests that God "let it be known this day . . . that I am your servant and that I have done all these things at your word" (v. 36).

The request just cited characterizes the miracle as a prophetic sign. From time to time, prophets would give signs along with their message to verify for the addressees that God was behind the prophecy.[25] Moses was given "signs" to be performed before the Israelites and the Egyptian pharaoh to demonstrate that YHWH had sent him (Exod. 4:1-9). Isaiah offers to perform any sign that Ahaz requests to verify his assurance that Ahaz's enemies would be overthrown (7:10-11). When Ahaz refuses out of pretended piety, Isaiah gives a sign of his choosing:

> Hear then, O house of David! Is it too little for you to weary men, that you weary my God also? Therefore the Lord himself will give you a sign. Behold, a young woman shall conceive and bear a son, and shall call his name Immanuel. He shall eat curds and honey when he knows how to refuse the evil and choose the good. For before the child knows how to refuse the evil and choose the good, the land before whose two kings you are in dread will be deserted. . . . (7:13-16)

What this sign was is a matter of continuing exegetical puzzle, but logically it would have to be some strange occurrence that verified the message before it came to pass. Usually signs were more obvious, as in Isa. 38:7-8, for example.[26]

---

24. Elijah's actions remind me of rituals a magician goes through to prove that there is no trick.

25. See chapter 2.

26. Which does not make them easier to believe!

The problem with signs is that they are not the monopoly of the true prophet. When Moses performed the signs YHWH had commissioned him to do, the Egyptian magicians were able to match them (Exod. 7:10-12). The Deuteronomic Moses must warn Israelites that a prophet of another deity might perform signs, but nevertheless "you shall not listen to the words of the prophet or dreamer of dreams, for YHWH your God is testing you, to know whether you love YHWH your God with all your heart and all your soul" (13:3). Only YHWH has the power to perform signs, but the sign itself does not guarantee the message or messenger.

There is an odd twist in Elijah's wording of his prayer that makes the people's conversion itself the sign:

> Answer me, YHWH, answer me, that this people may know that you, YHWH, are God, and that you have turned their hearts back. (18:37)

Nothing in the prayer explicitly names the miracle, the physical sign; it is the miracle's power to convert Israel that is a sign to Israel. An amazingly circular line of reasoning, yet a profound understanding of miracle: a miracle, or eruption of power, becomes a divine communication only in its rhetorical power.

The miracle itself carries symbolic significance: The sacrificial fire embodies the efficacy of the cult. Did YHWH's cult satisfy all of Israel's needs? The drought is in the background. In 17:1, Elijah announces a drought. A drought might be considered punishment, but in fact there is no indictment of Israel. Probably the text means to suggest that YHWH is withholding the rain to demonstrate that he has the power to do so. If he has the power to withhold, he is the power that bestows it. The latter claim is made good when the drought is brought to an end after the contest (18:41-46).

The challenge and contest in 18:17-40 are a play within a play. There is a contest over power: in the drought, it is over the forces of productivity; in the contest, whose cult is efficacious. This distinction is critical to the nation, for Israel cannot afford to honor YHWH exclusively if he is not the source of the productive power of nature, and his cult cannot show that it has access to this power.

The Contenders. To facilitate this decision for YHWH, the narrator represents the two contenders for the readers' hearts. Neither contender is depicted, but is presented through surrogates: for Baal, an indistinguishable mass of "prophets," and for YHWH a solitary, very sharply delineated individual. The prophets of Baal approach their god through a set routine, though it escalates into extreme measures; Elijah performs a minimum of ritual, approaching YHWH through an unadorned prayer formulated for the specific occasion.[27] Through the human approaches to their respective deities we glimpse the identity of the deity to which they are devoted.

The depiction of the performances of the prophets of Baal becomes progressively satirical. At the outset, they request their god to intervene in the same words as Elijah does, but as their cry goes unanswered, they "limp around [or 'upon'] the altar" (v. 26). Elijah had employed the same word (*psh*) to describe Israel's vacillation between YHWH and Baal (v. 21). Here the limping is probably a ritual dance, perhaps a technique for inducing a trance or arousing their god's passions.[28]

The silence of heaven after hours of supplicating gives Elijah an opportunity to ridicule Baal: "Cry in a loud voice, for he is a god. Either he is musing, or he relieves himself, or is out on a road. Perhaps he sleeps and awakens" (v. 27). What is the purpose for this rude behavior? It is the first time we have heard anything like this.[29] Elijah's ridicule is aimed at an audience sophisticated enough to find such a highly anthropomorphic image of a deity naive, perhaps even contemptible. Of course, he exaggerates the anthropomorphic images projected by the myths and hymns, which conveyed his identity to worshipers.

Elijah's taunt seems to have spurred the prophets of Baal to more desperate measures:

> They cried in a loud voice and cut themselves after their custom with swords and lances, until the blood gushed upon them. And as midday passed, they raved on until the time of the offering of the oblation, but there was no voice, no one answered, no one heeded. (Vv. 28-29)

One has to wonder whether self-mutilation was ever a "custom"; it sounds more like an extreme measure undertaken under dire circumstances. If they knew what awaited them (v. 40), they were quite right in their estimate.

27. Perhaps the portrayal of Elijah is an argument for a particular way of practicing Yahwism. The rituals of Israelite temples devoted to YHWH probably were similar in most respects to the rituals performed in temples devoted to Baal, Asherah, and others. Elijah's simple prayer, formulated spontaneously, projects a distinctive piety. He is, you might say, a precursor of "left-wing" Protestantism. By setting forth this model of worshiper as what is distinctive about YHWH, the text is at least encouraging readers to accentuate the direct, personal relationship with YHWH and downplay the formal ritual.

28. I am surmising this from 1 Sam. 10:5-6, 10-12, where a band is prophesying to music and dance in the name of YHWH.

29. There is nothing like it in the Pentateuch, not even in passages that warn Israelites to avoid serving other gods, such as Deut. 12:29-31; 18:9-14; Joshua 24. There is, however, a partial precedent in 1 Sam. 5:1-5, which dramatizes YHWH's superior power to Dagan by way of surrogates.

One has to ask how this extreme behavior fits the deity to whom they are appealing. Either it is calculated to move Baal to pity toward their self-sacrifice, or to arouse his passionate love for such devotion, or it seeks to enter through ecstasy into the source of supernatural power. In any case, Baal is thought to be subject to manipulation through the rituals of humans.[30]

The narrator portrays their failure in terms suggesting that no being occupied the receiving end of their pleas: "There was no voice, no one answered, no one heeded." In actual fact, they were not seeking a verbal answer; the narrator has phrased it this way to underscore the emptiness of Baal's throne.

Elijah's own actions are designed to underscore how deeply YHWH was implicated in Israel's identity. His first act is to "rebuild" the altar of YHWH (v. 30); YHWH had a historic claim on this place, while Baal had to have an altar built for the contest (v. 26). The act of rebuilding recalls the tribal confederation and YHWH's naming of the patriarch, Jacob. "Israel" has been YHWH's people since it came into being. When Elijah prays for a miraculous sign, he addresses YHWH as "God of Abraham, Isaac and Israel," and asks him to "let it be known that you are God in Israel . . . that you, YHWH, are God, and that you have turned their hearts back" (vv. 36-37). This issue is what Elijah understands the contest to be about: YHWH must reestablish the relationship that he has historically had with the people of Israel.

It is worth attending to the interweaving of particularism and universalism in this "argument." The chapter does not appeal to the obligation of the Israelite people to recognize YHWH alone; it seeks to convince them to do so. Their historical relationship is a reason to accept an obligation in the present. Elijah's prayer that YHWH show that he is "God in Israel" enunciates this nicely. Yet, to acknowledge the historical relationship as still in force, the people must be convinced that YHWH is God indeed. Hence, the second petition: "that this people may know that you are God." The sign by which they will become convinced of this is their own conversion: "that you have turned their hearts back." When the people witness the miraculous fire, they do not confess YHWH as "our God," as did the gathering in Joshua 24, but "YHWH, he is God. . . ." Because of YHWH's claim to exclusive recognition, Israel cannot recognize him as its national God unless it can recognize him as possessing all the powers of deity.

The argument for YHWH is an interlocking appeal to the people's memory, its identity as a people, and the power of their God to continue to

---

30. If they had Elijah's view of divine power, they would have declined to participate in the contest.

be all-sufficient. The argument is, in an important sense, an existential one. It has force only for the people who identify themselves as Israel, and the miracle has demonstrative power only as a confirmation of the relationship that gives Israel its identity.

The satire of YHWH's competitor, Baal, belongs to a particular, indeed cultural, conflict. It suggests that Baal was becoming unbelievable for the people of Israel, sufficiently so to be vulnerable to ridicule. For the reader, the conflict is all but over, Baal will not be a serious source of temptation. The lesson, so to speak, becomes the either/or itself. "Baal" becomes a cipher for all deities and, by extension, philosophical absolutes, that challenge YHWH's claim to Israel's undivided devotion.

Excursus. The killing of the prophets of Baal at the end of the account (18:40) is quite jarring. It reveals the violence and intolerance implicit in the first commandment. The narrative records this act deliberately: Israel's recognition of its obligation to serve YHWH alone requires the suppression of Baal worship, particularly cultic personnel who would lead and foster it. The killing of these representatives of Baal, thus, enacts the people's decision and, in a sense, "consecrates" them to continue to suppress Baal worship. It is this policy that erupted with virulence in Jehu's revolt (2 Kings 9-10).

Mount Carmel and Mount Horeb. 1 Kings 18 and 19 confront the reader with a paradox. The people renew their allegiance to YHWH, and nothing is said of a subsequent defection. It is Jezebel who seeks to kill Elijah (19:1-2), not the people. Yet, when Elijah arrives at Horeb, he seems to forget that Israel has renewed its allegiance   he alone is left (19:10, 14). Moreover, the accusations he makes against Israel refer to actions done before their renewal. The two chapters present clashing images of the situation of Israel before YHWH.

In 1 Kings 19, YHWH announces communal judgment:

> Those who escape Hazael's sword Jehu will slay, those who escape Jehu's sword Elisha will slay. Yet I will leave seven thousand in Israel, all the knees that have not bowed to Baal, and every mouth that has not kissed him. (19:17-18)

Elijah is commissioned to initiate this sequence of judgments by anointing its agents.

The reader is left to ponder the alternative scenarios of this critical moment in Israel's history with YHWH. Is this a case of two alternate "endings" to the crisis that came to a head during the reign of Ahab? How is the reader to reconcile them? Both in their way prepare the reader for the prophetic message of Hosea and the political crisis of the following century.

Idol Polemic

Elijah's ridicule of Baal foreshadows, if it does not inaugurate, an aggressive assault on the gods of the nations and their mode of representation. In Elijah's case, it was not really a "foreign" deity, but a deity with which Israelites were quite familiar. His satire is aimed at undercutting the attraction of this deity to the people of YHWH. Moreover, nothing is said about images of Baal, or Asherah for that matter, but of Baal's identity in the midst of his worshipers as represented by the mode of his supplication. What links Elijah's mocking to idol polemic is the "wicked" tool of satire.

It is not self-evident that idol polemic was directed primarily at deities Israelites were familiar with or attracted to. In its characteristic form, it is a broadside on all gods and their images. "For all the gods of the peoples are idols" (Ps. 96:5). It has a quasi-philosophical breadth and implies an argument about the nature of theological truth.

I would propose that idol polemic be classified as a rhetorical topos. Evidence for this classification is its frequency and rather limited modes of argument. It is distributed broadly through the books of the prophets and Psalms.[31] From this distribution, one can conclude that it was effective; it becomes virtually a cliché. In the Hellenistic era, it found an ally in philosophical ridicule of anthropomorphic religion.

The basic topos contained a few fixed points:

a. The image has the appearance of a living being with eyes, ears, mouth, and so on, but it cannot see, hear, or speak. Psalm 115 is typical:

> They have mouths, but do not speak;
> eyes, but do not see.
> They have ears, but do not hear;
> noses, but do not smell.
> They have hands, but do not feel;
> feet, but do not walk;
> and they do not make a noise in their throat. (vv. 5-7)

b. The image is a product of human labor, and the worshiper reverses the relationship, bowing before the image as his Creator. Again, here is Psalm 115:

---

31. Isaiah 40:18-20; 41:7, 21-24, 28-29; 44:9-20; 46:1-4, 5-7; Jer. 10:1-10; Pss. 96:5; 115:3-8, and elsewhere.

Their idols are silver and gold,
the work of human hands. . . .
Those who make them are like them,
so are all those who trust them. (vv. 4, 8)

The second couplet is not entirely clear to me, but I would hazard the guess that the point is that a person who bases life on an illusion is just as insubstantial.

c. The image is contrasted to YHWH, who is "for real."

Our God is in the heavens;
he does whatever he pleases. (Ps. 115:3)

Evidence for YHWH's reality is virtually always drawn from the conceptual matrix of creation and world lordship, almost never from saving history. The underlying contrast is between Creator and creature.

Idol polemic is put to several uses. Probably the most common is as a vehicle of praise for YHWH. The unreality of the idol is a negative term of comparison for YHWH, the "living God":

They are the work of the craftsman
and of the hands of the goldsmith;
. . .they are all the product of skilled workmen.
But YHWH is truly God,
he is the living God and everlasting King.
At his wrath the earth quakes,
and the nations cannot endure his indignation. (Jer. 10:9-10)

One frequently finds the theme of the incomparability of YHWH in conjunction with idol polemic:[32]

To whom then will you liken God,
or what likeness compare with him?
The idol? A workman casts it,
and a goldsmith overlays it with gold. . . . (Isa. 40:18-19)

The true God cannot be compared to any material conception realized by humans. The one is the creature of human imagination and skill, the other the creator and ruler of all.

Idol satire could also be used in more genuinely polemical ways—to discourage addressees from adopting them or to persuade non-Jews to switch

32. See C. J. Labuschagne, *The Incomparability of Yahweh in the Old Testament* (Leiden: Brill, 1966), 67, 74, 76, 111–12, 123, cf. 140–41.

allegiance to the true God. Isaiah 41:5-7 dramatizes the fearful response of the peoples to the advance of the conqueror from the east: they make images that presumably are intended to save them from the conqueror. Israel does not need to do that, though, because YHWH is with them to protect them (41:8-10). Later in the chapter, the gods are exposed as impotent (vv. 21-24, 29), which may be encouragement to the exiles not to succumb to the worship of Babylonian gods, but it could also be directed at non-Yahwists. The author of these chapters does look for a conversion of the remnants of the nations once the vanity of their deities is exposed (45:20-25).

Idol polemic raises questions that deserve our attention. The discussion of these issues will constitute a fitting conclusion to this chapter. First, it is worth our while to see how idol polemic grows out of the "chief commandment" of the Ten Commandments, or the first and second commandments by one common reckoning. Second, we need to consider how satire works as a rhetorical strategy, and the ambiguities that arise from treating other religions satirically. Finally, we need to consider how satire represents and perhaps betrays the first commandment.

Prohibition and Polemic. The content of the idol polemic can be logically derived from the prohibitions of other gods and of images. At first blush, one might derive it from the prohibition against images alone. That prohibition requires interpretation to be applied: the interpreter must infer the reason images are forbidden—why it is wrong to make and worship them—to apply it to cases. What constitutes a forbidden image? What sort of behavior toward it constitutes worship? The reasoning can then be used as a basis for an attack on religions that use images. To translate it into satire, one has to show that making and worshiping images is incongruous and unsophisticated.

Idol polemic seeks to do more than ridicule the making and worshiping of images, it seeks to discredit the gods that are so represented. Discrediting other gods requires the link we found in the chief commandment. The "other gods" are identified, by means of Exod. 20:5ab, with the images humans make and reverence. The thought may be that humans take creaturely powers—from heaven, earth, or below—and set them apart as deities by producing their likenesses in material and worshiping them. In any case, the "gods" that are excluded from recognition before YHWH are reduced to the status of human products.

Nothing in the Ten Commandments explains the human motives for producing creature images. It could be an utterly natural practice, involving no moral flaw, no sin. For Israel, however, it is a violation of an obligation, and that requires a moral reason, that is, it must be some sort of self-assertion against a known obligation. Hosea's analysis is an important step in the theological critique of idolatry:

> Take away all iniquity;
> accept that which is good
> and we will render the [fruit] of our lips.
> Assyria shall not save us,
> we will not ride upon horses;
> and we will say no more, "Our God,"
> to the work of our hands. (14:2-3)

This confession of sin—really a renunciation—was composed by Hosea for his people to make to YHWH. The parallelism between political policies and idolatry interprets the latter as Israel's effort to save itself. Rather than relying on their God for security in this period of crisis, the Israelites seek to guarantee their salvation themselves. This effort to control their destiny ends up making them playthings in the hands of the empires and the powers they have deified.

Hosea's analysis only concerns Israel. Indeed, Hosea has virtually nothing to say about other peoples and political states, except as they draw Israel away from YHWH and the protection he could give. Following the confession that Hosea inserts into Israel's mouth, he has YHWH say:

> I will heal their unfaithfulness;
> I will love them freely,
> for my anger has turned from them. . . .
> O Ephraim, what have I to do with idols?
> It is I who answer and look after [you]. (14:4, 8)

Idolatry is a sin for Israel, and it requires God's healing to be cured of it.

Idol polemic could be said to take Hosea's analysis of Israel's motives and apply it to all idolatry. To make this idea into satire, the author can describe how the image is made, and what its materials are, and then depict the maker as pleading for salvation from it (e.g., Isa. 44:12-17). To transfer the incongruity of seeking salvation from something humans have made to the god represented, the audience must infer that the god is the creation of the imagination analogous to the manual creation of the representation. In modern terms, the gods are projections of human desire to access power in order to stave off the threats to existence. The gods humans create have the power humans lack and yet need.

Satire. T. JemiClity has called attention to the presence of satirical qualities in many biblical texts, particularly in prophetic texts.[33] A great variety of subjects have been satirized through history, using various strategies for attacking. The satirist may plunge into images of brutality, employ obscene language, and mock ideas. What all satire has in common is its aggressiveness and use of exaggeration in rendering the subject contemptible or ridiculous. Satire may serve a number of different objectives. The satirist may be ingratiating himself with an audience that despises the object of attack, or may be offending an audience to shame it into changing or at least reexamining its certainties. Somewhere in between is the effort to persuade the audience that someone or some practice is unsophisticated, unworthy, or incoherent.

The satire of idols and idol making in itself is for persuasion, though it is frequently used to set off YHWH's uniqueness. For this type of satire to accomplish its suasive purpose, the audience must already be somewhat uneasy about the target. Satire seeks to heighten that unease, to generate contempt, or at least rejection. Evidence from Mesopotamia indicates that worshipers were somewhat uneasy about the fact that the image was the product of human art. A ritual for the consecration of an image for sacred use "unmade" the image after it had been finished, so that the deity could "make" it.[34] The satirist might be said to "expose" the truth—to deny the fiction the ritual was designed to construct.

A good many scholars have maintained that the polemicists misrepresent the meaning of idols for those who worshiped them. The "likeness" was not really the point of the image, and the worshiper did not regard it as the deity. Rather, it was a mode of presence for the deity; we might say a symbol of the reality it participated in.[35] If one regards idols in this way, the ark of the covenant was one. In the story of the ark's sojourn in Philistia (1 Samuel 5–6), the ark virtually acts on its own: it is obviously a vehicle of YHWH's presence.[36] It continued to play this role in Solomon's temple, only it was hidden away so the people did not have direct access.[37]

33. T. Jemiclity, *Satire and the Hebrew Prophets;* Literary Currents in Biblical Interpretation (Louisville: Westminster/John Knox, 1992).

34. See Th. Jacobsen, "The Graven Image," in *Ancient Israelite Reliigon: Essays in Honor of Frank M. Cross,* ed. P. D. Miller, P. Hanson and S. D. McBride Jr. (Philadelphia: Fortress, 1987), 15–32; also A. Horowitz, "Make Yourself an Idol," *Beit Miqra* 143 (July–September 1995): 337–47 (Hebrew).

35. An expression made famous by P. Tillich; see his Systematic Theology (Chicago: Univ. of Chicago Press, 1951) vol. 1, 106–26, 239–40.

36. See P. D. Miller and J. J. M. Roberts, *The Hand of the Lord: An Assessment of the "Ark Narrative" of* 1 *Samuel* (Baltimore: Johns Hopkins Univ. Press, 1977).

37. The uncarved pillars and trees forbidden by Deut. 16:21, 22 were probably idols, perhaps of other deities, though they were not images. Jeroboam's "golden calves" were images— probably of a being on which YHWH stood, or rode.

Idol polemic virtually ignores this aspect of idols, concentrating on the manufacture of a likeness. Hosea does condemn Israel for "inquiring of a thing of wood, and their staff gives them oracles" (4:12a). Whether these were images or not, it is their materiality, the tool-like character, that is incongruous. Jeremiah goes so far as to exclude the ark from the people's future worship (Jer. 3:16), and an anonymous prophet of the restoration after the Babylonian exile has YHWH assert that he does not need or want a temple (Isa. 66:1-2).

Despite this prophetic critique of all symbols of divine presence, their views never became normative for Judaism nor a part of the satire of idols.[38] It was the idols' origin in common material and human workmanship and their iconicity that was ridiculed; the real targets seem to be the deities they represent.

In the Hellenistic period, educated Jews made common cause, so to speak, with the monotheistic philosophical tradition, exemplified by Xenophanes.[39] The philosophers also employed satire to expose the superstitious religion of the masses.[40] A subtle but important difference separated philosophical and biblical polemic, however. For philosophers like Xenophanes, idols were a product of naive minds, and satire was meant to instill sophistication. In line with the prophetic tradition, biblical idol polemic ascribed the impulse behind the production of idols to the human effort at self-salvation. Although the anthropomorphic features of idols are subjected to ridicule, it is the effort to turn the creature, the product of human handiwork, into a saving power that makes them illusory. Idol making is a willful act, belonging to the category of sin. By implication, the deities represented are equally illusory and the product of the will to power. In these respects, the authors of idol polemic preserve the tradition of moral obligation involved in the first and second commandments.

Two questions arise from the biblical satire of idols: (1) Can one impute the category of willfulness that characterizes idolaters who are under the authority of YHWH's commandments to peoples who are not? (2) Does the use of satire supplant the moral relationship between God and Israel, constructed by commissives and exercitives, with an intellectual relationship (in which truth is equated with intellectual sophistication)?

As I already observed, the satire of idols misrepresents the transaction between images and those who relate to the holy through them in order to

38. Cf. B. Halpern, "'Brisker Pipes than Poetry': The Development of Israelite Monotheism," in *Judaic Perspectives on Ancient Israel*, ed. J. Neusner et al.,(Philadelphia: Fortress, 1987) 77–115.

39. Fragments of his writings are found in J. Burnet, trans., *Early Greek Philosophy* (London: A. & C. Black, 1920).

40. On the meeting and misunderstanding of Jews and Hellenistic philosophers, see Yehoshua Amir, "Die Begegnung des biblischen und des philosophischen Monotheismus als Grundthema des jüdischen Hellenismus," *Evangelische Theologie* 38 (1978): 2–19.

render them ridiculous. This misrepresentation may be effective at particular points in cultural history when specific symbols have become problematic, but it hardly represents a just and transformative critique. It may render the audience more sophisticated, but not more obedient.

The peoples were not under the prohibition of images or of serving deities other than YHWH. In theory, then, their manufacture of images and invention of myths are not under moral censure. In theory, at least, anthropomorphic thinking would be a natural, innocent expression of these peoples' relationship to the transcendent. The images may be subject to philosophical ridicule, but those who worship idols are not vulnerable to the charge of willful illusion. Naïveté is not a sin.

Perhaps motives were mixed, perhaps the use of idols in worship and the production of myths to understand the transcendent compounded the natural, innocent motives of the naive with the will to power. The imperial religions of Assyria and Babylon are fit candidates for such a critique. If this explanation holds up, "idolatry" can be condemned though the peoples involved are not under Yahwistic prohibitions. It would be a case of violating a natural morality to which the prophets assume that all humans are beholden (see passages such as Amos 1–2, Isaiah 10, 12–13, Ezekiel 26–32). This motivation, however, should not be confused with innocent imaging.

In response to the second question, the use of satire to weaken the attraction of YHWH's competitors may contradict the very foundation of YHWH's relationship with Israel. It seems rather contradictory for Elijah to pose an either/or between YHWH and Baal, and then ridicule Baal and his officiants. Does he seek to dissolve the choice he has set up? Yet how could Elijah honor Baal as a competitor without denying YHWH's exclusive claim on Israel? When the idol polemics expose the religious practices and beliefs of the Gentiles to ridicule, do they appeal to their audiences' desire to be sophisticated? If so, have they not changed the relationship from submission to God's will to adherence based upon pride of intellect—an assertion of self-will?

The commandment calls for a decision, an act of will on the part of addressees. However, the either/or is between obedience and disobedience, not two equally legitimate alternatives. The choice to obey includes reasoning; obedient reason gives an account of reality that corresponds to the commandment. It cannot float above commitment, as autonomous reason does. Satire is one mode, a powerful one, of dissolving the possible truth of disobedience. For the rhetor, it is a choice between life and death—for herself, and for the audience. Death seldom has advocates.

Irony. Although the biblical authors to whom we owe idol polemic would not have recognized it, the same critique they were applying to plastic images could be applied to "verbal icons."[41] After all, language, too, involves images and is crafted by humans. Language does allow for much greater fluidity and mediation than pictures and statues, but it does delineate an identity for God, one with anthropomorphic features, and the deity depicted is a source of power to those who worship him. L. Feuerbach can be said to have turned idol polemic against the deity it was meant to glorify and defend.[42]

Idol polemic gave biblical religions the "West,"[43] and now it has taken it away. What was once accepted as the accommodation of God to the capacity of human understanding has become the projection of humanity on the Unknown. Obedient reason has to absorb the consequences of its own aggressiveness and indiscriminate condemnation of the iconic in order to speak with power in the contemporary situation.

In Search of an Obedient Polemic. I propose that idol polemic be taken as prescriptive rather than apologetic, as setting forth the requirements for true God language rather than arguments for the truth of biblical God-language.

Idol polemic may well have come into being as an apologetic argument intended to bolster Israelite resistance to the religions around them. Jeremiah 10:2-10 makes this purpose explicit:

> Learn not the way of the nations,
> nor be dismayed at the signs of the heavens
> because the nations are dismayed at them
> for the standards of the peoples are empty. (V. 2)

The text then sets forth the typical contrast of idols—made from trees, overlaid with precious metal, clothed in fancy garments, carried about, but incapable of speaking or acting—to YHWH, "the true God, the living God and everlasting King" (v. 10).

This sort of polemic was also well designed as an apologetic for YHWH to other peoples. This point is salient in Isaiah 41–45, which is interspersed with debates between YHWH and the gods of the ancient Near East. Idol polemic would have had force particularly among those within these cultures that

41. See M. B. Dick, "Prophetic *Poiesis* and the Verbal Icon," *CBQ* 46 (1984): 226–46.

42. L. Feuerbach, *The Essence of Christianity*, trans. George Eliot (Amherst, N.Y.: Prometheus Books, 1989).

43. Idol polemic, broadly conceived, was the "heavy artillery" of the conquest of Europe and the Near East by the religions of the Bible. Naive polytheism dissolved before its onslaught.

were becoming too sophisticated to honor their anthropomorphic deities. It continued to have a powerful effect through the Hellenistic and Roman eras, and was even effective among the barbarians on the edges of medieval Christendom.

In fact, seldom do the passages actually offer any grounds for determining that YHWH is true; there is simply a contrast between the true God, the Creator and Lord of history, and the idols. Of course, an argument against the reality of idols (and the deities they represent) is implicit, which comes back to haunt the biblical God (in Feuerbach's argument). The identification of YHWH as the true God is simply asserted; at a logical level, what we have is a contrast between the idea of the true God and empty human representations of deity.

Idol polemic itself could lead one into complete skepticism or—if one is sure that something true must lie behind human religion—*via negativa*, that is, defining the ultimate by what it is not. It seems to me that this direction is the one indicated by Xenophanes and the religious strains of the philosophical tradition. Religious language is false because it naively ascribes human or other finite attributes to the ultimate source and ground of existence. A true conception of the latter can only be arrived at by purging all analogy and metaphor. At this point extreme rationalism may fade into mysticism.

The *via negativa* is obviously not the way to the biblical God; it would be an extreme form of "ascending to heaven" to procure the word of God (Deut. 30:12). The Deuteronomic Moses assures us that "this commandment" is not to be found in heaven or in some distant land, but that it is "very near you; it is in your mouth and in your heart, so that you can do it" (30:14). As a commandment, a performative utterance, the word of God comes from another—the Unique Other—but can be assimilated into one's culture and one's character. God accommodates to human addressees in the commandments.

Therefore, the prohibition of images is not a prohibition of all iconicity. Israel is prohibited access to God through visual images (though not symbols of presence), but to compensate God flooded Israel with "verbal icons," dramatic language, which mediate God's presence and identity. YHWH has an identity among his people, and can be known in no other way. If the verbal icon and the visual, spatial symbol are legitimate for Israel, the text cannot condemn the religions of the nations simply because they gain access to the Ultimate via visual icons.

Idol polemic is false and intolerant when it is used to satirize all visual iconicity; it expresses the prejudice of one group toward the means of grace enjoyed by another. The truth in idol polemic is the inevitable corruption of innocent iconicity by the will to power. This corruption is most salient in national and imperial politics, where religion becomes an extension and legitimation of the will of those who rule and control; patriarchal religion would fall under the same strictures. The choice of image for one's icon invariably invests sanctity in the creature. The Deuteronomic Moses warns Israel against making images "in the form of any figure, the likeness of male or female, the likeness of the beast . . . winged bird . . . creeping thing . . . fish" (Deut. 4:16-18).

This critique of idols does not stop at the borders; Israel's religion is as subject to it as others. The prophets, of course, had many words to say about literal violations of the prohibition of images by their fellow citizens, but they also had to condemn the "legitimate" symbols of presence, above all the temple (Jeremiah 7). Even the texts of divine law (Jer. 8:8-9) and the words of the prophets (8:11) were subject to falsification. While these latter are not "idolatry" strictly speaking, they manifest the same corruption that makes icons idols.

It was, and is, Israel's calling to relate to YHWH without visual icons. This calling had two effects: it heightened verbal iconicity and forced Israel to critique all iconicity. Those might be thought contradictory, but they are not. It forces Israel to qualify all its symbols and language with "My thoughts are not your thoughts, neither are your ways my ways" (Isa. 55:8, cf. Hos. 11:9). Yet these very texts are saturated with dramatic portrayals of God, beginning with the divine discourse itself. The God who transcends all human understanding accommodates to humans. God's otherness is preserved because the anthropomorphic language serves the performative transactions in which God is known.

If idol polemic is taken as stipulation rather than apologetic, it requires the audience to critique all religious language, beginning with its own. According to what criterion? Its sinful self-assertion. The true God, Creator, and Lord of history is a just and righteous God[44]—not the extension of the pride of power, intellect, or self-righteousness, nor the extensions of the resentment of the losers and victims.

Many theologians have taken the concept of idolatry in this way—including K. Barth, P. Tillich, D. Bonhoeffer, H. Richard, and Reinhold Niebuhr. E. Levinas speaks for this interpretive strategy when he summarizes the content of Torah as

---

44. See J. P. Miranda's exposition of idol polemic in *Marx and the Bible*, 84–85: it is distorted by a monomania about justice, but it is surprising how far that monomania can be confirmed by the text.

an invitation to follow at all times the highest path, to keep faith only with the Unique, and to distrust myth which dictates to us the *fait accompli,* the constraint of custom and land, and the Machiavellian State with its reasons of state. But to follow the Most High is also to know that nothing is greater than to approach one's neighbor, than the concern for the lot of the "widow and orphan, the stranger and poor."[45]

Summary

The first commandment is the only one of the Ten Commandments that forbids a relationship. It requires the recognition of the divine speaker alone. Political sovereignty provides the best analogy. The prohibition depends upon the exercitive force of the utterance; it contradicts the inclinations of the addressee. Even the monotheist is brought into a different relationship with God by the commandment. Hence, the knowledge of God communicated by the commandment is not available in any other way.

The first commandment seems to invite renewal in a way that no other commandment does. In times of uncertainty and crisis, the relationship between YHWH and Israel is reaffirmed and made effective. Joshua 24 depicts a rededication by the conquest generation. The people must choose which deity they will serve as long as they live on the land. It is a decision in favor of a particular reading of Israel's history and entails the acceptance of the consequences of this exclusive relationship. Like the account of covenant making at Sinai, the rhetorical force of the text is to persuade readers of the claim of YHWH upon them.

Elijah also elicits a renewal of the exclusive relationship between YHWH and Israel, but in a crisis when the people must be persuaded to recognize YHWH alone. They cannot decide between YHWH and Baal until YHWH demonstrates that he is their God. The contest concerns power, but power that has its particular rhetorical force from Israel's history. Neither deity in the contest is depicted, both are represented by officiants at the altar. The people are brought back into relationship to YHWH by the miracle that demonstrates his power as deity.

The chapter that follows this account of renewal (1 Kings 19) offers an alternative resolution of the situation. Rather than renewal, the people are sentenced to judgment. The reader is left to contemplate the alternative scenarios.

The account of the contest on Mtount Carmel introduces satire into the arsenal of apologists for YHWH's exclusive claim upon Israel. It seeks to dissolve the appeal of Baal to Israelites, and to be applied by readers to

45. E. Levinas, *Beyond the Verse*, 142.

whatever deity or philosophical absolute might attract them away from YHWH. Idol polemic is a more wholesale satirical assault upon competitors for Israelite loyalty. The popular rhetorical topos attacks the reality of other gods by portraying them as the product of human workmanship; image and the imaged are collapsed. This rhetoric has been highly effective, but it harbors ambiguities that have come back to haunt Judaism and Christianity. The best way to construe idol polemic is as a stipulation for true God-language rather than an apologetic for the truth of biblical God language.

5.
PROPHECY OF JUDGMENT

<hr />

CLASSICAL PROPHECY EXERCISED A POWERFUL APPEAL TO MANY IN MY generation. Our teachers had lived through great events of judgment on modern Western civilization—two world wars and the depression between—and found the prophetic condemnations of injustice, decadence, and idolatry palpably relevant to their own era. Our generation found a platform for critiquing American racism and imperialism, and the trivialization of Christianity in the churches. Then came a precipitous shift in evaluation, you might say a crash in the value of prophetic stock. A wide spectrum of scholars began to demur from the powerful divine-human encounter provoked by the prophets and to express a preference for the modulated, human voice of wisdom.[1] Probably it was the voice of prophetic rhetoric, its magisterial tone and disconcerting certainty, that aroused this reaction. Those of us who were guided by the prophets were at a loss for a reply and began to explore the literary structures of the prophetic books.[2] Perhaps rhetoric can vindicate our original investment in the unique and towering truth of classical prophecy.

What can rhetorical analysis do? Seek to uncover the peculiar power of prophecy. I will contend that prophetic utterances had and still have performative force, that is, the capacity to create the knowledge they

<hr />

1. It is hard to document a change in mood, but there are a number of books that sparked and fueled this interest in wisdom: G. von Rad, *Wisdom in Israel* (Nashville: Abingdon, 1972); W. Brueggemann, *In Man We Trust: The Neglected Side of Biblical Faith* (Atlanta: John Knox, 1972); J. L. Crenshaw, *Prophetic Conflict: Its Effect upon Israelite Religion*, BZAW 124 (Berlin: de Gruyter, 1971), followed up with a number of works on wisdom; both J. Barr, *Old and New Interpretation* and B. S. Childs, *Biblical Theology in Crisis*, raised up wisdom as a dimension of biblical literature that falls outside "revelation in history."

2. R. Rendtorff credits P. R. Ackroyd and R. F. Melugin for sparking the study of the final form of Isaiah: *Canon and Theology: Overtures to an Old Testament Theology*, OBT (Minneapolis: Fortress, 1993), 141–50. See Ackroyd, "Isaiah I–XII: Presentation of a Prophet," VTSup 20 (1978), 16–48; R. F. Melugin, *The Formation of Isaiah 40–55*; BZAW (Berlin: W. de Gruyter, 1976). Rendtorff devotes chapters 13, 14 and 15, 146–89 of *Canon and Theology* to Isaiah, and chapter 16 (pp. 190–95) to Ezekiel.

communicate—to modify the relationship between God and people, which is the subject matter of biblical theology. Although this monograph is entitled the "rhetoric of revelation," we have been focusing on one type of discourse—divine utterances with performative force—and have differentiated this type from the celebration of God's deeds, the evocation of God's presence in the cult, and the divine illumination of human understanding. All these communicate knowledge of YHWH, but in quite different ways. It is my contention that the prophetic utterances belong to the same category as the promises and commandments identified in previous chapters.

Prophecy shares with these other performatives the character of divine utterances. Indeed, one passage in the Pentateuch specifically characterizes prophecy as a continuation of the Mosaic office, so to speak.[3]

> A prophet from your midst, from your brethren, like me, YHWH your God will raise up for you; to him you shall hearken. In accordance with everything you asked from YHWH your God at Horeb on the day of the assembly, namely, "I cannot continue to listen to the voice of YHWH my God and to look upon this great fire any longer—let me not die." YHWH said to me, "What they have spoken is good. A prophet I will raise up for them from among their brethren, like you, and I will put my words in his mouth and he will speak to them all that I command him. The person who does not hearken to my words which he (or she) speaks in my name, I will hold accountable. (Deut. 18:15-19)

Just as Moses spoke for God in the law and in his decisions as leader, God promises to continue to speak with Israel after Moses' death. God will "put his words" in the prophet's mouth, and the audience will be held accountable by God for its reception of those words.

The fact that the audience is to be held accountable can only mean that the prophetic words have performative force. Yet a survey of prophetic utterances would show that the biblical prophets did *not* promulgate commandments and laws. Horeb was a once-for-all event, and thereafter it is a matter of interpretation and application. The prophets did interpret and apply what had been promulgated at Horeb, but they were not law givers, even in the restricted sense of Moses.

The prophets do communicate promises to Israel; indeed, in the popular mind, that is what they are chiefly known for. A case can be made that prophetic promises are in essence reactualizations, under new conditions,

3. James Muilenburg conducted a seminar on Covenant Mediator at the Graduate Theological Union in 1965, which began my interest in the subject.

of promises already in force.[4] However that may be, the conditions were so unprecedented and the status of the old promises sufficiently in doubt that it is legitimate, I believe, to speak of what prophets say as utterances with performative force. To repeat and extend a promise after all saving ordinances have been declared null and void requires divine authorization.

The declaration that all saving ordinances are null and void is the unprecedented word of the classical prophets. The prophecy of judgment is a different kind of performative than any we have studied, and in fact than any uttered before the eighth century B.C.E. This distinction is what attracts my interest in it; it provides us with an opportunity to extend the scope of performative discourse significantly. Judicial acts are set apart by J. L. Austin as a distinct type of performative utterance, "verdictive," and we hope to show that the prophetic word of judgment fits within it.

There are some other advantages to the study of the prophecy of judgment as well. The judgments of Israel that are preserved in the books of Isaiah (cc. 1–39), Jeremiah, Ezekiel, Amos, Hosea, Micah, and perhaps Zephaniah are, with rare exceptions, traceable to the prophet to whom they are ascribed, and their original setting can be reconstructed with reasonable certainty. Accusing the audience of punishable guilt in the name of YHWH is not an activity a person can do anonymously, but requires specific authorization, and an acceptance on the part of the prophet of responsibility before God and audience for what is alleged. Editors may augment and generalize, but not issue charges.

Moreover, the prophecy of judgment is hardly an audience pleaser; judgment of the audience seldom can be ascribed to the desire to win the audience through flattery. Indeed, it is hard to conceive of prophecy as a mode of persuasion, at least in the usual sense of the word. Discovery of the kind of rhetorical objective prophecies of judgment are designed to achieve is an important aspect of our study.

The prophecy of judgment was a revolutionary moment in the tradition. Nothing in the preprophetic tradition really required this turn of events. One can see concepts and developments that foreshadowed it, but the appearance of prophets of judgment was a leap, not a step. The tradition turns against itself; it holds its own embodiments up for scrutiny according to its own values and norms. Prophecy does not introduce new norms and values, but holds the audience accountable to its own. A sifting and refining of the tradition inaugurate a history of reexamination and

---

4. That seems to be the tenor of W. Zimmerli's essay, "Promise and Fulfillment," reprinted in *Essays in O.T. Hermeneutics*, ed. C. Westermann (Richmond: John Knox, 1963), 89–122.

reformation of what is received. What is true in the tradition must be won by vigilant deconstruction and reconstruction.

The prophetic books themselves represent formidable challenges, finally, to my quest for performative transactions between the extant text and its audience. Accusations of guilt belong to particular persons or groups, and cannot be reapplied without a new authorization. The prophecies of judgment preserved in the prophetic books are analogous to utterances within the narrative world of a story. They do not automatically, as it were, address the reader. If this is so, how can the prophecies retain their performative force for the readers of the book in which they are preserved? If they cannot, the thesis of this monograph must be substantially qualified because we would have to admit that prophecy makes claims upon later readers of a different kind than it made on the original audience.

Prospectus of the Argument. We have already foreshadowed the argument of the chapter. Our primary contention is that the classical prophecy of judgment is a type of performative utterance, in particular, a "verdictive," to use Austin's terminology. We will call upon Claus Westermann's genealogy of the basic form of the prophecy of judgment to support this contention. Form criticism will be supplemented by an exploration of the rhetorical strategies of the first prophet of judgment, Amos, strategies designed to persuade the audience that a judicial transaction can be extended to the entire people.

While the prophecy of judgment is, according to this analysis, a transaction between YHWH and Israel; it is also a transaction between a human speaker, the prophet, and his or her audience. The prophet employs a form—actually various forms—to achieve a particular result in the audience. The challenge for the prophet, as rhetor, was to persuade her audience that the message derives from God, indeed, that the audience is hearing God's verdict on the audience's collective existence. The prophets of judgment could not rely upon the form to carry authority; auditors could doubt the authenticity of the prophet, and had good reason to do so. Authority had to be constructed by the power of prophetic rhetoric.

Lurking in the background is the question of the purpose, the rhetorical objective, of the prophecy of judgment. Conventional interpretation has taken recourse to "repentance": the prophet exposes his audience's sin and threatens divine punishment to motivate it to repent. This construal, unfortunately, overrides the verdictive form and many explicit statements of the prophets, and also makes out the prophets to be rather poor psychologists. Perhaps a better model can be found, one that takes its clue from some types of "deconstructive" discourse. Perhaps the prophet seeks to shatter the confidence of the audience, to unsettle and disorient it so that it will be malleable in the hands of God in the course of coming defeat and exile.

The chapter cannot end with the original transaction between prophet and audience; the prophecies have been preserved in books to communicate to later generations. Are the books designed to enter into a performative transaction with the audience or is the audience to generalize from them about the nature of God and human destiny? If the latter, the readers of the book experience revelation second hand. To avoid this conclusion, the interpreter must find a way to fuse horizons. How can accusations designed for one particular audience be applied to another? How can the interpretation of one specific set of international developments be applied to another? How have interpreters through Jewish and Christian history sought to appropriate prophecy of judgment? Have they been successful?

Pioneering Rhetoric

Yehoshua Gitay deserves credit for calling biblical scholarship to attend to the rhetoric of prophetic discourse and for devising a method of analyzing it. To be sure, other scholars had begun to apply the type of rhetorical criticism advocated by James Muilenburg, but he and his students depend exclusively upon stylistic features to signal structure; Gitay seeks to follow the train of thought and how it is designed to persuade.[5] To uncover the argument, the scholar needs to consider the rhetorical situation, with its rhetor, the audience, what the rhetor seeks to accomplish with the audience, and how the discourse is calculated to accomplish the objective.[6] I will be doing something in the same vein.

The prophet must consider the beliefs and attitudes of the audience in formulating the message she feels called to deliver. In the construction of a speech, the prophet must devise appeals to the audience's reason and

---

5. See P. Trible, *Rhetorical Criticism: Context, Method, and the Book of Jonah*; GBS (Minneapolis: Fortress, 1994), 25–48, for her classification. Gitay's view of Muilenburg's and Trible's method is stated in *VT* 33 (1983): 215.

6. Y. Gitay, *Isaiah and His Audience: The Structure and Meaning of Isaiah 1–12* (Assen/Maastricht, The Netherlands: Van Gorcum, 1991), 6; *Prophecy and Persuasion: A Study of Isaiah 40–48* (Bonn: Linguistica Biblica, 1981); "A Study of Amos's Art of Speech: A Rhetorical Analysis of Amos 3:1-15," *CBQ* 42 (1980): 293–309; "Reflections on the Study of the Prophetic Discourse: The Question of Isaiah 1:2-20," *VT* 33 (1983): 207–21; "Rhetorical Criticism," in *To Each Its Own Meaning: An Introduction to Biblical Criticisms and Their Application*, ed. S. L. McKenzie and S. R. Haynes (Louisville, Ky.: Westminster/John Knox Press, 1993), 135–49.

emotions, and establish personal credibility. These devices are called, in classical rhetoric, modes of *invention*.[7] The discourse itself needs to be structured to prepare the audience to hear the thesis, to refute opposing views, and then to wrap the address up with the main points and application.[8] The rhetor will employ literary formulas and figures to make the speech interesting and effective. At this level, Gitay's analysis converges with the method proposed by Muilenburg.

Gitay adopts classical nomenclature and definitions for his study of prophetic discourse. He admits one could devise a new scheme, but considers the Greco-Roman one to be sufficiently universal to apply to prophecy.[9] He even adopts the tripartite division of the rhetorical situation: forensic (argumentation in judicial cases), deliberative (debating over policy), and epideictic (praising and blaming).[10] Isaiah of Jerusalem, according to his analysis, falls under deliberative and epideictic.

Gitay himself is faced with a hard sell. To analyze prophetic texts as oral discourse of a deliberative or epideictic character, he must persuade scholars that the methods with which they have analyzed the texts are flawed and lead to misconstruals as to what the speaker is getting at. Standard operative procedure in the study of preexilic prophets has been to break the text into small, stylistically and formally homogeneous units ("oracles"), and to challenge the authenticity of clauses, sentences, or larger textual segments on the basis of style and subject matter. Gitay considers these small units too small for persuasive discourse, and challenges the idea that a rhetor must organize his entire speech in a homogeneous style. Thus, to analyze the prophetic text as persuasive discourse, Gitay believes that he has to defend a "maximal conservative" view of authenticity: it must be the speech the prophet delivered.[11]

Though form criticism starts from the same premises about the oral setting of prophetic discourse and seeks to understand the "communication code" shared by prophet and audience, Gitay finds it to be a false friend. It has been too dependent on formal characteristics, conventional modes of expression, and institutional setting to notice the persuasive design of the discourse. H. Gunkel was convinced that the prototype of every primary genre was brief and stereotyped, so texts that were long, complex, and inventive were relegated to the status of imitations and secondary mixed forms. Subsequent form critics have tended to agree with

7. Gitay, *Isaiah and His Audience*, 7.
8. Ibid.
9. Ibid., 5–6.
10. Ibid., 7.
11. Ibid., 1–3; "A Study of Amos's Art of Speech, 293–96.

him on the evolution of genres, though they sought to appreciate the more elaborate compositions. Moreover, they have tended to read texts not for their rhetorical objectives, but their conformity or deviation from conventional patterns.[12]

In recent years, Gitay has devoted his efforts to analyzing the prophetic discourse of Isaiah of Jerusalem, but previously he examined several other prophetic books, including the book of Amos. He argues that chapter 3 of the book is one speech, and that the five units into which scholars have divided it (vv. 1-2, 3-8, 9-11, 12, 13-15) are constituent parts of an organic whole.[13] Various references within these segments, such as "your sins" (v. 2) and "on the day I requite Israel's offenses . . ." (v. 14), must be filled out by textual context. Verse 2 is related to vv. 3-8 by the use of cause and effect. One must await vv. 9-11 for a description of the "sins" for which the people will be punished.[14] He outlines the speech as follows:

1. Vv. 1-2   Introduction
2. Vv. 3-6   Refutation of opponents
3. Vv. 7-8   Establishment of prophet's credibility
4. Vv. 9-12   Description of sins and punishments
5. Vv. 13-15   Epilog underscoring thoroughness of punishment

Gitay centers his analysis on vv. 3-6. The point of the unit is to prove that YHWH does evil. "The prophet is not concerned here with the people's sin, but with the fact that God is going to punish them and in the form of major civil calamity."[15] The passage is noteworthy for its use of rational appeal through a series of analogies to make its point. It is also stylistically clever, using anaphora in vv. 3-5, breaking the pattern for its climax.[16]

This review should be sufficient to grasp the way Gitay applies his method of rhetorical analysis to a prophetic text. Now I want to indicate how my approach differs. Let us begin with the status of the written text. I think we are on firmer ground regarding the written text as a presentation of Amos' prophecies for a later audience—the reading audience. We cannot infer Amos's own speeches from it, because it is quite possible, indeed likely, that textual material has been arranged for the literary presentation. We can either regard the extant arrangement as a structure worth contemplating in its own right, claiming nothing about Amos's

12. Gitay, "Reflections on the Study of the Prophetic Discourse: The Question of Isaiah 1:2-20," *VT* 33 (1983): 208–14.

13. Gitay, "Amos's Art of Speech," 194.

14. Ibid., 294–95.

15. Ibid., 197.

16. Ibid., 203–04.

relation with his original audience, or we can piece together Amos's argument from all over the book, constructing Amos's understanding of his audience along with the burden of his message by what he says.

I share the view of the scholars who determine units by homogeneity of style, formulas, and formal structure. While a prophet might well construct larger units out of these, we should interpret homogeneous units as self-contained discourse first, then consider their fit with contextual units. Gitay's actual practice is approximately the same, only he seems to be guided in his micro-exegesis by his perception of the larger argument. From my point of view, Gitay is allowing the editorial presentation to determine what the prophet was arguing, perhaps imputing a connectedness that the editors did not intend.[17]

My most important departure from Gitay is on the value of form criticism. In my opinion, when Gitay adopts the classical categories of rhetorical situation, he is importing a genre from a culture with quite different institutions and religious and cultural traditions. Form criticism has sought to discover genre from the biblical text and the ancient Near Eastern milieu. From a form critical point of view, Gitay has ignored the most important dimension of prophetic discourse: it is presented as divine discourse. Actually, not all of the text of Amos is, and that is an important rhetorical feature. When does the audience hear God addressing it? The authority of such words is quite different from the prophet's own words. How does the prophet formulate words for God, which will convince the audience that they are hearing God? Gitay does not consider such questions.

When we speak of God's discourse, we want to know not only what God says, but what God *does* in the saying. That is, what is the illocutionary stance God is taking in these words? I will argue that passages such as 3:9-11, 12, 13-15 are verdictive-forensic, the one classical category Gitay does not attribute to Isaiah (and Amos). Amos 3:3-8 is the prophet speaking on his own authority, but the whole is, I shall argue later, a defense of his right to speak on God's behalf.[18] I take 3:1-2 to be a disputation, spoken by God, directed at an objection of the audience; the argument is complete in itself.

This review and differentiation should be sufficient to prepare the reader for the approach of this chapter to prophetic rhetoric.

17. He is also stuck defending authenticity of passages that most scholars rightly question; I happen to agree with him regarding Amos 3, but I would not do so regarding many chapters of Isaiah.

18. Gitay's idea that the main point of the argument is found in v. 6b seems far-fetched to me; ancient Israelites naturally ascribed calamity to deity and, if they were "exclusivists," to YHWH. The laments of the Psalms ascribe the supplicant's troubles to God as a matter of course, and great consternation.

Form-Critical Genealogy of the Prophecy of Judgment

Form criticism is the scholarly method specifically designed to discover the conditions for linguistic transactions within ancient Near Eastern society. It was originally designed to identify the conventions for speaking in particular social settings, especially social settings in which form was essential to performance. Unfortunately, in the effort to obtain assured, objective results, form-critical scholarship has tended to become "formula" criticism, and to play down the opportunity for invention within traditional society. Some types of linguistic performance do consist of formulas—rituals and ceremonies, legal instruments—but others foster invention for the purpose of persuasion. ANE society certainly afforded the opportunity for deliberation, forensic argument, and epideictic effusion, which are the classical threesome of Greek rhetoric. In such cases, form criticism invites supplementation by rhetorical analysis. The rhetorical analysis of the originating moment of discourse, in turn, needs to understand the tradition that provided the need, opportunity, and limits of invention.

To understand the rhetoric of the prophecy of judgment, one must appreciate the conceptual framework that gave it effect and limited its practice. The authority of the speaker was an essential ingredient in its efficacy, and the utterance itself may have had the force of an authoritative pronouncement—a performative act. That, at least, is my contention. Our primary task is to identify this performative force, and to show how rhetorical invention served to strengthen it, indeed, in classical prophecy to construct it.

One way to identify the performative force of prophecy is to trace the lineage of prophetic forms. Early or "primitive" stages in the development of a form tend to reveal the type of exigency the form was generated to meet. Once the genre becomes a part of tradition, utterances build upon the shared understanding and expectations of speaker and audience. As crises develop in the conventions of the transaction—anything that would produce doubt as to its efficacy—the speaker must take recourse to rhetorical invention to reconstruct that efficacy.[19]

For this task, I am adopting C. Westermann's genealogy of the prophecy of judgment.[20] The danger of doing so is that it makes this argument a "hostage to fortune." If the genealogy is not acceptable to readers, the thesis that I base upon it will undoubtedly not be persuasive.[21] However, if we

---

19. This description was formulated with prophecy, particularly prophecy of judgment, in mind. The development of some other forms, say, lament, may be different.

20. As set forth in *Basic Forms of Prophetic Speech* (Philadelphia: Westminster, 1968) 129–176.

21. Gene Tucker's Foreword to the 1991 reprinting of the translation demurs from the genealogy; see xii.

try to protect all theological exposition from vulnerability to scholarly critique, we will not be able to pursue biblical theology as a part of the discipline of critical biblical scholarship. While scholars on the right and the left may say that it does not belong within the critical discipline, I certainly believe that it does.

Westermann's Genealogy. The prophecy of judgment of the people can be traced back, according to Westermann, to the prophecy of judgment of individuals. The latter has two roots, the ANE tradition of humans delivering messages of particular deities and the judicial process governing crimes.

Israelite prophecy has antecedents in ancient Semitic culture; a set of texts was discovered at the Mesopotamian city of Mari which record the messages of deities to the king and magistrates of Mari, mediated by individual humans. These mediators, or prophets, reported experiences of revelation, the content of which was a commission to bear a message, followed by the words of the message. In content, these messages were conditional promises of salvation: if the king or magistrate would perform some specified act of a cultic or civil character, the god would reward the person with victory, prosperity, and successors.[22]

While one can trace connections between the content of the Mari prophecies and early biblical prophecy, one has to look within Israelite tradition for the antecedents of the prophecy of judgment against individuals. Westermann cites Elijah's condemnation of Ahab as a paradigm:

> Go and say to Ahab . . .
> Have you killed and taken possession?
> Thus says YHWH:
> Where dogs licked up the blood of Naboth shall dogs lick up your
>   [own] blood. (1 Kings 21:18-19)

We have a commission by YHWH to deliver a message, an accusing question (one might say a bill of indictment), and the pronouncement of the punishment (or sentence). It corresponds to the legal formulation, known as *mot yumat*, in the Book of the Covenant:

> Whoever strikes a man to death shall be put to death. (Exod. 21:12)

The law corresponds in its parts to the accusation and sentence of the prophecy of judgment against individuals; it is reasonable to surmise that the latter was designed to carry judicial force.[23]

---

22. Westermann, *Basic Forms*, 115–28.
23. Ibid., 130–36.

What would call forth this development of prophetic messenger speech? The situations themselves suggest the answer. A king or high official has committed a crime or offense that has gone unpunished because no human court would have the temerity to bring the offender to trial.[24] YHWH, as the source and guardian of the legal community, intervenes to enforce the justice the human court system is incapable of maintaining. Because God does not need the judicial process to determine guilt, the accusation is sufficient to establish guilt and justify the sentence. The decision does need to be announced, because judgment is a performative transaction; the prophet is the agent of this announcement.

What factors in this transaction require rhetorical invention? The addressee certainly knows the act of which he is accused. It only needs to be formulated with sufficient power to touch the conscience of the addressee and convince him that the prophet does not act on his own authority and that the Judge cannot be silenced by killing the messenger. When Nathan confronts David with his adultery and murder (2 Sam. 12:1-15), he takes precautions by telling a parable that elicits David's condemnation of an offender, and using the prophecy to convince David he has condemned himself. This cunning rhetorical invention is rare among the biblical texts of judgments of individuals.[25]

The prophecy of judgment against individuals continued to be employed by the prophets of national judgment.[26] When the prophet encountered official resistance or witnessed egregious official actions or policies, he would single out the culprit. The first of the prophets of national judgment, Amos, was expelled from Bethel by Amaziah, the priest in charge of this national shrine. As a parting shot, Amos issued the following:

> Now therefore hear the word of YHWH:
> You say, "Do not prophesy against Israel,
>   and do not fulminate against the house of Isaac."
> Therefore thus says YHWH:
> "Your wife shall be a courtesan in the city,
>   and your sons and daughters shall fall by the sword,
>   and your land shall be parceled out by line;
>   you yourself shall die in an unclean land,
>   and Israel shall indeed go into exile away from its land." (Amos 7:16-17)

---

24. Ibid., 133.

25. Cf. Westermann's list and discussion, *Basic Forms*, 137–42. 1 Kings 20 is the only other example of such invention.

26. An important piece of evidence in favor of deriving the judgment of the people from the judgment of the individual. Note how Amos 7:16-17 fuses the two.

Amaziah's offense was the act of silencing the prophetic word. As an authorized agent of the king, Jeroboam II (7:10-13), he probably enjoyed legal immunity. Moreover, his offense would not have been judiciable; only the divine speaker would be in a position to judge Amaziah's action a serious delect. Law is, in a sense, being invented on the spot. The sentence, moreover, is a reiteration of the punishment announced in Amos's prophecies against the people, applied to the particular case. Amaziah's fate would vindicate the truth of Amos's message and the reality of his sin in trying to silence it.

The prophecy of judgment against individuals falls firmly within Austin's category of performatives termed *verdictive*. When a duly authorized court finds a person guilty of a crime, the accused *becomes* guilty before the law and within the society under that law. The linguistic act changes the person's status. The decision is, of course, a finding, so the person was in fact an offender before the decision; or the court may make a mistake, imputing guilt to an innocent person. Nevertheless, the judicial act changes the relationship of the convicted to her community and to the authority governing that community.

Of course, the religious skeptic can object that YHWH is not a real person, but a fiction of the community. That same objection would apply to the law itself, and to all the institutions and traditions binding ancient Israel into a national society. If YHWH is a fiction, he is a fiction without which this people could not exist. It would be inconsistent to deny the performative force of prophecy and accept the judicial system, monarchy, and family as "real" transactions.

According to Westermann, Amos created the prophecy of judgment against the people by extending the prophecy of judgment against the individual. The two parts of the judgment of the individual, namely, accusation and announcement of punishment, continue to be found in the judgment of the people. The change of addressee prompted a subdivision in each, but this change does not alter the continuity of function.[27] The alternative against which Westermann was arguing, namely, that the judgment against the people is a combination of "reproach" and "warning,"[28] is much less plausible. The issue is whether prophecy of judgment against the people is a diatribe against general corruption or wickedness, followed by a warning of dire consequences if the addressees do not repent, or a divine verdict on Israel for concrete actions and habitual behavior. Westermann has made

---

27. This effort to systematize the augmentation of the judgment against individuals in the judgment of the people has not proven very convincing: see Tucker, 1991, xiii.

28. Reviewed in Westermann, *Basic Forms*, 14–89.

the case that it is the latter, establishing collective guilt and inaugurating a course of events that will bring national life to an end.

It was Westermann's contention, moreover, that this structure of accusation and announcement of punishment was not just one of a number of speech forms employed by the prophets of national judgment, but the basic or underlying structure of most of their prophecies. The basic form could be augmented, varied, and "clothed" in other forms, but the performative act of declaring a verdict remains the same. While this contention has met a mixed reception, it fits nicely with the idea that the prophecy of judgment against the people required and facilitated an explosion of rhetorical invention. It is to the exigencies that faced Amos and his rhetorical invention to meet them that we now turn.

The Rhetoric of Amos's Prophecy of National Judgment

In order to base my case on actual texts and to respect the intellectual integrity of each prophet of national judgment, let us turn our attention to one. Amos of Tekoa is the obvious candidate. There is good reason to believe that he originated the speech form;[29] he is certainly the first to have his oracles committed to writing, collected, and passed on under his name. The book of Amos is relatively small, homogeneous, and textually trustworthy, yet quite enough for constructing a picture of the rhetorical invention of a prophet of national judgment.

The decision to base the analysis of the rhetoric of a text on form criticism—a strategic decision based on the idea that form criticism provides access to the original oral setting of texts that originated as oral address—entails source and traditional-historical criticism. Prophetic books are not the transcriptions of speeches, but collections of speeches that have been put into writing, arranged, and supplemented by "traditionists" in order to communicate with reading audiences. Traces of each stage in its formation have been left for tradition history to analyze. To approximate the original oral prophecies, say, Amos's addresses to the crowds at the northern shrine, Bethel, we must "deconstruct" the extant text, removing all nongenuine material.

As prophetic books go, Amos is relatively unproblematic. To be sure, some critics have deconstructed the book rather radically,[30] and if this were a work of primary criticism I would have to review and evaluate their reconstructions. As a theological work, that should not be necessary; it

29. Westermann, *Basic Forms*, 169–81.
30. E.g., R. B. Coote, *Amos among the Prophets: Composition and Theology* (Philadelphia: Fortress, 1981).

should be adequate to state a reasonable and rather common judgment as to what can be ascribed to Amos. All the discourse in the book that bears the stamp of the same author, speaking to an audience of Israelites during the later years of the reign of Jeroboam II (ca. 789–748), can be accepted as belonging to Amos.

There is a relatively broad agreement that the heading (1:1), the fragments of a praise psalm called the *doxologies* (1:2, 4:13, 5:8-9, 9:5-6), the oracle against Judah in the cycle against the nations (2:4-5), and the concluding oracles of salvation (9:11-15) are questionable. Scholars do occasionally defend their authenticity. However, I do not consider these defenses compelling enough to include them in the exposition of Amos's message of national judgment.[31] A few other verses scattered through the book sound intrusive, such as 5:15, which appears to be a reader's response to the foregoing message. 5:26-27 does not match anything else that Amos says, but S. Paul is fairly persuasive in his defense of its originality.[32] A few other editorial additions may exist in the book, but they are so well integrated into their context that it makes little difference to interpretation.

The arrangement of the book probably belongs to the post oral stages of its history. Even if Amos were instrumental in some of the arranging, it is not an element of the oral rhetoric. Each prophecy can be taken as a communication in its own right. The first two chapters of the book do represent one address, and will be treated as such. Even though the book contains a few other "composite" addresses, prudence suggests reserve in tracing unities where connecting devices like refrains are lacking.[33]

My objective in this section is to substantiate the characterization of Amos's utterances as verdictive. It is not really a question of fact, but a matter of judgment regarding how the facts, or the utterances of the book, fit together into a coherent picture. Moreover, showing that this prophet of national judgment pronounced a verdict on the people of Israel is not my sole objective; just as important is to understand the challenges he had to face to make his message effective, and how he met them. The result will be an interpretation of Amos's message, which has a performative force realized through imaginative, effective rhetorical invention.

---

31. Only 2:4-5 is a prophecy of judgment, so the rest fall outside the scope of this discussion anyway. Of course, one could take a clue for interpreting the whole book from one of these, as M. Polley does in *Amos and the Divided Empire: A Socio-Historical Approach* (New York and Oxford: Oxford Univ. Press, 1989), but one certainly makes oneself a "hostage to fortune" by doing so.

32. S. M. Paul, *Amos*; Hermeneia (Minneapolis: Fortress, 1992), 194–98.

33. This sidesteps whether one can determine the beginnings and endings of oracles, but Amos is not particularly problematic in this regard, unlike the book of Hosea.

While it would be possible, and perhaps advantageous, to expound the oracles in commentary fashion, displaying how each is structured and designed to convey its message, I will work through the form-critical elements, drawing from all parts of the book. This approach is congruent with the objectives of my analysis: to show that Amos was conveying YHWH's verdict on the people of Israel and how he employed rhetorical invention to make it effective. It produces a composite of Amos's message, which is a message no particular audience would have actually heard, but the composite gives us a better sense of his range.

The Accusation. Let us begin with some theoretical considerations. When Amos changed the addressee of the prophecy of judgment from the individual to the people, he changed the nature of the transaction substantially. Collective guilt is much different from personal; whether it is a legitimate concept is still a controversial issue.[34] Likewise collective punishment. Prophecies of judgment against individuals were a coherent part of the judicial process of a legal community, a compensatory measure to rectify deficiencies; collective judgment "springs" this framework. Amos's project was a daring analogical extension of verdictive utterance, and required imaginative, constant rhetorical invention to succeed.

The prophecy of judgment against an individual concerns one crime or, as in the case of Amos 7:16-17, nonjudicable offense. It can be located and described quite concretely. Because the accused knew what he had done, the accusations were short and pointed; little effort was spent convincing the addressee. When the prophecy was taken up into tradition for a general audience, it was invariably supplied with an account of the offense, which was designed to convince readers that the accused was guilty as charged.[35]

The prophecy of judgment against the people concerns a pattern of offenses that add up to a general characterization of the people, its institutions, powerful classes, and the underlying spiritual tone of its life. If it were a matter of particular offenses that had not been remedied, the prophet could exhort the audience to find the culprits and punish them, or to show remorse for the past offenses and renew their efforts to live holy and just lives. What Amos had to do was to show that the particular offenses were manifestations of a corruption of power, a bondage to vice, and an ideological distortion of reality so deep and pervasive that an intervention of God is required to break the pattern.

---

34. There is a debate over whether the entire German people are guilty for the crimes committed under Hitler: cf. the recent best-seller, D. J. Goldhagen, *Hitler's Willing Executioners: Ordinary Germans and the Holocaust* (New York: Vintage, 1996).

35. See "Forensic Narration" in *Rhetoric and Biblical Interpretation*, 57–79.

The first accusation against Israel in the book, 2:6b-8, is a paradigm of Amos's rhetorical strategy:

> Because they have sold for silver the innocent
>   and the needy for a hidden gain—
> they who trample the heads of the poor into the dust of the ground
>   and thrust the humble out of the way—
> a man and his father cohabit with the same young woman,
>   thereby profaning my holy name.
> Upon garments seized in distraint
>   they stretch themselves out beside every altar,
> and the wine of the fined
>   they drink in the house of their God.[36]

The refrain preceding this accusation, "For three transgressions of . . . , and for four, I will not revoke it," encourages an enumeration of offenses suggestive of corporate, recurrent behavior. Each charge is a description of a particular act, a miniature "forensic narration," but the cataloging points to a pattern of behavior, habitual and pervasive, rather than particular acts in the past. The particular scenes form a larger picture: the rich and powerful oppress the innocent, particularly the poor and vulnerable, at every turn. Hence we find a generalization, couched in metaphors, in v. 7a. It is also possible that v. 7b, "thereby profaning my holy name," is not an allusion to cultic prostitution, as it is often taken to be, but a transfer of a cultic category to moral behavior.[37] In the same vein, the cult is itself described as a scene of oppressive behavior (v. 8).

Amos's accusations are not a shotgun blast at the ills of Israelite society, but a construction of a pattern of offenses that can be generalized as injustice and oppression of the poor and marginal. This fundamental accusation concerns the condition of the people as a whole. It generates further accusations: the oppressive class is decadent, and the religious life and faith of the nation are corrupt.

Condemnations of oppression and injustice constitute a leitmotif running through the book. The most salient articulation is in Amos's charges regarding the judicial system:

> [Woe] to those who turn justice into wormwood
>   and hurl righteousness to the ground.
> They hate the arbiter in the gate

---

36. Trans. S. M. Paul, *Amos*, 44, except for "out of the way," which he renders "off the road."
37. Paul, *Amos*, 83.

and abhor one who testifies honestly. . . .
You persecutors of (the) innocent,
    takers of bribes,
    who subvert the cause of the needy in the gate. (5:7, 10, 12b)[38]

The corruption of the court is particularly grievous because it is the institution devoted to rectifying injustice. When the instruments of justice become the vehicle of injustice, the victim has no recourse but God.

Elsewhere in the book we find general accusations of injustice and oppression associated with commercial greed (8:4-6) and luxurious living (4:1-2). The audience is expected to fill in the connection. Probably the violence portrayed in 3:9-10 alludes to class warfare, for that is the only conflict evident in the book.

Amos had a point of contact with his audience when he charged Israel with oppressing the poor and marginal. The audience knew that it was supposed to protect and enhance the lives of those without power, and that failure to do so would incur the wrath of YHWH. Provisions in the legal tradition[39] and in laments and praises instructed Israelites on this subject. Amos, thus, draws upon norms well known to his audience to condemn his audience. The challenge was to convince it of the seriousness of the problem.

All societies pay "lip service," as we say, to norms and ideals they do not fully, or even adequately, embody. Moreover, the citizens of ancient Israel would have considered protecting the poor as only one requirement among many, hardly decisive for maintaining divine favor. Amos must show that it could be decisive. To do so, he appropriated a form of discourse probably belonging to the priestly administration of the cult,[40] inverted, it and inserted his famous dictum that social justice is the key to amicable relations with God:

I hate, I despise your festivals,
I take no delight in your solemn assemblies . . .
But let justice roll on like water,
    righteousness like an ever-flowing stream. (5:21, 24)[41]

The prophet takes recourse to the language of authority rather than rational argument to introduce this radical revaluation of what is important to

38. Trans. Paul, *Amos*, 157. I follow H. W. Wolff, *Joel and Amos*, 229–30, in inserting "woe" at the beginning of v. 7 (originally proposed by G. A. Smith). Both Wolff and Paul regard vv. 8-9 as an insertion.

39. Cf. Exod. 22:21-27; 23:6, 7, 9, 11, 12.

40. Wolff, *Joel and Amos*, 260–62.

41. Trans. Paul, *Amos*, 188–89.

God, but it does build upon the very tradition it changes. Rhetorical invention can take many forms, and the prophet has in his arsenal the authority
to speak performatively as long as the audience recognizes the continuity
with what it is familiar with.

Amos found other occasions to highlight the seriousness of Israel's sin.
In the prophecy already discussed, 2:6-16, YHWH sets his demonstrations
of gracious power on behalf of Israel (vv. 9-11) in contrast to its oppres-
siveness.[42] This juxtaposition characterizes the oppression of the poor as
response to God, an incongruous response, an inversion of aiding the pow-
erless. The recitation goes beyond the events of the credo—exodus, wilderness, and conquest—to include the good offices of Nazirite and prophet (v.
11), which generates another accusation of rejecting God's gift (v. 12). This
little contrast motif within the contrast motif underscores the significance
of Israel's crimes against the poor, and introduces the accusation of silencing the word of God.

Amos did not have established norms to appeal to for his other accusations. For Amos, the counterpart to the oppression of the poor is the decadent lifestyle of the rich. No laws or moral traditions condemned luxurious
living. Feasting, drinking, and singing were quite acceptable, even desirable,
to Amos's audience. Yet Amos finds reason to condemn the well-off for living in this fashion (4:1):

> Hear this word, you cows of Bashan
>   on the hills of Samaria,
> who oppress the poor,
>   crush the destitute,
> who order their lords,
>   "Bring so that we may imbibe."[43]

The description of the women asking for a drink is offered as a concrete
example of oppression. The audience would hardly have made this connection; Amos is forcing it to recognize that its indulgent ways are
financed, as it were, by the scarcity of the poor. Amos 6:4-7 blames luxurious living for blinding them to their condition: the revelry of the ban-
queters anesthetizes them to the tragedy encompassing the society they are
leeching off of (v. 6c).

One other accusation against the ruling classes may be found in 6:8 and
6:12-13. Verse 8 sets "fortresses" in parallel to "pride of Jacob," both objects

---

42. See Westermann, *Basic Forms*, 182–85, on the "contrast motif." There are two other
recitations of YHWH's deeds for Israel, 3:1 and 9:7, but they serve a different rhetorical
purpose.

43. Paul, *Amos*, 128.

of YHWH's hatred. Perhaps it is an accusation against reliance on military strength. The epithet applied to YHWH, "God of hosts," intimates at his military prowess, and the punishment that follows corresponds nicely. The next prophecy, 6:12-14, may be in the same vein. Verse 13 quotes the accused as saying, "Have we not by our own strength captured Karnaim for ourselves!" Within biblical religion, taking credit for victory is usually false pride and a prescription for humiliating reversal (so v. 14).[44] If we take v. 12—

> Can horses gallop over rocks?
> Can one plow [the sea] with oxen?
> Yet you have turned justice into poison
> and the fruit of righteousness into wormwood—

as a general accusation, Israel's pride in its recent military conquests is an instance of Amos's fundamental charge of oppressing the poor and marginal. Again, the audience has to fill in this enthymeme.[45]

The cult seems to be the target of accusations primarily because it mirrors the culture of the rich and powerful.[46] In 3:13-15, the sanctuary at Bethel is placed in parallel to the mansions of the rich. Amos 4:4-5 sounds like a parody of the current cult: sacrifices and dues are multiplied exponentially. Only the well-to-do could afford to fulfill these new obligations, so only they could please God and secure his blessing. It is no wonder that YHWH rejects a cult life by and for the rich (5:21-25).

Amos must confront another aspect of Israel's religious life: it is a source of delusion and denial. Amaziah's expulsion of Amos from Bethel because he was upsetting worshipers (7:10-13) is indicative of the denial of the prophetic truth. Amos cites such denial as a reason to single out those who utter denials for punishment (9:10). Amos declares a woe on those who looked forward to the "day of YHWH" (5:18-20), when YHWH would destroy Israel's enemies once for all, in a kind of polemic against false hope. He does not dispute that a "day of YHWH" is on the horizon, but insists that Israel will be subject to the same judgment as its enemies. The final verse (v. 18) dramatizes with wry dark humor how inevitable this judgment is.

Amos engages in a theological dispute with his audience regarding the meaning of election, of Israel's unique relationship with YHWH, the Lord of history. In one, he qualifies Israel's favored status:

---

44. See Paul, *Amos*, 218.

45. Perhaps the peasantry had to finance the military, submit to the courts of the walled cities, but was not protected during times of attack.

46. There are two cryptic passages that can be taken as condemning idolatry, 5:26 and 6:13.

> Are you not like the Ethiopians to me, O Israelites?
> declares the Lord.
> Of course I brought Israel up from the land of Egypt,
> but so, too, the Philistines from Caphtor
> and the Arameans from Kir (9:7).[47]

If Israel is not unique to YHWH, if other nations are equally his concern and beneficiaries of his saving power, Israel is just as subject to his judgment as they are (v. 8). Amos's audience would have believed that these other nations were subject to YHWH's judgment, but they would not have thought them precious to YHWH; rather, Israel was special and therefore would never be destroyed.

In the other passage, Israel is accorded a special status:

> You alone have I chosen *(yd')* from all the families of the earth.
> This is why I shall call you to account for all your iniquities (3:2).[48]

This time it is what chosenness means that is disputed. Amos's audience would have thought that election meant special favor, protection against threats to its existence, perhaps a degree of indulgence toward its moral failures. After all, YHWH needs his people to witness to his power and righteousness.[49] Amos insists that, to the contrary, election involves special obligation; a witness, which brings ill-repute on its God by its injustice and oppression, must be brought to task. It is not so much a pronouncement of judgment as it is an argument for the possibility of judgment.

In summary, Amos had to convince his audience of the possibility and necessity of YHWH's verdict. He could not single out just one offense in the past that would require judgment of the entire people; rather, it was a pattern of offenses, embedded in class structures and institutions, which added up to the accusation of injustice and oppression of the poor and marginal. This disobedience was serious enough to deserve corporate punishment, and the efforts to deny this condition before God compounded national guilt. The construction of this case against his audience was rhetorical invention at the highest level.

Announcement of Punishment. Just as in the case of the accusation, there are fundamental differences between individual and corporate punishment, so the extension of the prophecy of judgment to the people entailed an

---

47. Trans. Paul, *Amos*, 282.
48. Ibid., 100.
49. This sentence, and the reply, are my imagination of their thought process; it may be beyond Amos and his audience, but we do get something in this vein in Ezekiel.

analogical leap, realized through extensive rhetorical invention. The logic of punishing an individual offender is retribution; the offender should suffer to the same degree that she caused suffering. This definition is the meaning of the poetic *lex talionis*: "a life for a life, an eye for an eye . . ." (Exod. 21:23-24). The execution of retributive justice vindicates the legal order that governs the community, and thereby benefits the community. Two motive clauses running through the Deuteronomic law spell out this conception of punishment: "you shall purge the evil from your midst" (Deut. 13:5) and "all Israel shall hear and fear and never again do any such wickedness among you" (Deut. 13:11). The same logic applies to prophecies of judgment against individuals. When God judges offenders who are invulnerable to judicial process, he vindicates his law, removes evil from the people, and inspires fear of retribution for wrongdoing.

Corporate punishment would also vindicate YHWH's law and reestablish his sovereignty. If the punishment was a setback to the people, but left them and their institutions intact, it could benefit them in the long run, converting them into a just and holy society. However, if judgment was the obliteration of the people, destruction of their institutions, and the death of their collective memory, as Amos seems to announce, it loses the rationale it has for the punishment of individuals. It would not seem to serve any divine purpose, indeed would seem to be the abandonment of the purpose served by the election of Israel. Perhaps God has given up on the human race in frustration.

How would Amos convince his audience of such disastrous news? Does he really announce a sentence of death to Israel? Was his message calculated to elicit repentance, more of a warning or threat than a settled divine decision? What is to be made of the calls to repentance and intimations of a remnant?

Let us begin with Amos's invention to convince the audience of God's verdict of death. Amos had precedents for the message of collective punishment in Israelite tradition, and builds upon these to make his message credible.

(1) The announcement by a god that he will destroy the enemies of a king is as old as the Mari prophecies.[50] These are not exactly judgments, but verdicts, because the enemy is not accused of offenses; enmity with the addressee is enough.[51] In Israelite tradition, there was the oracle of the war

---

50. Discussed by Westermann, *Basic Forms*, 122–23.

51. Westermann, *Basic Forms*, 204–9, classifies all judgments of foreign nations as a type of prophecy of salvation, for the defeat and destruction of an enemy is salvation to the addressee.

of YHWH, "I will give x into your hand."[52] Alongside of these, or developing later, there seem to have existed prophecies that pronounce YHWH's
assault on nations independently of Israel. Amos's cycle against Israel's
neighbors, which begins the book (1:3—2:3), builds upon this tradition. He
modifies the form by adding an accusation, making the punishment a genuine verdict for violating an international moral order under YHWH's gov-
ernance.[53] The audience would have recognized the legitimacy and cogency
of these judgments, for the majority of the offenses had Israelites as victims.[54] A part of the shock that would have come when he began, "For
three transgressions of Israel, and for four . . ." (2:6), would have been the
force of analogy itself. Amos was transferring to them the concept of collective judgment from those the audience would consider appropriate
(enemies), and making the transfer seem so simple and natural.

Amos follows a similar train of thought in 9:7-8, except that he enunciates its presupposition: Israel is vulnerable to judgment just like foreign
nations because YHWH's relationship to Israel is no different in principle
than his relationship to others; everyone is playing by the same rules, so to
speak. Perhaps this same argument is hidden in Amos's insistence that the
"day of YHWH" will be dark (5:18-20).

(2) The wrath of the deity could be stirred up against a nation because
some serious offense had gone unpunished. This invention is more on the
order of a warning, but it would cause suffering. It seems to have been a
common concept in antiquity; we even meet it in the Greek tragedy *Oedi-
pus Tyrannus*. It is by this logic that David massacres the family of Saul in
response to a famine (2 Sam. 21:1). Amos 4:6-12 would seem to be a further
development of this idea. Instead of particular guilty actions that need to
be remedied, the series of warnings were directed toward compelling Israel
"to return to me" (4:6, 8, 9, 10, 11). Perhaps there was already a tradition for
that type of collectivization.[55] Amos constructs a "history of warnings," so
to speak, in order to demonstrate to his audience that they were given a
chance, but that now it is too late.[56] One warning after another had failed

---

52. Identified by G. von Rad, *Heilige Krieg im alten Israel* (Göttingen: Vandenhoeck &
Ruprecht, 1958). For prophecy, see D. L. Christensen, *Transformations of the War Oracle in
Old Testament Prophecy: Studies in the Oracles against the Nations;* HDR 3 (Missoula, Mont.:
Scholars, 1971).

53. Probably an "imitation" of his prophecy of judgment against Israel.

54. All but 2:1-3. It is often suggested that the audience would have approved of them; they
might even have aroused nationalistic fervor.

55. Some scholars believe that he had a full-blown form of "history of warnings to repent"
at his disposal, such as Lev. 26:3-45. This curse is exilic in its present form, and I doubt that it
could have arisen without the concluding judgment—Amos's own creation.

56. Probably the warnings were from events in audience's memory.

to make an impression, so now they face a final, qualitatively different, encounter with God (v. 12). It is left to the audience's imagination to visualize what this will be,[57] but clearly it will not be another warning.

(3) Finally, a tradition of "ruler punishment" involved corporate suffering.[58] To punish a ruler, the deity might strike a blow to his subjects, thereby weakening him. When David takes a census, he incurs YHWH's wrath, and must choose between kinds of divine assault, two of which will kill off a portion of his subjects (2 Samuel 24). This choice would certainly be experienced by the populace as a form of collective punishment. Indeed, throughout history subjects have had to suffer for as well as benefit from the policies of their rulers.

Amos does not specifically single out Jeroboam as an offender, though several occasions in the book mention the judgment that will overtake him and his house (7:9, 10). Amos 6:1-3 does single out the capital cities of Israel and Judah, and identifies the governing officials as the specific culprits.[59] Their specific offense is a false sense of security, a denial that Israel is as vulnerable as her neighbors to blows of a mighty foreign power.[60] It does not quite fit the description of ruler punishment, but an audience familiar with the concept would be able to imagine suffering for the policies of its rulers. Indeed, the victims of the injustice of Israelite society would suffer along with the perpetrators; Amos's message would not have been good news for them, though they would receive the satisfaction of witnessing the punishment of their oppressors.

Amos's employment of these traditions of corporate punishment and suffering would have forced the audience to face realistically the possibility of national demise, and his grounding of the announcement on accusations of systemic evil made it sound inevitable. He had other inventional resources at his disposal to reinforce his message. Several features stand out in the first prophecy against Israel, 2:6-16. The announcement of judgment is signaled by *hinneh*, "behold," and a first person pronoun, setting it apart from the accusations and contrast we have heard so far in the oracle. Although 2:6-16 is designed to build upon the analogy between YHWH's judgment of foreign nations and of Israel, the announcement itself breaks the rather formulaic announcements against the others (1:5, 8, 10, 12, 14,

---

57. There is a reference to a gesture, perhaps some movement suggesting a deadly blow; now the audience has to imagine that as well.

58. D. Daube, *Studies in Biblical Law* (New York: KTAV, 1969), 161–66.

59. This passage, along with 5:5, shows that Amos considered his verdict to apply to the whole people of YHWH, Judah as well as Israel. History, however, differentiated them.

60. Some of the references in this woe are to events that happened after Amos's mission to Israel.

2:2). This final prophecy is not only the climax of the series, but the message needing the most forceful language. Amos employs metaphors to depict the divine intervention. Unfortunately, the verb he uses is so unusual that translators have had to guess as to its root and meaning.[61] Is this ambiguity deliberate, or did Amos's language communicate a specific image to his audience? If it were deliberate, even his audience would have been drawn into the project of visualizing how a cart in the mud might evoke God's assault on it. If one, for example, opted for the meaning of "press down," an analogy could be made between it and the accusation of "trampling the heads of the poor into the dust of the earth" (v. 7). YHWH would be doing to Israel what its ruling classes are doing to those under their power. Images of poetic justice, of a correspondence between the offender's actions and God's action against the offenders, are common in the prophecy of judgment.[62] In Amos, the accusation of violence within Samaria will be punished by violent assaults from enemies (3:9-11). Those who have accumulated houses and vineyards by injustice will not enjoy them (5:10-12). A time of famine and drought of the prophetic word (8:11-12) will form a fit punishment for a people who silences and denies the prophecy of judgment.

The other thing to note about 2:13 is that it announces a divine intervention, emphasized by the first person pronoun. It was certainly standard to speak of God's intervention against foreign nations, as the oracles in 1:3—2:3 do. However, the prophecy of judgment against an individual seems not to have.[63] A judicial verdict focuses on what will happen to the offender, not on the agent of the punishment. When a prophecy of judgment against an individual conforms to this pattern, we can with justice use our modern term *sentence*. However, the prophecy of judgment against the people frequently announces God's intervention to bring punishment about. Something about the superlegal situation invites strengthening. That God is pronouncing a verdict in the words of the prophet seems to require that God back it up in the announcement, as though God were saying, "I myself will enforce this."[64] Given the background of the divine intervention to defeat and destroy, the audience would also hear, "I will intervene against you as I intervene against enemies."

---

61. Paul, *Amos*, 94–95.

62. Hosea is famous for them—cf. 4:4-10, 13; 8:7-10; 9:1-3; 10:1-2, 9, and so on. See P. D. Miller, *Sin and Judgment in the Prophets*. SBLMS 27 (Chico, Calif.: Scholars, 1982). Although not an image of divine intervention, there is a poetic justice involved in Ahab's sentence: "In the place where dogs licked up the blood of Naboth shall dogs lick up your blood" (1 Kings 12:19).

63. Nathan's against David does (2 Sam. 12: 7-8), but neither of Elijah's.

64. Occasionally he actually says that—the divine oath.

When Amos describes the consequences of YHWH's intervention to punish, he frequently employs images of military defeat, death and destruction, and exile. His century was a violent one; great empires were competing with each other for the subjugation of the smaller states, and the latter were attempting to maintain their independence by strategic alliances and as much of an army as they could muster. The walls of Assyrian palaces celebrate precisely the horrors Amos evokes in his poetic images. The most effective way for the prophet to depict such horror was to break it down, give an impression of how it will feel to live through it. In 2:14-16, Amos flashes a set of seven images of military defeat across the mind, all based upon the idea that a particular virtue will fail the test. In 5:1-3, Amos appropriates the dirge—lament for the dead—to announce the annihilation of the army and people.

While Amos evokes images of destruction and exile that reflect his century, images that would be all too real for his audience, he says almost nothing of the imperial politics itself. Assyria is not even named in the book, though it introduced the policy of mass deportations to which Amos condemns the survivors of his audience. Amos seems to have been unconcerned about international politics per se, and only drew upon imagery of war.[65] His fellow eighth-century prophets of national judgment would underscore their announcements of punishment by depicting very specific international threats and the vain efforts of king and counsellors to avoid disaster.[66]

Did Amos announce his death sentence on Israel as a foregone conclusion or could it be averted by repentance? This question has confronted interpreters of the book throughout history, and it divides interpreters to this day.[67] Amos does exhort his audience to seek God (5:4-6) and good (5:14-15), and in the context of the book this exhortation would constitute a call to repentance. Because, however, these exhortations have an ironic, qualified cast to them, as we shall see, those who interpret Amos as offering hope must build their cases on theoretical considerations. Why would the prophet go to such lengths to convince his audience of impending disaster if it could do nothing about it? Moreover, if divine wrath is an expression of divine love, as surely it is, vindication of divine justice (the legal order) cannot be for its own sake.[68] The announcements of punishment must be, it is proposed, threats of what will happen if the people do not change their ways.

65. N. K. Gottwald, *All the Kingdoms of the Earth: Israelite Prophecy and International Relations in the ANE* (New York: Harper & Row, 1964), 94–103.

66. Ibid., 119–208.

67. See Zechariah 1:2-6 on preexilic prophets of judgment.

68. See A. Heschel, *The Prophets*, Part II (New York: Harper & Row, 1962), 59–78.

However, the actual words of Amos thwart the effort to classify him as a "prophet of repentance." The exhortation to "seek me and live" (5:4) is turned against the cult:

> But do not seek Bethel,
> nor go to Gilgal!
> Nor cross over to Beer-sheba!
> For Gilgal shall go into galling exile
> and Bethel shall become a nullity (5:4b-5).[69]

These words are followed by an exhortation referring to YHWH in third person:

> Seek the Lord that you may live!
> Lest he flare up like fire against the house of Joseph
> and consume Bethel with none to quench it (v. 6).[70]

Here, perhaps is a glimpse of hope, but its juxtaposition with the unconditional condemnation of the shrines at which YHWH is available leaves the audience wondering where and how to seek its God. Perhaps by design, the next oracle (5:7, 10-12) deals with the gates of justice.

The exhortation to seek good (vv. 14, 15) turns on the popular belief that YHWH is with Israel. For Amos, this basis of national confidence and hope can only be true if the people give undivided devotion to the good. What the good is is explicated in the second exhortation:

> Hate evil and love good!
> And set up justice in the gate.

Here we have the norm against which Amos has measured Israel throughout his prophecies. By implication, the people, or at least its judiciary and wealthy classes, have loved evil and hated good. Hence, the serious qualification of the hope that follows:

> Perhaps the Lord, the God of hosts,
> will show favor on the remnant of Joseph.

The hope is couched as a conditional possibility, and it only reaches to a portion of the people. The "perhaps" indicates that the people are guilty and have been sentenced, so to speak. If Amos were warning the people of

---

69. Paul, *Amos*, 157.
70. Ibid., 157.

a judgment that will come if they do not "return" (4:6, etc.), the "perhaps" would be confusing and a weak motivator. In the Deuteronomic tradition, God's favor is set forth as a certainty, a promise, for those who choose faithfulness and obedience (Deuteronomy 11, 29; Joshua 23). A call to repentance in conjunction with a warning should guarantee advantage to the audience. The "perhaps" of Amos, however, assumes, in contrast to the Deuteronomic tradition, that the people stand convicted before their divine judge; the judge is free to show clemency, but is not obliged to do so. Repentance must be done for its own sake, so to speak, out of genuine compunction, not as a way to manipulate God.[71] The "perhaps" underscores the uncertainty of the outcome.

In addition, God's favor—in this case forgiveness[72] that maintains the intimate, empowering relationship articulated in the slogan "YHWH is with us"—is held in prospect for a remnant, not all Israel. It is one further indication that Amos announced punishment of the whole people as an irrevocable decision. The whole people will pass through events of defeat, destruction, and exile; some may survive to bear the memory of divine judgment and fulfill the divine vocation. Who, where, how is left unsaid.

The prospect of a surviving remnant itself was a dangerous idea because the audience might seize upon this shred of hope. "It will happen to the wicked, but I will survive." An isolated verse in Amos 3 seems to be directed at such evasion: "As a shepherd rescues out of the mouth of the lion two shank bones or a tip of an ear, so shall the Israelites dwelling in Samaria be rescued, only with the head of a bed or the foot of a couch" (3:12). This remnant may only have to do with the capital city, but certainly the idea of *remnant* is satirized.

Again and again, the direction of Amos's announcement of punishment is to close escape routes. When the addressee has escaped a lion and a bear, he is bit by a snake in his own house (5:19). The vision of judgment in 9:1-4 sums it up: there is no escape, YHWH is bent upon visiting evil on his audience, an evil that is the fruit of its own oppression.[73] Amos's message of punishment is not designed to answer abstract questions about what will happen to Israel, but to make the audience face the darkness, accept its inevitability and rightness. Perhaps he envisaged a remnant of the innocent and repentant surviving, to carry on the tradition and incorporate the judgment, but his rhetorical task was to bring the people, his audience, under judgment in his very proclamation.

71. Ibid., 178. Note repentances of David, Ahab; Ninevah in Jonah.
72. Ibid., 177–78.
73. K. Koch, "Gibt es ein Vergeltungsdogma im Alten Testament?" *ZThK* (1955), 1ff. [ET = "Is There a Doctrine of Retribution in the Old Testament?" in Theodicy in the Old Testament, ed. J. L. Crenshaw (Philadelphia: Fortress Press, 1983).]

The Rhetorical Effect of the Prophecy of National Judgment. If the people could not avert punishment, why would Amos expend such efforts persuading them of the depth and breadth of oppression and decadence in Israelite society and of the inescapability of defeat, massacre, and exile?

Let us begin with a meditation on why verdicts are announced as the conclusion of criminal trials. Why not simply carry out the punishment? The defendant cannot avert the punishment by remorse and repentance, though clemency might be shown a compunctious offender. I would suggest that the declaration of a verdict and sentence changes the status of the accused before the law and society. The accused and the society need to employ language that defines and puts the new relationship into effect. It also inaugurates the execution of the sentence. Not only does the punishment entail actions of authorities against the guilty, it also entails subjective appropriation by the guilty of the new status and its consequences. The offenders should feel remorse for their violation of trust and the harm they have done, and anguish over the suffering they must undergo. The community, for its part, needs a public confirmation of the power and majesty of the law; its punishment of the offender consolidates the community around its values and collective interest in order.

Do such considerations fit the prophecy of judgment against the whole people? Here the accused and the legal community that is under the law and enforces it are the same. The law giver and judge, however, is above the accused community, and not only renders the decision but enforces it. The prophet is only his spokesman. The prophecy changes the status of the accused vis-à-vis the law giver and judge—who also happens to be the community's benefactor and defender. The people need to know that their status is changed, that they have violated the very order they live by and enforce, and therefore they must themselves have it enforced against them. As they undergo defeat and exile, they need to realize it is their own doing, so to speak.

Convincing a whole people of its guilt and the possibility and inevitability of destruction as a people would be a monumental rhetorical challenge. Indeed, it would be insurmountable. The prophecy of judgment cannot have the formal, official performative force of an actual court verdict. In a certain sense, the trial takes place after the verdict is announced: it is not the judge who must be persuaded, but the guilty. And they must be persuaded of a deep, pervasive evil, an evil the members of society take for granted; they may bemoan its harshest aspects from time to time, but they accept it as the price of survival. Anyway, Israel is supposed to be in a privileged relationship with God, and they are filled with thankfulness and deference to God. Surely he would not betray them or treat them like an enemy. He needs them because they honor him, feed him sacrifices, and witness to his greatness.

If Amos's task was to convince them of their guilt and punishment, and motivate them to show remorse and to reform their society, he was bound to fail. If he were to succeed, YHWH would have shown grace to a remnant. Punishment of a nation is not quite like punishment of an individual. The people is guilty not only of a series of offenses that should be rectified by "an eye for an eye . . . ," but of a corruption of the institutions, a pattern of power arrangements, and a spiritual malaise that must be broken. If the systemic evil could be broken, God could mitigate the punishment for past offenses. But first they must have their consciences redeemed; they must be brought out of themselves to see the enormity of their guilt in the eyes of God. The prophecy of judgment is at once an effort of getting the people to see themselves as YHWH sees them, and a kind of test to see whether they can be reformed rather than destroyed.

Amos's task, so conceived, is bound to failure. The audience is going to attack the messenger, or at least deny his authority and expel him. The authorities cannot tolerate such a disturber of the peace. He must be a plant of their enemies, or some sort of prank.

We can, however, view his task from another angle, and from it we can regard him as a success, indeed, a brilliant performer and thinker, whose effect on his own time and subsequent history is incalculable. His message itself inaugurated judgment. It unsettled, disturbed, rendered certainties uncertain, turned the traditions by which the audience justified its existence into an accusation, weakened resolve, intensified the people's (and rulers') fears about the course of political events, stirred up social and political conflicts, and touched symbolic nerves (like nightmares). While the people resisted his message, they could not repress it entirely; the foundations of their world were swaying like the earthquake he predicted (8:8).[74]

What purpose would this serve? While I doubt that Amos could have articulated it, he was shattering the people's entrenched oppressive way of life and blindness to their evil so that they would be malleable clay again in the hands of God (cf. Jer. 18:1-11). At least some could be shaped by the coming events of defeat and exile into a shape pleasing to God.

---

74. This may seem a rhetorical exaggeration, but it is noteworthy that the prophets themselves describe themselves as weapons and tools in the hand of God, as in Hos. 6:5: "Therefore I have hewn them by the prophets, I have slain them by the words of my mouth. . . ."

Amos the Rhetor

So far I have been arguing that the prophecy of judgment is a transaction between YHWH and Israel, a transaction borne by the speech form. Now we can look at it as a mode of human discourse. To treat prophecy solely in terms of the transaction it sought to elicit between God and people is to "mythologize" it, for it was equally a vehicle for the communication of a human speaker to his audience. The rhetorical challenge for the prophet was to convince the audience that he does indeed convey the message of God.

The office of prophet, if we can call it that, was unlike the other positions of power and responsibility in ancient Israel. The prophet's authority was entirely dependent upon his capacity to persuade audiences that he conveyed the word of God. Kings, priests, and judges carried institutional authority; their institutions were founded by God, and officials were responsible to God for their performance, but the community recognized their actions as long as they acted within their institutional competence, using sanctioned means of enforcement. While prophets were also recognized as legitimate, and sought after in times of decision and crisis, they had to persuade their audience of the divine origin of what they said, or they had no effect; they had no power of enforcement.[75]

The wise woman or man, the counselor, was the only other Israelite "office" to rely so heavily on persuasive power. The authority of the wise depended on their capacity to persuade their audience that a particular policy or strategy or mode of life would succeed. In a sense, wisdom's guiding principle was prudence—the action to take that will attain the end the actor desires. The prudent action, according at least to scriptural wisdom, was also the just and honest and pious action, but there is no recourse in classical wisdom to God's revealed law or his demand in the particular case.[76]

Thus, prophets and the wise were equally dependent on rhetoric, but at opposite poles on how they sought to persuade their audience. The prophet had to frame a message that convinced the audience it was hearing God. This challenge was relatively unproblematic when the prophet was experienced as charismatic and the message corresponded with the audience's expectations or desires. The public was happy to support prophets at sanctuaries, and kings supported them at the palace. They were thought to be odd, and could be the objects of ridicule, but they were also feared for their power and holiness.

75. Some early prophets incited coups, but it was their power to persuade usurpers to act that made them effective.

76. Intertestamental wisdom began to identify wisdom and revealed Torah.

The rhetorical challenge for prophets of judgment was much greater. Those that condemned kings and high officials took their lives in their hands. The addressee had to be persuaded that killing the messenger would compound his troubles with the Judge. It was left to narrators to persuade a larger audience of the culpability of the offender. The prophet of national judgment had an even greater challenge, as I argued in the last section. To a large extent, the prophet's apologia for his genuineness converged with the task of convincing the audience of its guilt and impending punishment.[77] Naturally, an audience that rejected the latter would deny that the prophet spoke for God: If God says it, it must be true; if it is not true, God must not have said it.[78]

The prophet could also mount a defense of the genuineness of his commission and personal goodwill, and the congruence of his message with God's past revelation and even human wisdom. Such apologia could not make up for a lack of rhetorical power in oracles, but it could block certain psychological ploys the audience might devise to discount the message. In this section, I will review Amos's apologia. My thesis is that he did not rely on divine authority to mask personal invention, but took recourse to invention to give power to the word he had, he believed, received.

Public Apologetics. Two passages in the book of Amos (3:3-8, 7:10-17) contain defenses of his authority to speak. In both the authority lodges in the act of God that calls forth prophetic discourse. While each implicitly argues for the prophet's personal integrity, Amos's own character is not appealed to as a reason to believe him.[79] Because he is charged with conspiracy in one case, he might be expected to defend his own integrity, but he simply refers his interrogator to YHWH. It is as if he were saying, if you cannot believe the message, check it out with the Sender.

Both Amos and his audience shared a religious worldview in which God spoke to humans, both individuals and the community, by calling and commissioning human spokesmen. Amos's claim was not, thus, to a unique status, but to a culturally recognized one. A person who makes a claim to speak for God in a cultural milieu that does not recognize such a status is considered deranged; it has no rhetorical power, to say the least. In a culture that recognized such a claim, it has unique rhetorical potential.

However, the claim to such a status did not guarantee that the audience would confer it. As the people of YHWH, Israel was obligated to receive the

77. Thus, the exposition of the last section could be repeated here.
78. This logic would not necessarily have applied within polytheism, with its diffusion of powers, but it would in exclusivistic Yahwism.
79. Classical rhetoric knew of the argument from *ethos*, of the character of the speaker.

prophetic word as God's (Deut. 18:18-19), but not all the words purported to be from the deity were (18:20). The audience had to make a judgment, to practice discernment. Ultimately this judgment came down to the persuasive power of the prophet. The truth of prophecy could not be established by an appeal to authority, the discourse had to persuade the audience that God could and does say what he is purported to be saying. Prophetic authority is being constructed rhetorically.

The hitch in the prophetic transaction is that the audience may not be competent to make a sound judgment. The book against rhetoric is that speakers can gain assent not only by speaking the truth with power, but by speaking the semblance of truth, speaking what the audience, in its injustice and self-will, wants to hear. If the prophet, or other rhetor, speaks an unpleasant or disturbing truth, it will be deemed false or at least overly pessimistic, in comparison to soothing words. Consequently, the truth of prophetic discourse cannot be identified with its immediate power to persuade. Deuteronomy 18:21-22 offers the test of accurate prediction. If one takes this criterion figuratively—that is, that the message offers the profoundest, most realistic understanding of the course of human events[80]—it holds up well, and was the basis for the inclusion of the prophecies of Amos in the canon.[81]

If Amos knew that his audience would be hostile and would not, or probably could not, accept the truth of what he had to say, he had to devise a rhetorical strategy for generating the possibility of offense. He could not afford to have his message dismissed, even if it could not be accepted. In one apologetic, he draws the audience into a process of analogical reasoning, which forces it to acknowledge that there must be something behind what he says. In the other, he undercuts his interrogator's effort to ascribe dishonorable motives to his disturbance of the peace.

Amos 3:3-8 can be treated as an independent unit. The speaker is not YHWH, but an observer of life. There is no first person reference; Amos does not explicitly claim anything about his own message or call. The string of analogies starts "far away" from the point to which the passage argues. The audience is to be caught unawares. The analogies are a set of perceptions of causal relations: when someone sees two individuals walking together, the observer assumes they must have arranged the meeting; of course, this inference is not a necessary one, it is just a natural one. Likewise when one hears lions roaring, or sees a bird caught in a trap. The analogies are subtly approaching the target. Next comes a trumpet blast in a city. The

<hr/>

80. This is approximately how Jeremiah applies it in 28:8-9.
81. See Th. C. Vriezen, *An Outline of Old Testament Theology,* trans. S. Neuijen (Newton, Mass.: Branford, 1960), 40–42, on the exile as the criterion for inclusion in the canon.

connection changes: it is not what caused the trumpet to be blown, but the effect the call to alarm has on those who hear it. Why the change? Perhaps the analogies were becoming too predictable. Perhaps Amos is suggesting how the audience should take his message.

Verse 6b exposes the rhetor's subject, but not his point. "If evil happens in a city, does not YHWH do [it]?" This question appears to return to the analogies that infer a cause from an effect. When one observes or experiences a disaster, one surmises that YHWH was behind it. Amos assumes that his audience shares that connection; he is reminding them of it. If the audience is accustomed to ascribing disaster to the deity, it should not dismiss a message that warns of such an event.

Amos needs another premise, one the audience may not believe. The grammatical structure changes. Of the two *ki* clauses, the first does not seem to be a logical connector, but on the order of an interjection. "*Now* Lord YHWH does not do a thing [word] *unless* he reveals his counsel to his servants, the prophets." Prophets are privy to the plans of God. Why? So that they can prophesy, and the people can know what is happening to them. What the people are to do with the message is not stated, it is left to the audience to decide. They should, at least, respond to it as they would a trumpet sounding an alarm.

Amos brings his argument to its point in v. 8. Verse 8a returns to the image of a roaring lion, this time with the effect it should cause (fear), not the inference. In fact, if one surmised that the lion had already caught its prey, one would not fear. Now Amos is suggesting that the lion is on the prowl; his roar quite naturally arouses a sense of danger. Now comes the analogical leap: "God has spoken, who can but prophesy?" It is not exactly what one would expect. Why not: God has spoken, should not the people fear? Amos takes us, in the surprising conclusion, into the recesses of prophetic experience. The prophet is compelled to speak, it is as normal as shuddering at the roar of a lion.

This argument does not lead the audience directly to the conclusion that the message is true, but that the messenger is speaking out of an experience they can understand and confirm. He does not recount his call, nor even refer to his own message, but he asks the audience to put itself in his shoes. His prophecy has an encounter behind it. Even if the audience cannot accept the validity of the message, it must acknowledge the legitimacy of the prophet's speaking it. Of course, if it meditates on the reasoning that led to this conclusion, it would realize that it had better take it as possibly true.

Amos 7:10-17 is a much different speech form from the foregoing, a narrative rather than an address. We have already had occasion to explore the unit as a prophecy of judgment addressed to an individual. What is note-worthy in the present connection is the exchange between priest and prophet before Amos's prophetic pronouncement. How was Amos's prophecy perceived? How did Amaziah discount its claim to be from YHWH? What status did Israelite officials ascribe to prophecies? How does Amos expose these perceptions and strategies of denial?

Amaziah sends a message to King Jeroboam II passing on a digest of Amos's message and a characterization of the speaker.[82] His summary consists of a prophetic sentence, formulated as a prediction of Amos, not an act of God. Indeed, Amaziah makes no mention of YHWH in anything he says to Jeroboam or to Amos. The Mari parallels make it a point to name the god speaking, for that is the true sender. Amaziah assumes that Jeroboam knows, I should think, that Amos speaks in YHWH's name, but he leaves it out to "de-legitimize" Amos's prophecy. Amaziah also characterizes Amos's activity: he is causing a disturbance, indeed the land is about to explode under the pressure. From the point of view of governing authorities, such activity is cause enough for action. Moreover, Amos's disturbance is not innocent, it is some sort of "conspiracy" to upset the political order.[83]

We discover more of Amaziah's thinking when he addresses Amos. He tells him to return to Judah where he belongs. Actually, Amos is told to "flee": Amaziah pretends to offer him a chance to escape with his life. Amos is addressed as *seer*, perhaps in disparagement. When he is told to "eat bread there and prophesy there," Amaziah is most likely classifying Amos as a prophet who lives at a sanctuary and is fed from sanctuary revenues. If we combine what Amaziah says to Amos with what he wrote to Jeroboam, he thinks that Amos was sent up here by southerners to cause a disturbance and perhaps spark some public revolt.

Amaziah does not question Amos's formal compliance with prophetic discourse. He speaks in the name of Israel's God and Amaziah assumes that he serves as a cult functionary at Yahwistic shrines. Amaziah sends him away as one who has not performed his function at the "temple of the kingdom" properly, and is indeed undercutting the institution and its royal patron; but he could serve at a southern sanctuary fine.

Why did Amaziah believe that he could discount the message from the God whom he too served? If YHWH has provided prophets to his people to announce decisions for their ongoing life, how can authorities who are

---

82. Rather similar to the reports of Mari officials.

83. He makes no effort to prove this charge. He has only one slim piece of evidence for conspiracy: Amos is from the Southern Kingdom, probably evident from Amos's accent. Amaziah's surmise is most likely an effort on his part to discount the truth of the message.

justified by their superintendence of the people silence messages that meet the formal criteria of legitimacy? Perhaps the fascinating story of authorities and prophets told in 1 Kings 22 can provide the answer.

Whatever the historicity of 1 Kings 22, it vividly depicts the ambivalence of Israelite authorities toward prophets. The kings of Israel and Judah have decided to go into battle to recover some historic Israelite territory from the Arameans. The king of Judah wants the decision ratified by prophecy, so the king of Israel calls in four hundred court prophets. They answer the inquiry by announcing YHWH's support of the expedition. The king of Judah is skeptical; he evidently is aware of the possibility that prophets can trim their message to their benefactor's wishes. The king of Israel reluctantly calls in a prophet known to be antagonistic to him. While they await his arrival, the four hundred, sensing that their "objectivity" has been impugned, work up a frenzy to convince the kings of the truth of their message. When Micaiah ben Imlah appears, he delivers a favorable message. The king of Israel senses something fishy, and exhorts him: "How many times shall I adjure you to speak nothing but the truth in the name of YHWH?" Well, that is a new one. Then Micaiah delivers devastating news, and then the king of Israel turns to his cohort and says, I told you so, he is out to get me. Micaiah attacks the credibility of the court prophets by telling a satirical story about a decision in the divine council to deceive the king of Israel into self-destruction. Now YHWH himself is playing the game! Micaiah is arrested and held hostage to the truth of his message.

The "truth" of the prophetic word seems to be alternately evaluated on its derivation from God and its capacity to bolster the morale of the authorities and their armies. The authorities plan to act, but they seek to manipulate God into supporting them, giving them added certitude and courage. Yet they must be able to believe that the prophets speak truly for the desired effect. When the kings of our story go into battle, they go with doubts, and these themselves may have turned the tide against them. Amaziah may have entertained the possibility that Amos was speaking the truth, but it was a truth he could not accept if he was to perform his office. He must suppress his doubts, explain away Amos's message as well as he can, and proceed with a resolve to be confident in God's support because any hesitancy will undo their cause.

Amos undoes Amaziah's effort to explain his message. He does not have the support of any institution, he is not for hire. While it weakens his official legitimacy, it increases his credibility. He is an honest worker whom God has seized ahold of and sent forth with a message. The more the recipients try to silence him and block out his message, the greater the likelihood that it will come true. Elsewhere Amos adds silencing prophecy to the accusations against the people (2:12) and singles out deniers for special punishment (9:10).

Amaziah might have tried another explanation of Amos's message, a psychoanalytic one. Perhaps Amos is being driven not by some prospect of gain, but by some inner need or conflict. He may be speaking in good conscience, but still not be communicating a message received from the Other.[84] Any psychology of prophecy would be distorted, however, if it were not a psychology of audiences as well. Why does the audience identify the truth with favorable words, falsehood with unfavorable? Why should that be considered any more sane than pessimistic prophets?

Behind the Public Apologia. We have an autobiographical narrative of revelations in chapters 7 and 8. I do not think that these passages were a part of Amos's public message. The only reference in his public discourse to his encounter with YHWH is his reply to Amaziah, where it certifies his honesty (7:14-15). Amos 7:10-17 was probably inserted into the series of "showings" (7:1, 4, 7, 8:1) to establish the connection: his reply to Amaziah is, as it were, "documented."

If the autobiographical narrative was not formulated for public presentation, for whom was it composed? One can only speculate that Amos told disciples; some might actually ascribe the narrative to disciples. In any case, this "private" tradition about the "secret" of Amos's prophecy was made public for the presentation of Amos's message in book form.

The role of these accounts in the book is fairly obvious: to certify Amos's message. They correspond to the commission of Moses. Like the commission of Moses, the representation of the exercitive action is shaped apologetically. The first two showings (locusts, fire) exhibit intimacy between YHWH and the prophet, dramatize Amos's goodwill toward the people, and the general bent of YHWH's mind from the outset, namely, toward judgment. Amos does not desire the judgment of God; his message does not arise out of animosity to his people or anger arising from personal injury. He pleads on their behalf on the basis of Israel's vulnerable condition. YHWH is twice moved. Yet when we read the second showing, we know where God is headed; it is as if God is breaking down Amos's resistance.

The third showing is the turning point. Unfortunately, it is uncertain what Amos saw. The Hebrew word, *'anak,* probably does not mean a *plumb line*, as it has been translated for centuries. What it does mean, though, is

---

84. Jeremiah begins to probe such psychological explanations for the apparent honesty of at least some prophets who opposed him. That is how I take Jer. 23:23-32: the prophets speak lies of their own hearts/minds.

hardly settled among linguists.[85] The context still suggests to me an instrument of measure, but it could be an instrument of destruction. The upshot is, we only know of its import, destruction of cult and state. The fourth showing, based upon a pun in Hebrew, heightens the destruction to encompass the populace at large.[86]

These four showings leave out some things typical of call narratives, prompting some scholars to deny them that status. Most importantly, Amos is never told to go to the people of Israel and say. . . . If one is a literalist, the showings do not document Amos's claim in 7:15. Because we have so many prophetic calls—from Mari as well as the Hebrew Bible—to compare it with, the absence of a commission does stand out. Perhaps the connections Amos makes in 3:7-8 between being admitted to God's counsel and prophesying explain how the showings led him to infer a commission.

Amos is not told the reason God has decided to judge his people. He is told the sentence. The verdict is implied by the statement, "I will never again pass by them" (7:8, 8:2): I will not continue to pardon them, my days of forbearance are over; Amos can stop interceding. Clearly a decision has been made. But the reason for that decision is not given.

How different the prophecies of judgment against individual offenders: what the addressee has done is a part of the commission, and is the subject of the forensic narration (2 Samuel 12, 1 Kings 21).

I infer from the way Amos is called to prophesy that the exercitive action, the verdict and sentence, imposes on the prophet the responsibility for discovering and formulating the accusation. Amos knows a reason exists because YHWH has told him he will not "pass by" them again. It is not a blind fate; it is a moral transaction. Now he must discover and persuade.

How would Amos discover the accusation? Once Amos knows God's decision, and has become attuned to his angry mood, he looks at the life of the people from a new perspective, literally through God's eyes.[87] What has God seen in the life of this people that would compel him to decide against them? The injustice that he had observed, but also taken for granted as a part of doing business, now suddenly "shouts" at him.

It is Amos's task as rhetor to communicate the same perception to his audiences. He seeks to open their eyes to what he, instructed by YHWH's

85. See Paul, *Amos*, 250.

86. Amos 9:1-4 has often been added as a fifth "vision," but it is not a showing and there is no dialog between YHWH and Amos. Whether it was a public proclamation or private story passed down among disciples is hard to say.

87. A. Heschel, *The Prophets*, Vol. 2, 87–103, 206–26, 263–68, sees the communication through emotional rapport.

wrath, sees. What the people could not know without the prophetic word is the divine verdict. It puts what they know, and repress, of themselves in a new light, and changes their relationship to God and their future prospect.

Between Text and Audience

If the illocutionary action of the prophet is to pronounce YHWH's verdict on Israel and to persuade the people that it is deserved and certain, what performative force does the book of prophecies have for the audience? Because verdicts apply only to the guilty, Amos's words cannot be "transferred" to the audience of the book. The oral prophecies were designed for a particular moment in Israel's history, and within a few decades the addressee of the verdict, the Northern Kingdom, was no more, or at least, no longer a political state with a national cult. The message of Amos had been confirmed. But what purpose would be served in preserving that message? Is it a kind of tombstone erected over the grave of the nation with the epithet: "I told you so"?

Not too many years ago scholarly interest was focused entirely on the original message of the prophet, in its historical context, and the books were treated as pieces of evidence with which to construct the original message. The only way one could spark interest in the extant form was to ascribe it to the prophet, or offer proposals as to the history of collection and redaction. What was missing was an interest in the book as discourse addressed to the reading audience. In the last few decades, the interests of scholars have changed dramatically. The study of the organization, redaction, and supplementation of the prophecies has become as important as the study of the original.[88] This new development is quite justified.

Certain aspects of the transaction between text and audience, however, escape the analysis of structure and theme, and it is these that concern me here. The structure does not of itself indicate how the world of the text is fused into the world of the audience, if it is. We must reflect upon our own transaction with the text, and look for confirmation of our introspective insights in the structuring of the text and in the way the text has been interpreted through history.

The World of the Text. Let me start with an analogy regarding the relation of the textual world to the world of the audience. Perhaps Amos's oracles to the Northern Kingdom in approximately 750 B.C.E. constitute the narrative

---

88. Cf. Rendtorff, *Canon and Theology*, 141–50.

world for the reader of the book. They belong to a story, an interaction between prophet and various people in various places at various times, which is implied, not told. Enough of the story is told in the book to evoke the story that is not. Moreover, it contains references to persons in the oracles that also hint at the story, and some of the passages themselves evoke images in the reader's mind of how they might have been delivered and received. The cycle against the nations, for example, projects a crowd that is enthusiastically seconding these judgments until Amos comes to Israel. This mental picture may not be accurate at all, but it serves a purpose in the act of reading.

The analogy suggests a particular way of regarding the audience's relation to the words of the text. What we said about the call of Moses and the textual audience's relation to that call fits here. The proclamation of the commandments at Sinai is different, for the audience is among its addressees. However, the accounts of covenant making are like the call of Moses. In all these cases, the audience overhears exchanges of another "world."

Analogies contain differences as well as similarities, and that is true of the proposed analogy. The narrative is designed to be "overheard" by the textual audience. The exchanges within the narrative world must be realistic, convincing enough for the audience to entertain their reality, but they are designed to do various things to the reader. Not so the oracles of the prophet. They were designed for the addressees. To the degree that we have the original words of Amos, they are shaped to pronounce God's verdict on Israel, on a particular kingdom, cult, judiciary, social and economic hierarchy. The reader of the book is overhearing discourse literally designed for others.

The book was not designed for the original addressees. It probably did not exist until after the addressees had been killed or exiled or absorbed into a province of the Assyrian Empire. The book is designed, then, to present discourse for one audience to another audience. For this very reason, I did not give a final form reading of Amos: its rhetoric is not, like a narrative, designed for the reading audience. To be sure, certain passages are, but I judge these to belong to the presentation of Amos's message to the reading audience and that they should be treated as an aspect of presentation.

The arrangement of Amos's prophecies belongs to the presentation level, but their message is still applicable to the original addressees, not the reading audience. The editors of the book have the object in mind of representing for a later audience the message of Amos to his audience. No actual audience would have known the full scope of his message, its subtle juxtapositions and recurring themes. The book presents a comprehensive overview of Amos's message, and allows the reading audience to discover meaning that the addressees could not have discovered. But it is not addressed to them. The audience is presented, that is, with an ideal image of a past event of discourse.

Message to Readers. The reading audience is directly addressed in the two concluding oracles of salvation (9:11-12, 13-15). I follow the majority of critical scholars in regarding these oracles as an exilic addition.[89] Not only do they assume the exile of Judah and the end of the Davidic kingship, they are not imaginable in the mouth of Amos and would be utterly inappropriate in a message designed for the Northern Kingdom. If Amos had said anything of this sort, Amaziah would be quite right in judging him an agitator sent up from Judah to serve its political purposes. The Northern Kingdom did not recognize the legitimacy of Davidic claims to rule it, and Amos would have to respect its traditions to exercise the office of prophet responsibly.

The book is designed for an audience that does recognize the legitimacy of the Davidic scion, but which is not being ruled by a Davidide. At least in its present form, the book is designed for a Judean audience after 587 B.C.E.[90] We can call that the "reading position" the book communicates to the audience. The event of judgment announced by Amos is passed, restoration is future.

How is the reader to take the past event of divine discourse? The question is complicated by the fact that Amos addressed the Northern Kingdom during the Assyrian heyday, but the audience is Judean and experienced its exile at the hands of Babylon. The reader must, it seems to me, "telescope" the two exiles and two kingdoms. Amos probably did consider Judah to be under the same verdict as the Northern Kingdom (6:1), but when Israel fell and Judah survived for a century and a half, it was natural to "narrow" his addressee to the Northern Kingdom. When Judah fell later, Amos's accusations against one generation had to be extended to subsequent generations and reapplied to Judah. The sixth-century prophets' insistence that the early accusations still applied (cf. Jer. 5:1-5, 10-17) undoubtedly shaped the reading of Amos.

The book of Amos, in my estimation, expects readers to regard Amos's message of judgment as applying to their people, their "fathers," and hence to regard their own exile (or depressed condition under foreign rule in

---

89. Max Polley is to be commended for defending them as powerfully as they are capable of being defended: see his *Amos and the Divided Empire: A Socio-Historical Approach.*

90. It might, of course, address people living within the territory of the ancient Northern Kingdom as well.

Palestine) as the punishment meted out by YHWH for the offenses pre-sented by Amos. This line of thinking is so natural within the horizon of biblical prophecy that it would be hard to imagine how the book of Amos could be taken in any other way. Amos's message retains its verdictive force, but the audience has a significantly different relationship to the discourse than the original addressees. The audience is engaged in incorporating an aspect of national identity.[91] It is similar, I think, to the force of the accounts of murmuring and rebellion in the wilderness (Exodus 15–17, 32, Numbers 10–20, 25), and within a canonical horizon the Pentateuch and Prophetic texts reinforce each other.

The audience could justly object that its present condition was not its own doing, that it has as it were inherited "guilt," or at least the conse-quences of guilt. Both Jeremiah and Ezekiel cite a saying of their audiences to that effect: "The fathers have eaten sour grapes and the children's teeth are set on edge" (Jer. 31:29; Ezek. 18:2). Both prophets seek to refute the implied charge of injustice, but they have to invent a "utopian" world to do it. The Israelites in exile have indeed been "fated" to suffer for past wrongs, just as earlier generations were "fated" to belong to YHWH, live under divine law, and experience the benevolence of God.

The reading position established by the book of Amos does not exhaust its rhetorical power. The voice one hears throughout the book is Amos's, addressing us as if we were his audience. The boundary between the narra-tive world and our own is not well guarded, you might say. The addresses press the textual audience, as they pressed the original oral audience, to examine itself, to view its society from the perspective of God. The book disturbs complacency, makes readers look seriously at what they take for granted and subjects what we take pride in to the test of justice and simplicity.

The verdict holds only for the original addressees; the accusations and undercutting of certainties now accost the reader as warnings, a call to repentance and reform. Many interpreters read Amos as calling his original audience to repent. This interpretation, in my opinion, projects the later impact of the language back onto the narrative exchange itself. This reeval-uation of the illocutionary force of the prophets of judgment can already be found within the prophetic canon itself: Zechariah characterizes the message of the preexilic prophets as calls to repentance (Zech. 1:2-6).

For the prophecies of Amos to be pronounced with their original per-formative force to a later audience, the interpreter would have to be called

91. Although Brueggemann's *Hopeful Imagination: Prophetic Voice in Exile* (Philadelphia: Fortress, 1986) concerns Jeremiah and Ezekiel, it identifies the wording position evoked by Amos as well; Brueggemann's thesis ignited my reflections on this question.

by God to do so. Indeed, it would be a new act of prophecy, even if Amos's words were used. The movement from possible guilt and punishment to actual requires the verdictive action of the Judge. It would be interesting to ask whether the peasants' revolts in the Middle Ages and Reformation drew upon Amos's message for their condemnation of their societies for oppressing the poor.[92]

Amos's message was rediscovered in the modern era by various streams of social Christianity. Seldom did Social Gospelers actually pronounce a divine verdict on industrial capitalism, but texts like 3:1-2 and 5:21-25 were read as if they had been spoken in their hearing.

Intertextuality. In the course of this reflection, I have several times cited texts to provide what might be called leverage on the text of Amos. Amos's message is to be incorporated into the people's identity like the judgments in the wilderness. Jeremiah's accusations against Judah transfer Amos's accusations to another segment of the people of God at a later time. The people's complaint about suffering for the sins of their ancestors responds to the way the prophecies of judgment and their confirmation in the exiles of Israel and Judah are designed to be appropriated. In citing these texts, I am interpreting texts through other texts. This "cross-pollination" of texts is what I mean by intertextuality.

This phenomenon is much more important to the interpretation of texts than scholars are comfortable with. Just when we think we have pinned down a text to a determinate meaning, that interpretation is upset by association with texts that mean something else. In a word, intertextuality destabilizes our classifications and concretizations. Our response has been to protect determinate meaning by banishing intertextuality to the Gehenna of allegory; it is not really interpretation.

Then we discover that intertextuality is deeply embedded in the texts themselves. M. Fishbane has traced the networks of verbal intertextuality running through the Hebrew Bible persuasively. He concludes:

> The whole phenomenon of inner-biblical exegesis requires the latter-day historian to appreciate the fact that the texts and traditions, the received *traditum* of ancient Israel, were not simply copied, studied, transmitted, or recited. They were also, and by these means, subject to redaction, elucidation, reformulation, and outright transformation. Accordingly, our received traditions are complex blends of *traditum*

---

92. Although a revolt is not the same thing as a prophecy, a revolt under a leader claiming divine authority regards the oppressive system as under God's sentence of death.

and *traditio* in dynamic interaction, dynamic interpenetration, dynamic interdependence.[93]

Of course, one could still control the phenomenon by requiring demonstrable linguistic connections before one grants recognition. Intertextuality operates, however, on other levels as well. The incorporation of Amos's prophecies into a prophetic canon is a case in point. Amos's message now becomes a voice in a chorus singing a part in God's great prophetic oratorio. That is, the assumption of the prophetic canon is that God does not speak in contradictions, so all these spokespersons are consistent with each other. Moreover, the prophets are all announcing the same event of God, each providing a different perspective on it. The event involves judgment and then salvation, so that one provides the conditions of the other, and the effect of the two together will be a transformed Israel in a transformed world. Not every book covers the whole event, so interpreters must read them synthetically.[94]

The historical critical interpreter can protest this homogenization of prophecy, insisting on the particular message of each prophet and the differences between them. One can even say that it is a fiction to regard them as speaking of the same event. One can expound Amos's message to the Northern Kingdom fairly well within these "nominalistic" constraints. However, it will not do for the *book* of Amos. The concluding oracles of salvation draw the message of Amos into the message about the "one event." There may be other traces of cross-fertilization: the judgment of Judah in the cycle against the nations, the accusations against idolatry (5:26-27) and heterodoxy (8:14), and the doxologies, which evoke epiphany to depict YHWH.[95]

What significance does intertextuality have for the performative transaction elicited by the text? For both practical and theoretical reasons, exegesis must stay within the borders of the book and biblical theology should probably restrict its exposition to the actual texts and perhaps the scope of their possibilities. It does behoove us, however, to be aware of the explosive possibilities of intertextual reading.

93. M. Fishbane, *Biblical Interpretation in Ancient Israel* (Oxford: Clarendon, 1985), 542–43.

94. Cf. R. E. Clements, "Patterns in the Prophetic Canon: Healing the Blind and the Lame," in *Canon, Theology, and Old Testament Interpretation: In Honor of B. Childs*, ed. G. M. Tucker, D. L. Petersen, and R. R. Wilson (Philadelphia: Fortress, 1988), 189–200.

95. Critical scholars have defended these as by Amos; and they could be. I have just noted that they could be examples of this transfer of the messages of others to Amos.

6.
LAMENTATION
OVER THE EXILE

<hr>

THE PROPHECIES OF NATIONAL JUDGMENT DIFFER FROM DIVINE PROM-
ises and commandments in several significant respects. The latter create the knowledge they communicate, for that knowledge is of the terms of
a relationship between speaker and addressee. The verdict pronounced in
Amos's prophecy of judgment—and by Amos's successors[1]—also creates
the knowledge that is communicated, but it modifies an already existing
relationship. To judge someone as a violator of law, the accused must be
obligated to the law.

The relationship also involves interchange, the human voice responding
to God's utterances and acts, and provoking God's response. The interchange goes back to the very beginnings, and continues unabated through
the history of the relationship.

It is the lament on which I propose to focus in this chapter. Israel and
Israelites had, you might say, certain "rights" within the relationship: They
had access to the divine sovereign by virtue of the institution of the divine
name. In the presence of YHWH, Israelites had the right to petition grievances and call for aid against enemies.[2] If the grievance was with God,
either for hostility or indifference, they had the right to accuse God.

Individual and communal laments do not have verdictive force, as do
God's declarations of judgment. An accusation against a third party does
not effect guilt, an accusation against YHWH does not put God in the
wrong. Are the words of lament, then, only expressions of feeling? Obviously they are that, but they have more force than that. A petition with a
specification of grievances is a claim on authority, which the authority, if it
is just, will assess and respond to.

<hr>

1. This extension goes beyond the argument of the last chapter. I actually believe that it
holds, but I do not want to claim that I have established that; I might well discover that it
would have to be modified in the extension.

2. W. Brueggemann's "The Costly Loss of Lament," *JSOT* 36 (1986): 57–71, taught me to
recognize this dimension of lament.

Now let us turn to the human response to the prophecy of judgment. Amos met denial and expulsion by the addressees, who offered no lament to God for the message of judgment. The people do not respond to Amos's utterances as God's, but as suspicious human words. Lament will not arise from their lips until they experience calamity. Their laments may have preceded 733 and 722, but when the decisive blows fell in those years, dismembering the Northern Kingdom, slaughtering, exiling, or subjecting its citizens to Assyrian rule, all communal laments arising in other events would now refer to the exile. Judah too may have lamented their reduction to Assyrian vassalage, and their near annihilation by Sennacherib, but the memory of destruction and exile by Babylon in 598 and 587 would overshadow any other reference.

Virtually all the communal laments in the Psalter, then, are unreflectively taken as responses to events known collectively as *exile*. This reference is reinforced by the reading position communicated by the Hebrew Bible. Although individual passages, even larger segments of the text, may speak to the audience as settled in the land of Canaan under Israelite rulers, several strategically placed passages speak to the textual audience as in exile. Moses speaks to the audience throughout the book of Deuteronomy as settled in the land in control of its own institutions, but then in 30:1-10 he addresses the generation in exile. This "latest" reading position qualifies all the Pentateuch.[3] The historical narrative accorded the name Former Prophets ends with Judah's exile (2 Kings 25). The book of Amos addresses its audience as looking back on judgment, forward to restoration and salvation. Approximately the same is true of the other prophetic books, though some are postexilic; the latter may see their present as the dawning of restoration, yet the period of judgment lingers and full salvation is a future hope. The Writings are not fixed in some temporal framework and cannot really be said to characterize the reader as in exile. Only Ezra and Nehemiah, however, assume that the exile is over, and neither of them really regards the present as the messianic age. As if to underline the exilic reading position of the Hebrew Bible, when the Writings were finally given a fixed order in the Hebrew canon, 1–2 Chronicles was placed after Ezra and Nehemiah; the Writings, thus, now end with the exile. It is not accidental that Judaism has characterized the era since the Diaspora as "exile."

By far the dominant interpretation of exile is as divine judgment: Israel had sinned and God punished it, and this condition of punishment lingers on into the present. Some passages spell out the reason for judgment and how the exiles can get back into the good graces of God (Deut. 30:1-10).

3. While interpreters try out all sorts of dates for 32:1-43, it now invites an exilic reading.

Some prophetic books assume that God's people are so mired in their rebellious ways that the exiles will not be able to turn to God with a whole heart without "prevenient grace."[4] Thus, there is no uniform teaching about what the reader can do about their exilic status, nor a delineation of salvation to come. The hidden understanding, though, is that readers live after judgment and under its conditions.

Now we might ask whether there are any other witnesses. Is there another version of what brought about exile? In fact there is: the book of Lamentations and the communal laments scattered through the Psalter. Not all of these dispute the accusations of the prophets, but they so focus our attention on the pain and loss, and the sense of divine betrayal or indifference, that blaming the supplicants would be shameful.

The communal laments of the Psalter show that biblical monotheism is not authoritarian. The people articulate their own perspective on the disaster. They demand that God see and hear what they are going through; in that, they preserve their integrity in the face of overwhelming power. The very stubbornness that made them resist the prophetic condemnation becomes a virtue in the time of suffering.

The prophets themselves incorporate the people's lamentation in their divine discourse. God is moved by their passion and identifies with them in their sorrow. It has a truth of its own that cannot be suppressed by the judgments of moral standards. The story of their relationship is not as simple and clear-cut as the prophetic word makes it out to be; it can just as well be seen as a case of divine betrayal. The exile does not resolve the tension in their relationship, it brings it to a crisis that requires resolution.

The crisis is, as it were, passed on to the textual audience. The reader is provided with a script with which to approach God, some of which protests God's decision to execute judgment. The interchange between God and his people is not over.

Communal Laments over the Exile

Between the book of Lamentations and the communal laments preserved in the Psalter we find a rather broad range of responses to the exile. The book of Lamentations is not strictly speaking, except for chapter 5, a communal lament; rather, it is a dirge over what is lost and apparently gone forever. Only Lamentations 5 has petition and complaint.[5] The communal

---

4. Jeremiah 31:31-34 and 32:36-41, and Ezek. 36:22-32 and 37:1-14 are the most explicit.

5. Lamentations 5 has very little petition and complaint: v. 1 requests God to observe what is being described and v. 21 petitions for restoration; there are a few tentative accusing questions (vv. 20, 22).

laments of the Psalter complain, accuse, and plead forthrightly, and some directly contest the prophetic account of the exile.

Prophets too could use the dirge. Amos 5:2 does:

> Fallen, no more to rise, is the virgin Israel,
> forsaken on her land, with none to raise her up.

The first verse of Lamentations employs the same figure for city or country:

> How lonely sits the city that was full of people!
> How like a widow she has become,
> she that was great among the nations!

In the latter case, the female figure is not herself the victim to be mourned, but the mourner of the loss of inhabitants, greatness, commerce, and so on. A more significant difference is found between Amos's dirge and Lamentations: a difference of illocutionary stance. Amos is announcing the fate of the people, depicting God's judicial punishment from the point of view of the addressee. Lamentations rises up from the ruins of the city. The author has survived the killing and destruction, and evidently avoided deportation; the writing is an expression of deep grief and dismay over these horrible events. By tradition, this speaker was Jeremiah, though that is not in fact very likely. The speaker does accept the prophetic account of why this happened: it was the people's sin that brought it on (Lam. 1:8, 9, 14, 18, 2:14, 3:42, 4:13, 22). Yet, even the sin that provoked God's judgment is a subject of sorrow and shame. It compounds the pathos. The powers the people had counted on for protection—whether deities or foreign nations—had abandoned her to her fate (Lam. 1:8-9, 18). The people's only recourse is to accept their judgment (3:37-42) and trust that God will strengthen them and eventually restore their national life (3:19-33). We might call this a "doxology of judgment," a response to judgment in remorse and contrition. It maintains its integrity by its insistent witness to the carnage, the pain of the survivor, the dimensions of the loss. The exile is a great tragedy, not a melodrama.[6]

Psalms 44, 74, 79, 80, and 89 are a different story. These communal laments manifest no remorse and contrition, they petition God to take full cognizance of their suffering and to show the compassion with which they are

---

6. Psalm 106 is a doxology of judgment, much more distant than Lamentations from the event of exile; judgment is figured for the wilderness period. It reminds one of Ezekiel 20, and matches Psalm 105 in a dialectical fashion.

familiar.[7] Their question is: What has happened to you? Why have you turned cruel? Why are you betraying us?

Psalm 80 begins with an extended petition (vv. 1-3) to give the people a "hearing" and to do something. This plea is juxtaposed to a series of accusations against God: he is indifferent to their cries, and has turned cruel. The most powerful statement in the lament is a rehearsal of God's action toward the suppliants, under the figure of a vineyard:

> You brought a vine out of Egypt;
> You drove out the nations and planted it.
> You cleared the ground for it;
> it took deep root and filled the land.
> The mountains were covered with its shade,
> the mighty cedars with its branches;
> it sent out its branches to the sea,
> and its shoots to the River.
> Why then have you broken down its walls,
> so that all who pass along the way pluck its fruit?
> The boar from the forest ravages it,
> and all that moves in the field feed upon it. (vv. 9-14 [Eng. 8-13])

The first four bicola depict YHWH as a wise and benevolent vine-tender, but the idyllic story is broken by an accusing question: Why has God abandoned he vineyard to the depredations of whatever comes along? God's action is incoherent, out of character. The petition that follows (vv. 15-16) seeks God's attention on the assumption that if God took the care to observe what is happening to them, he would surely act to save them.

This psalm makes a perfect match with Isa. 5:1-7:

> My beloved had a vineyard on a very fertile hill.
> He plowed it and cleared it of stones,
> and planted it with choice vines;
> He built a watchtower in the mdist of it,
> and hewed out a wine vat for it.
> And he looked for it to yield grapes,
> but it yielded wild grapes.
>
> "And now, O inhabitants of Jerusalem and men of Judah,
> judge, please, between me and my vineyard.
> What more was there to do in my vineyard

---

7. I am following C. Westermann, *The Praise of God in the Psalms*, trans. K. R. Crim (Richmond: John Knox, 1965), 52–64, for the identification and description of the category. Psalm 79:8a mentions forgiveness, but it is for the sins of the fathers, not their own.

that I have not done in it?
When I looked for it to yield grapes,
why did it yield wild grapes?

"Now I will tell you what I will do to my vineyard.
I will remove its hedge,
and it shall be devoured.
I will break down its wall,
and it shall be trampled down.
I will make it a waste;
it shall not be pruned nor hoed,
and briers and thorns shall grow up.
I will even command the clouds not to rain upon it."

It is as if Ps. 80:9-14 (Eng. 8-13) were composed to invert Isa. 5:1-7. The two agree as to the first part of the story, God's gracious care of the vineyard; they give opposite versions of the break, God's abandonment. Each blames the other. For the people, God has stepped out of character, and the rhetorical task is to get him to realize that. It is really amazing how blunt the supplicants are in the presence of the divine majesty. That says a lot about the freedom afforded by the relationship and the intimacy they shared despite the inequality of power.

Psalm 44 also juxtaposes the story of God's past benevolence and present betrayal. The contrast is put in terms of God's empowerment of his people on the battlefield. Once God gave them victory over mighty foes, and they were able to secure their place on earth; now God does not accompany the army into battle, and they are defeated, despoiled, and disgraced [vv. 2-9/10-17 (Eng. 1-8/9-16)]. Is this happening to them because they have betrayed the relationship? To the contrary, they have been true though God has been false:

Our heart has not turned back,
nor have our steps departed from your way,
though you have broken us in the place of jackals
and covered us with deep darkness. (vv. 19-20 [Eng. 18-19])

There follows an oath of clearance, then this most poignant charge of all:

Nay, for your sake we are slain all day long,
and accounted as sheep for the slaughter. [v. 23 (Eng. 22)]

Their faithfulness to God and adherence to the covenant is the very reason they are suffering; they are persecuted for their faith. This sounds like a foreshadowing of the later history of the Jews. The pleas that follow are shocking:

Rouse yourself! Why are you sleeping, O Lord? Awake! (v. 24 [Eng. 23]).

Such pleas echo Elijah's taunt of Baal in the contest on Cape Carmel (1 Kings 18:27). Here it is said within a relationship the speakers take pride in maintaining.

The protest of innocence in this psalm is diametrically opposed to the prophets, beginning with Hosea and Micah, who accused Israel of breaking faith with YHWH. There is an irreconcilable disagreement. The Israel that speaks here is not about to appropriate the exile in remorse and contrition. It is God who must vindicate the trust and devotion they have accorded him.

Hovering in the background is another doubt: that God has "lost" his power, that "his arm has been shortened." To the theological mind that may be an illogical doubt, but the experience of the people is illogical. The communal laments go no farther in stating this than Psalm 44's suggestion that God is asleep.[8] It occurs to me, though, that the rehearsal of God's act of creation within a lament is designed to counteract the doubt. Psalm 74 begins with accusing questions about God's loyalty to his own (vv. 1-2), describes how the enemies desecrate the sanctuary and shame the people (vv. 4-11), ending with the telling: "Why do you hold back your hand . . . ?" There follows in vv. 12-17 a rehearsal of a creation myth, which highlights the aspect of subduing other powers. The logic seems to be: if you can do that, surely you can overthrow our conquerors. Psalm 89 also has a full-scale creation psalm (vv. 5-18), along with an account of the promise of God made to the Davidic house (vv. 19-37), before we come to the lament over the fall of the monarch (vv. 38-51). The promise to David is juxtaposed to what is happening to the Davidic king. Perhaps the creation psalm is intended to assure the supplicants that God is capable of doing something about it if he wills.

The preservation of these communal laments within a tradition that interprets the exile, under divine authority, as judgment is quite noteworthy. What is the purpose of these psalms within the teaching of Scripture? Someone might suggest that they are an exhibit of why Israel had to be judged. Certainly, they challenge the biblical theologian to search for supple theological categories, some way of modeling scriptural communication as a dialog, or in this case a shouting match.

---

8. At least one individual lament broaches the possibility: Ps. 77:10.

Toward a Theology of Lament. Biblical theologians have normally considered their task to be the abstraction of concepts and principles concerning God, humans, and the created world from texts that were originally formulated for practical purposes. If the theologian demanded discourse designed specifically to teach concepts and principles, there would be precious little on which to construct a biblical theology. Quite rightly, it has been assumed that narratives, liturgical texts, prophecies, and so forth have implicit or "understood" theological conceptions, and that an interpreter can articulate these.[9]

When, however, one applies this theological method to the communal laments, the result is odd and without much insight. The laments in question assume that God is the direct or indirect cause of all events in time, including evil; that God can enter into special relationship with one people, and has; that the people can move God by prayer to change decisions; that some evil events are unjust and false to the relationship. What is the status of such an implicit conceptual scheme? Would any theologian, sitting in her study or lecturing to students, want to assert this as a normative scheme? Would one then dismiss it as conceptually inadequate?

There should be a way of according theological import to the act of speaking and the rhetorical shaping of that act. G. von Rad designed his *Old Testament Theology* to correspond to the Bible's own presentation.[10] It was, I believe, a conceptual breakthrough of great importance for the practice of biblical theology. Its genius was not in its actual organizing of ideas, though von Rad was a superb exegete with an uncanny sensitivity to textual rhetoric, but in its redirection of our attention. Now the theological interpreter was to seek after the "kerygmatic intention" of each text.[11] I am proposing to reformulate it as the "illocutionary force" of the text.

For the laments we have discussed, I propose that we define and test out the categories of testimony, petition, and accusation. What is it to testify? One asserts something to be the case, usually some event. In judicial situations, such testimony usually refers to the act of some person and how the witness knows. In cases where the witness is either the beneficiary or the victim of the action in question, the witness will report how it affected him.

---

9. N. Wolterstorff's "second hermeneutic" fits this description: *Divine Discourse,* 202–22.

10. See G. von Rad, *Old Testament Theology* vol. 1, 355–56, 383–418, on individual laments and related material; he has no section on communal laments. W. Brueggemann's *Theology of the Old Testament: Testimony, Dispute, Advocacy* (Minneapolis: Fortress, 1997) 317–403, is the most serious effort to incorporate the theological witness of lamentation that I know of; the book appeared, unfortunately, after I had finished the text of this chapter.

11. W. Brueggemann and H. W. Wolff, *The Vitality of Old Testament Traditions* (Atlanta: John Knox, 1975), set forth this theological method.

Theological discourse would not be considered judicial in modern culture, but biblical literature recognizes God as law giver and judge. A judicial model is frequently buried in texts, and occasionally quite explicit. Perhaps we can say that the judicial model is a "root metaphor" or guiding analogy for biblical God language. However, it should not be overextended; there are nonjudicial uses of the idea of testimony and witness. One may *witness* some scene that one takes as paradigmatic for a person or group; one may undergo an experience that prompts one to *testify* to others, say, as to the effectiveness of some medicine or the quality of some person.

In a court of law, one's testimony is taken as evidence and weighed against other testimony and material evidence. One's testimony is presumed to be honest, the truth as the witness knows it, but the judge or jury must decide what is true. Outside the courtroom, there is no arbiter of truth. The witness simply stands on what was seen and heard until other experience or argument disconfirms it.

Biblical literature has forms of religious expression that fit the description of testimony in the nonjudicial sense. When Moses meets his father-in-law after the exodus, he reports to Jethro what YHWH has done (Exod. 18:1-12); this witness would certainly qualify as testimony. The psalms of thanksgiving have a testimonial component along with praise. We might say that testimony can undergo a kind of unfolding toward praise (crediting and honoring God) and proclamation (persuasion of the religious community of the truth of what one testifies to).

Is lament a form of testimony, a kind of inversion of praise? There are some aspects of testimony in lament. The dirge form of Lamentations 1–4 is a picture, or series of pictures, of what happened to Jerusalem and Judah during and after the Babylonian assault. It is not testimony to what Babylon did so much as it is to what God did. It is depicted as an event of divine judgment for infidelity, self-will, and oppression of the people.[12] The overall import could well be called a *doxology of judgment.*

The communal laments in the Psalter are a different story. They contain descriptions of what happened, and what the supplicants are going through, and the character of the enemy, but these have a different illocutionary force: they are designed to move God to change his decision and act to save Israel. I would classify communal laments as *petition.* Everything in these laments is aimed at procuring a favorable hearing on a request. Perhaps the word *request* is not strong enough; *plea* probably comes nearer, sometimes bordering on a *demand.*

---

12. Confession of sin is not testimony, it is more like praise: blame of self.

The impression that the plea borders on a demand comes from the *accusations* made against God. God is charged with injustice, negligence, mercilessness, uncontrollable anger, irrationality, and is asked—in rhetorical questions—why and how long. This kind of "persuasive" discourse belonged to a distinctive rhetorical culture.[13] It is not the way most cultures advise petitioners to approach authorities. Deference and servility are usually more in order.[14] The language of biblical petition, whether between humans or a human and God, is meant to put the addressee on the defensive. The petitioner accuses and presents the request as the way the authority can rectify his or her mistake.[15] If the addressee is "stung," so to speak, the petitioner wins.

A petition is much more than an expression of desire. It has a public status, a quasi-legal standing, which is dramatized powerfully in Job's wish:

> O that my words were written down!
> O that they were inscribed in a book! (19:23)

By uttering them, they are. The addressee may suppress them, just as the addressee could destroy a written message (cf. Jeremiah 36). The attempt to suppress or destroy is in fact an indication of their public character, their claim on the addressee. Job entertains the possibility that an advocate will intervene after his death and force an inquiry into its cause; God might be found culpable!

The communal laments have a claim on God's consideration. If God is a just ruler and judge, he will give them "cognizance," so to speak. They are a part of the record. They must be weighed in the decision. Maybe God's condemnation will be reversed, or the sentence mitigated, or new measures adopted to effect reconciliation.

Responses of God

Israel's pleas do not go unheeded. We begin to hear them taken up into divine discourse as early as Hosea. As the Northern Kingdom sank into oblivion, the people made efforts to propitiate YHWH and tap into his power. Hosea cites a resolution to return to YHWH in 6:1-3:

> Come, let us return to YHWH,
> for he has torn, that he may heal us;

---

13. Nicely set out by T. Frymer-Kensky, *In the Wake of the Goddesses: Women, Culture, and the Biblical Transformation of Pagan Myth* (New York: Fawcett Columbine, 1992), 128–40.

14. As the woman of Tekoa approaches David (2 Sam. 14:4-20); also as David prays to YHWH (2 Sam. 7:18-29).

15. Frymer-Kensky shows the similarity of Sarah's approach to Abraham to Moses' approach to YHWH: *In the Wake of the Goddesses*, 131–32.

he has stricken, and he will bind us up.
After two days he will revive us,
on the third day he will raise us up,
that we may live before him. . . .

YHWH's answer is a cry of frustration:

What shall I do with you, O Ephraim?
What shall I do with you, O Judah?
Your love is like a morning cloud,
like the dew that burns off early.
Therefore I have hewn them by the prophets,
I have slain them with the words of my mouth. . . .
For I desire steadfast love and not sacrifice,
the knowledge of God rather than burnt offerings. (6:4-6)

Israel's resolve is ephemeral, enduring no longer than the sense of crisis. And the people's idea of regaining YHWH's favor seems to have been, judging from the Torah enunciated in v. 6, a sacrificial rite. The prophetic word of judgment will continue until they abandon their religious and political efforts to save themselves.[16]

Hosea 11 contains a strange inner dialog of God that sounds like a lamentation and response. In vv. 1-7, YHWH recounts his gracious and nurturing efforts on the behalf of his child, but Ephraim continually strayed. YHWH cannot see any alternative but to turn the people over to tougher taskmasters. Then he suddenly has second thoughts:[17]

How can I give you up, O Ephraim!
How can I hand you over, O Israel!
How can I make you like Admah!
How can I treat you like Zeboi'im!
My heart recoils within me,
my compassion grows warm and tender.
I will not execute my fierce anger,
I will not again destroy Ephraim;
for I am God and not man,
the Holy One in your midst. . . . (Hos. 11:8-9)

16. I say this on the basis of the prayer of repentance that Hosea formulates for the people in 14:2-3.

17. Whether God here reverses his previous sentence, or is vowing not to allow the people to be destroyed in exile, is hard to say. The following verses from a postexilic author/editor construe it as the latter.

What does this have to do with lament? It seems that God is formulating a lament or dirge for Israel, and is so moved by compassion that he answers his own words with a saving assurance. God can be inconsistent like that; it is a prerogative of deity.[18]

Jeremiah's prophecy is permeated with lament. YHWH laments over Judah, Jeremiah laments over Judah, Judah laments to YHWH, Jeremiah laments to YHWH. There are passages where the voices speaking are hard to identify:

> My grief is beyond healing (?)
> my heart is sick within me.
>
> Hark, the cry of the daughter of my people
> from the length and breadth of the land:
> "Is not YHWH in Zion?
> Is not her king in her?"
>
> "Why have they provoked me to anger
> with their graven images and their foreign idols?"
>
> "The harvest is past, the summer is ended,
> and we are not yet saved."
>
> For the wound of the daughter of my people
> is my heart wounded,
> I mourn, and dismay has taken hold of me.
>
> Is there no balm in Gilead?
> Is there no physician there?
> Why then has the health of the daughter of my people
> not been restored?
>
> O that my head were waters,
> and my eyes a fountain of tears,
> that I might weep day and night
> for the slain of the daughter of my people! (8:18—9:1 Eng.)

A few statements clearly belong to Israel, one to YHWH, but the first person running through the other verses could be either Jeremiah or YHWH.

---

18. There is another passage that sounds like the reverse: 13:12-14; but I am quite uncertain as to how to construe this passage. I have imagined it as a cry of despair after 722.

Perhaps the boundary is purposely faint. Even YHWH's accusation is formulated as a "why" question characteristic of lament. God is taking a double attitude toward judgment: anger at his people's betrayal, pity for the suffering they are bringing on themselves. Their sin and its consequences have also been strangely fused. YHWH seems helpless to do anything about the tragedy unfolding between them.

In Jeremiah 30 and 31, lamentation receives a saving answer. In 30:12-15, God composes a lament in the people's behalf:

> For thus says YHWH:
> Your hurt is incurable . . .
> There is no one to uphold your cause,
> no medicine for your wound . . .
> All your lovers have forgotten you . . .
> for I have dealt you the blow of an enemy . . .
> because your guilt is great . . .
> because your sins are flagrant,
> I have done these things to you.

Then comes the reversal:

> Therefore all who devour you shall be devoured . . .
> For I will restore health to you,
> and your wounds I will heal, says YHWH,
> because they have called you an outcast:
> "It is Zion, for whom no one cares!" (vv. 16-17)

The one thing you can count on from YHWH is pity for the downtrodden and outcast. The very judgment that YHWH felt compelled to execute against his people now renders them fit candidates for his mercy and restorative powers. The old relationship has not been forgotten either:

> I have loved you with an everlasting love;
> therefore I have continued my faithfulness to you.
> Again I will build you, and you shall be built,
> O Virgin Israel! (31:3b-4a)

There is one other prophet who weaves lament into oracles, the anonymous prophet of the Babylonian exile known as Second Isaiah. In chapter 40 she offers a hymn to YHWH the Creator and Lord of history (40:12-26) as a foundation for answering a lament of the people. The lament is quoted in v. 27:

Why do you say, O Jacob,
and speak, O Israel,
"My way is hid from YHWH,
and my right is disregarded by my God"?

The people are complaining that God is not defending the cause of his people. The expression "my way is hid . . . " may be a complaint that the Creator is so concerned with cosmic and world-historical matters that he has no time for them. In any case, in their view, the result has been unjust.

The prophet does not answer as one might expect, saying, God still cares for you and will defend your right. Rather, the audience is assured of God's power and the availability of this power to those who entrust themselves to God (vv. 28-31).

None of the prophets acknowledges the charges of the communal laments against God's justice and loyalty to Israel. By implication, the people's charges against YHWH are rebuffed. Divine judgment is not unjust nor a repudiation of the unique relationship between them. If Israel will surrender itself to the power of YHWH, it will sustain them and turn their fate around. YHWH is moved by the suffering of his people and will not give up on the relationship between them, but he refuses to be put on the defensive by the people's accusatory petitions.

There remains, thus, an irreconcilable gap between the people, to the degree that the communal laments articulate their stance, and YHWH, as represented by the prophets. The first prophetic oracle in Jeremiah rehearses the history of YHWH's gracious acts and Israel's contradictory response, and then pronounces a "sentence" not of punishment but of interminable debate:

> Therefore I will contend with you, says YHWH,
> and with your children's children I will contend. (2:9)

As long as Israel's perspective is at variance with God's, the debate will continue. The promise in this is that God will not destroy his people nor suppress their petition; their perspectives must be reconciled. Only true reconciliation can terminate it. This is also Israel's judgment.

Between Text and Audience

To understand the implications of the preservation of the communal laments we have been discussing, it is necessary to step back and reflect on the way the book of Psalms engages the textual audience. The Psalms stand out from the rest of biblical literature as discourse *for* the reader, the textual audience, not *to* the reader.[19] One could say, figuratively, that the Psalms are handed to readers to provide authorized words for formulating petitions and praises as they approach the throne of God.

Let us try a model. In the concluding chapter, we will consider an idea proposed by N. Wolterstorff of "appropriated discourse," discourse by one author which another person adopts as his sentiments. The whole industry of greeting cards is based upon appropriated discourse. It seems to me that the psalms fit that category perfectly: the worshiper prays through the words of others. Because the words are someone else's, they are not the way the worshiper would formulate the prayer herself, and there may be some statements in the appropriated text that the worshiper would not identify with. The worshiper is saying to God, catch my meaning in these words.

There is, we should remember, more than one way to "use" the psalms. If one were to push the greeting card metaphor a bit further, the worshiper would read through the psalms to find one closest to his sentiments, and then "send" it. In doing so, one would try to imagine how each psalm would "fit." This effort would move in the direction of the actor who re-creates the action of a character; each psalm can be reenacted as dialog. Benedictine monastic practice is to chant all 150 psalms in a cycle, say, every two weeks. The actions of separate psalms tend to be blurred into the larger movement and mood. While this breaks down the distinctive utterance of each, the monk becomes an intimate of petitioners and celebrants in a vast range of moods.

The Psalter has also been a text for meditation, which transforms the language of illocutionary acts into images, ideas, and mysteries. The images and patterns of thought antedate the composition of the Psalms and Yahwism itself, and carry a power of their own. One might say that they are ripe candidates for a Jungian analysis of archetypes.[20] Christians have often felt that they could use the psalms of lament only if they listened for the voice of Christ in them.[21] Those whose piety and theology preclude the kinds of accusation and petition of the laments have found it necessary to internalize, or spiritualize, the transaction.

---

19. This distinction should not be applied too rigidly: there are divine words and some liturgies within the Psalter that are *to* rather than *for* the reader, and there are psalms scattered about in narratives for the reader to respond to the event depicted, for example, Exod. 15:1-17. There is also the book of Lamentations. The Song of Songs is also for the reader's use, but probably not for worship.

20. The Mount Angel scholar, Jeremy Driscoll seems to subscribe to this idea: "The Psalms and Psychic Conversion," *Cistercian Studies* 22 (1987): 91–110.

21. For example, the common complaints and petitions against enemies are not acceptable for most Christians without some reconfiguration.

If the interpreter seeks to understand and use the psalms as praises and petitions, as the illocutionary acts they were composed for, the presence of communal laments presents a difficulty. The individual laments, which vastly outnumber communal laments and indeed all other psalmnic genres, deal with concerns of persons no matter when and where they live, but the communal laments assume a nation that has suffered a complete destruction of its political, cultic, and social order. Jews were never again to live as a nation, so communal laments were no longer applicable.[22] They do not apply to the church in principle.[23] How can they be prayed?

My contention is that they were referred to the exile, even centuries later. The Ninth of Ab has continued to memorialize the fall of the Temple— actually, both First and Second. Lamentations is used on that occasion. The consequences of the event continue to shape the conditions of Judaism: it is a nation in exile, dispersed among the nations, looking forward to the Messianic Age, when Jews will return to their land. It, of course, is now more a matter of theory, or received doctrine, preserved in liturgy and commentary, than it is a living mode of consciousness. Nevertheless, the communal laments have an illocutionary force for that understanding. If a Jew understands the present as exile, the experiences under the conditions of exile can be incorporated into the communal lament. The travail of Jews in Christian and Muslim countries, reaching a climax in the twentieth century, gives new cogency to the accusations of these psalms. Israel has been surrounded by vicious enemies, and God seems all too often to abandon it to its fate.

The communal laments authorize the stance of protest, authorize resistance to the message of the prophets. Actually, the Psalms and Lamentations taken together authorize a range of stances. Not only is Israel authorized to protest, it is also authorized to acknowledge God's righteousness in his judgment. It establishes no one "orthodox" position, at least not one in Hebrew Scripture. Israel's debate with God must continue, not in a frozen position, but by adopting a range of stances. Israel is to appropriate these contradictory words to send its prayer to God.

22. The Second Temple period was fairly similar for Jews in Palestine, especially during the Maccabean century. After 70 C.E., all Judaism was in diaspora.

23. They may have been applied to the church, but the church is not a political entity. No Christian country could seriously claim to embody God's people, though the communal laments might have been applied at times. Thomas Tallis uses Lamentations for the breakup of church/Christendom during the Reformation.

7.
DIVINE DISCOURSE AND
THE KNOWLEDGE OF GOD

IT IS TIME TO TALLY UP OUR FINDINGS, SO TO SPEAK, AND TO REFLECT ON the conceptual scheme that would encompass the kinds of performative transactions identified and expounded in the foregoing chapters. First we need to survey what has been found, or constructed if you prefer. Then we can formulate an agenda for bringing these findings into the discussion of the hermeneutics of the Bible.

Retrospect. The burden of the book has been to identify and expound passages with different kinds of performative utterances. The call of Moses was expounded as a promise of God, the proclamation of the Ten Commandments as an exercise of authority, and Amos's message of judgment on Israel as a divine verdict. In each case we examined the illocutionary act within the narrative world, then considered how it engaged the reading audience. Within the narrative world we expounded the performative within its network of illocutionary acts and supporting argumentation. These discussions were designed to persuade and instruct the reading audience as well as carry the narrative action forward.

The revelation to Moses at the burning bush begins with a theophany evoking the presence of the holy. Once the event has been set off as an encounter with the supernatural, the divine speaker identifies himself with reference to tradition, promises deliverance to the enslaved Israelites, and commands Moses to act as his agent. Each of these performative acts is followed up in the ensuing exchange with Moses. God divulges his name, explains his plans, and equips Moses with demonstrative signs. Moses resists the commission until compelled to obey.

The promise to the people has been formulated to persuade the addressees of its truth. God expresses feeling for their suffering and shows how the pharaoh's resistance can be broken. The recipients can know whether the words are true only by believing that the speaker is true and playing their part in the struggle. Moses becomes their leader, with the authority to speak and act for God, by obeying God's command. The utterances of God make up a network of performative and assertatory acts with the overall force of promise.

The reading audience is included among the addressees of this discourse by ritual reenactment. It is the command to perform the Passover that addresses readers directly. By obeying this command, addressees receive the promise of ongoing relationship inaugurated in the promise of deliverance. The narrative of fulfillment highlights the power of YHWH and gives the reader—the Passover celebrant—ways of confirming this power in the reenactment of the event.

The promise of constancy implied in the Passover commandment generates a promise of a new exodus when the future of their relationship comes into question in the message of the prophets of judgment, and in the exile. An event that started as promise and inaugurated a history under promise becomes a figure of the promised resolution of history.

The issuance of the Ten Commandments is the premier exercise of the power to command in the Hebrew Bible. An exercitive act presupposes the authority of the speaker to command and the duty of the addressees to obey. The narrative of the Sinai event constructs the hierarchical relationship that the commandments presuppose. Within the narrative world, the promises and commandments of YHWH elicit Israel's acceptance of the relationship in a pledge to obey all that YHWH says. Even after the people break the chief commandment and provoke God's wrath, the relationship is reconstructed with the added provision of divine forbearance. The narrative seeks to persuade the textual audience to accept this past transaction as binding on it.

The Decalog is addressed not only to the Israel of the narrative world, but to the reading audience as well. The exercitive act of God creates obligation for the addressees. It expresses God's concern for the good of the addressees and imposes responsibility on them to interpret and do what is commanded so as to please the speaker. The text of the Ten Commandments centers on the chief commandment, which protects God's unrivaled authority; the other commandments construct and protect the human community on the understanding that any violation is a breach of the addressee's relationship to God.

The prohibition against recognizing any God but YHWH makes unique claims on addressees and calls for periodic renewal. It creates an obligation that cannot be known in any other way and is decidedly at odds with the addressees' own natural inclinations. It calls for an obedient reason that gives no recognition to any deity or power beside YHWH. At several junctures in Israel's history, according to the biblical narrative, Israel renewed its pledge to recognize YHWH alone. The narratives of these renewals seek to persuade readers that they belong to this relationship their ancestors entered. It is a relationship that requires decision and the acceptance of responsibility for defection.

A new mode of argumentation arises in one of these accounts of renewal: the satire of the gods competing with YHWH for Israel's recognition. Elijah ridicules Baal and his personnel during the contest over which deity can light the sacrificial fire. One might call this a surrogate combat of deities in a narrative tradition which allows only YHWH to be rendered. Idol satire becomes a popular mode of theological disputation. By its very nature, satire distorts in order to dissolve the power or prestige of its target. Its cogency and legitimacy is limited to an audience under the prohibition of other gods and images, though in fact it has been used as a powerful apologetic weapon through history.

If God exercises the unconditional authority to obligate addressees, what happens when the command violates the addressee's sense of right or the common judgment of morally competent humans? If the addressee is required by ethics to subject God's commands to personal or communal moral judgment, they lose exercitive force. Divine commandments call for obedient reason, a reason that accepts responsibility for interpreting God's commandments and commands in the light of the moral character of God and in discussion with the community under the same authority.

The third type of performative expounded was the discourse of a court rendering a decision regarding innocence and guilt. The identification of prophecies of judgment as divine verdicts is more controversial than the other two. I had to argue *that* this is the case as well as *how* it is. Prophecies against individuals can be seen as extensions of the judicial system to cover cases that escape the human courts. Prophecies against the people as a whole stretch the concept of judicial discourse to the extreme, but continue to have a verdictive illocutionary force. In fact, it was the prophet's rhetorical burden to persuade addressees that the prophecy they were hearing had verdictive force.

Amos's utterances to the citizens of the Northern Kingdom provided ample evidence of divine accusation and sentencing. Amos had to draw up accusations of collective behavior that the addressees would recognize as wrong and as prevalent, and to convince them that God could and would hold them accountable as a nation. This prophecy called for rhetorical invention on a broad scale.

Amos's task was to convince the people that they deserved the verdict that he knew, by private revelation, YHWH had rendered. Because his addressees were so invested in the very practices that were condemned, he could not expect them, at least not many of them, to acknowledge their new status. At most his words would unsettle them and erode their confidence in their piety, righteousness, and God's favor.

The book of Amos is designed for an audience other than the Israelite people in 750 B.C.E. The reading audience is looking back on the divine verdict on a previous generation. The book ends with words of promise designed for an audience that has experienced the fulfillment of the prophecies of doom. It has the force of persuading this audience that the judgment was deserved but that God has preserved a remnant—the addressees—for a future.

Hebrew Scripture also preserves the voice of the people regarding the exile. In the words of lamentation, the people raise up their experience of suffering to move God to mercy and action. Some of these—Threni in particular—acknowledge the speakers' guilt, but some insist that God has betrayed Israel, or that he has grown too feeble to save. Thus, Scripture preserves a debate that must continue until the parties are reconciled.

Prospect. What agenda follows from this exposition? If the reader concurs in the identification of the performative transactions in our three primary texts—the call of Moses, the proclamation of commandments at Sinai, and Amos's proclamation of national judgment—then the next question is how the performative transactions can be formulated in general theological or hermeneutical terms, or formulated as an answer to theological or hermeneutical questions.

Revelation is at a junction, so to speak, where biblical theology and hermeneutics intersect. It is a standard topic within the systematic presentation of the teaching of the Hebrew Bible about God, creation, and human existence. The subject of revelation in such a systematic presentation would draw attention to the many and various ways God communicates knowledge and power to humans, and seek to mesh them together. In the course of the exposition, the theologian would be expected, I would think, to delineate the relationship of what is revealed by God to the knowledge humans can attain through reason, affections, and practical experience.

The hermeneutical path leads into philosophy. Here the question is whether it is possible for humans to be recipients of divine communication, and if so, how such communications relate to the other modes of human knowing and being. Because we are dealing with the interpretation of texts, the question of revelation concerns how the texts might communicate knowledge and power that cannot be attained by autonomous modes of knowing.

Although the rhetoric of revelation could assist us along either path, it seems to me to be of more immediate import to hermeneutics. Rhetoric concerns the transaction of a text with its audiences, its readers, its community of interpreters. One might say that rhetoric is the biblical text's movement toward a future, toward a community that endures through time, a community that seeks power and truth from the text to live by from generation to generation under changing political and cultural conditions. How does the text deliver what is expected of it? What is there in the text of the Hebrew Bible that makes it capable of empowering the community of interpreters to continue to live by it? How does it convince readers of the truth of what it communicates?

Recently, Nicholas Wolterstorff has published a philosophical study, *Divine Discourse*, employing Austin's theory of illocutionary discourse. His book is obviously of the utmost importance for understanding the import of the three primary passages examined in this monograph. Where he converges and diverges from my use of Austin's theory should be quite instructive.

Wolterstorff's *Divine Discourse*

Nicholas Wolterstorff's *Divine Discourse* is a sustained and multifaceted argument for ascribing discourse to God, based upon Austin's theory of speech acts. It forms an ideal dialog partner for applying the findings of this book to theological hermeneutics. In this discussion, I will adopt some of Wolterstorff's theses and differentiate my position from his on others.

Wolterstorff's argument has Austin's theory of speech acts as its center, so to speak, but he has to advance, on more than one front to achieve his objective of defending the ascription of discourse to God. To clear the way for the formulation of a coherent conception of divine discourse, Wolterstorff differentiates speaking from revealing. Here we have a significant parting of the ways from the very outset.

To ascribe discourse to God, one is not only ascribing a propositional content, but an illocutionary action to God. By saying things, God is doing things—promising, commanding, judging, expressing states of mind, divulging and authorizing the divine name, describing, informing, and the like.

How can God execute a speech act? Wolterstorff's answer is multifaceted. He proposes the model of mediated discourse to justify the idea that humans can speak for God. He sets out the conditions for participating in a community of discoursers and describes how God could meet these conditions. Finally, he argues that nothing in modern science and philosophy precludes divine intervention.

Wolterstorff arrives at his objective in two chapters on hermeneutics. He proposes to regard the Bible as human discourse that has been "appropriated" by God. As human discourse, it is subject to the same interpretive practices as any other body of literature. As divine discourse, interpreters must make a judgment—according to one's understanding of God's character and purpose—as to what God was saying in and through the human discourse God has appropriated.

The book ends with a consideration of the apologetic issues of entitlement and justification of belief. Here his Anglo-American philosophical roots evidence themselves most vividly.

In the following paragraphs, I will expound aspects of this argument that are most relevant to the interpretation of the specific performative transactions we have identified and expounded in the course of this book. After expounding his thesis, I will assess it and set forth my own solution to the problem.

Speaking and Revealing. The first question is whether we should be speaking of a "rhetoric of revelation" at all. Wolterstorff believes that we should not. To begin with, the verb *reveal* does not have the same force as verbs for illocutionary actions—to promise, command, and so on. To reveal a command is not to command. Revelation occurs when ignorance is dispelled, with or without the act of the agent. The most likely candidate for what is revealed is the inwardness of the self. Not all such revelations are intentional. One may consciously express, say, an attitude toward someone or one may exhibit, even "betray," it in one's speaking. The direct expression can be called *propositional*, the betrayal *manifestational*.

If speaking were considered a species of revelation, it would be a species of "agent self-revelation" of a "propositional character." However, an illocutionary act does not, according to Wolterstorff, *transmit knowledge*, it does not *communicate*.[1] The promise that "I will do something" cannot be taken by the addressee as knowledge that it will be done; the occurrence may not be in the power of the speaker to bring about, or the speaker may not intend to do it.

Wolterstorff maintains a rather strict formal difference between the illocutionary act of the speaker and the act of reception, called the *perlocutionary* act. The latter is the effect of the speaker's act, but the speaker's act does not depend on whether the addressee received it according to the intended effect. An utterance may be designed to produce knowledge in the addressee, but whether it does so is not within the power of the speaker to

---

1. *Divine Discourse*, 19–36.

determine. What happens in an illocutionary act is the implementation of the rights and duties of speaker and addressee inherent in the act. One who has been promised something has the "right" to expect its performance, the speaker a duty to do so; these facts are normative rather than conceptual.

Wolterstorff's personalistic model of revelation does not match the biblical use of terms for appearances and other revelatory transactions. God does indeed communicate in words and actions what God thinks and feels; in fact, we found the expression of God's attitude toward Israel in all three of our passages—compassion in the call of Moses, a gracious yet demanding disposition in the offer of covenant, and anger in the call of Amos. These expressions of the divine disposition, however, are not the object of revelational terminology.

Wolterstorff does incorporate what I take to be biblical usage, namely, the perceptible means by which the recipient knows that God is the one speaking or acting.[2] This definition fits the theophanic aspects of the call of Moses, the proclamation of commandments at Mount Sinai, and the call visions of Amos. Wolterstorff brings up the "signs and wonders" performed in Egypt; he describes them as "manifestational revelation . . . a *natural sign* of the actuality revealed."[3] They display the power of God and the capacity of God to focus coercive power discriminately. Because God announces each plague beforehand and explains their significance periodically, Wolterstorff would classify them as "agent self-revelation."

I would argue that the divine discourse that occurs in theophanies can be said to be *revelation*. The framing of an exchange between God and humans as a theophany lends another type of rhetorical force to the discourse. The framing may be no more than a report, and then its function is to locate the scene and perhaps certify the claims of the commandments or promises that come out of it (as in Gen. 17:1). However, when the appearance is depicted in graphic detail, as in Exod. 3:2-6, Exod. 19:16-20, and Amos 7:1-10, 8:1-3, the text has the rhetorical force of evoking revelation for the audience.[4]

The case of Amos raises some interesting questions about how far the mantle of revelation is to extend. Amos is commissioned in a series of divine appearances to deliver a message to Israel. These experiences included

---

2. On p. 21 of *Divine Discourse*, Wolterstorff speaks of a "*revelational correlate*, consisting of God's revealing that He was performing the act." Though he makes little of this, it is the basic idea of the theophanies and wonders of the Bible.

3. Ibid., 28.

4. The audience can say: we know it happened because we ourselves have experienced it.

verbal exchanges (even a pun). When he fulfilled his commission, he was speaking as God's "deputy," his utterances carried divine authority. However, they do not depict or build rhetorically on his experience of revelation.[5] His message to the Israelites depends for its "authority" on the power of his discourse to enact the transaction of judgment, of being declared guilty and sentenced for the offenses depicted. This transaction is divine discourse, by Wolterstorff's definition, but not revelation. It seems to me that category boundaries are extremely porous in such cases.

It is my contention, to summarize to this point, that the discourse that takes place within a theophanic event, or that derives its authority from one, falls under the category "revelation" in its biblical sense. I would even go farther: the discourse is usually the point of a theophanic event.[6]

The theological concept of revelation that still shapes much contemporary usage is not biblical, but seems to have emerged in the medieval discussions of the relative weight to be given divine communication and philosophical reasoning in the attainment of the knowledge of God.[7] In that context, it meant the knowledge of God transmitted by God. It could be identified with Scripture, or Scripture as interpreted in a certain, divinely guided tradition. Parallel to it was the division of the knowledge of God into what humans are capable of knowing of God by unaided reason and what they must accept on God's authority mediated through Talmudic discussion, church teaching—some institutional structure and interpretive practice.

The need for revelation was understood to be, in Christian theology, the fall of the human race. Humans were created in possession of the knowledge of God, rooted in an obedient relationship with God, but of their own free will the progenitors of the race disobeyed and defaced the knowledge of God. Revelation must not only make up for human ignorance (due to finitude), it must restore the capacity to know God, transforming the distorted knowledge humans have in their fallen condition.

The medieval usage perdures when we use revelation in contrast to reason, or some other faculty, even if the larger framework of the medieval discussion has been replaced. When philosophical arguments become locked in interminable debates and theological knowledge is denied public status, the term *revelation* is bound to take on a different valence. It does,

---

5. He does defend the freedom of prophecy (3:3-8) and his own authenticity (7:12-15) by allusions to the call, but this has only a defense-removal function in his rhetoric.

6. There is another kind of narrative that looks a lot like theophany, which is associated with God's deeds: I follow C. Westermann, *The Praise of God in the Psalms*, 93–101, distinguishing "theophany" from epiphany.

7. This is a surmise; I do not have a study at hand.

nevertheless, retain the memory, as it were, of past usage.[8] I have used the term *revelation* to mean the knowledge of God communicated by God off and on in this monograph, and am proposing a model of this communication that makes the communicative transaction essential to the knowledge communicated. This argument might be open to a formulation that does not employ the word *revelation*, but I do not see any compelling reason to do so.

It is against this definition of the word that Wolterstorff aims another argument: he denies that illocutionary actions communicate knowledge. He distinguishes between the propositional content of an utterance and its illocutionary force. "Saying x *counts as* doing A."[9] "Saying x" is a proposition that has conceptual content and reference. By speaking appropriately within the conventions of the discourse community, the proposition becomes an illocutionary act (A) of a particular sort. The same proposition can be the subject of different illocutionary acts. The illocutionary act does not add, shall we say, to the knowledge communicated in the proposition. Moreover, the intention to communicate knowledge in the speech act does not guarantee that it has indeed been learned by the addressee.

While these conceptual distinctions may be valid at an analytical level, a performative utterance—that class of utterances that construct the propositional content in the act of speaking—synthesizes the knowledge to be communicated inseparably with the act of speaking. One must know the illocutionary force of the utterance to grasp how the utterance is to be taken and hence how it can be judged to be true or false.

Let us consider the case of YHWH's promise to Israel addressed to Moses: "I have come down to deliver them out of the hands of the Egyptians" (Exod. 3:8). Wolterstorff notes that one does not know from this utterance whether the speaker intends to or is able to do what he says; he may be dissembling or not up to it. But Moses knows that YHWH has obligated himself to do so. Moreover, to receive the promise as promise, Moses must trust that YHWH is both honest and capable. If Moses is not willing to do so, he cannot know whether the deliverance would actually have taken place. The promise must, to use Austin's terms, have the proper perlocutionary effect to have its illocutionary force.[10] Many promises and agreements are performative *transactions*—all parties must play their assigned role for the action to succeed.

8. A memory certainly maintained in the study of the texts that use the term with the medieval definition.

9. This section is covered in chapter 5 of *Divine Discourse*, 75–94. Wolterstorff diverges from Austin on the definition of locutionary: see n. 1 to chapter 5, 304.

10. Cf. D. Evans, *The Language of Self-Involvement* (London: SCM, 1963), 150–51, 170–73.

The subsequent narrative depicts how YHWH has to overcome Moses' initial resistance and subsequent doubts, and Israel's uncertain faith. It seems that YHWH needs only a certain degree of compliance to accomplish his purpose. Nevertheless, both Moses and Israel must venture trust and obey the directions given them at crucial points for the truth of what has been promised to be experienced.

The Jewish interpretive community cannot know whether this story of past deliverance is true if parents do not comply with the command to celebrate the Passover. If the Passover is celebrated, it depends upon the power of the God of the exodus to maintain a witnessing community from generation to generation. If external and internal forces destroy this witnessing community—as they have threatened to do in every era—the promise to Moses will be proven false. Its truth can never be known except in the mode of trust and obedience. No other measure of its truth is sufficient without this one.

Do performative transactions like the promise to Moses and the command to perform the Passover yield "knowledge"? I suspect that an argument over definitions would prove inconclusive. If one decides it is not, the argument of this monograph is for naught.

How Can God Speak? This seemingly naive question requires a sophisticated exploration of what it means to speak and what would have to be predicated of God to ascribe speaking. Wolterstorff devotes three chapters to different aspects of this question, all of which reward the study. The issue is, from beginning to end, not the locutionary or perlocutionary aspects of utterance, but the illocutionary. The question is not how God authors speech, but how God authorizes discourse with particular illocutionary forces.

In pursuit of analogies for the biblical phenomenon of God's speaking through human speakers, Wolterstorff sketches the various ways humans speak in the words of others. When an executive has a secretary take dictation or compose a letter for him, the communication is executed by one person with the authority of another. The same thing happens when one tells someone to say something to a third party. Wolterstorff names this type of transaction "double agent discourse." When an ambassador has the power to formulate words in the name of her government, even to negotiate agreements that obligate her government to specific actions, we have what Wolterstorff calls "deputized discourse." Finally, there is "appropriated discourse" when a person subscribes to the words of another—sending greeting cards, quoting poetry in speeches, citing an authority in a scholarly work.

These three ways humans speak in the words of others are, in Wolter-storff's opinion, fit analogies for how God can speak through the variety of biblical texts. Mosaic and prophetic speech certainly purports to be "deputized discourse." Psalms and wisdom could be understood as God's "appropriated discourse."

For God to speak with illocutionary force, God must be subject to the obligations and conventions of a discourse community in order to acquire the normative standing necessary for effective communication. Wolterstorff disputes those divine command theories that accord God exercitive authority without corresponding obligations. Without the latter, the former would be purely arbitrary. A sovereign who does not abide by his own laws is a tyrant. Wolterstorff proposes that certain actions are required of God because they befit God's character, but God is free to transcend the law in works of supererogation, for example, to forgive the sinner and give life to the dead.[11]

If God is to participate in a community of discoursers, it is necessary to speak of divine intervention. Despite the analogies of deputized and appropriated speech, there must be acts of authorization. Various attempts to avoid this conclusion have been made, but they either require a world of complete predictability or they end up denying the capacity of God to generate discourse. Modern apologetic theology has taken the latter course in an effort to avoid conflict between religion and the scientific worldview. Wolterstorff, who has written in the area of science and religion before, believes that the scientific concept of law does not preclude divine intervention, which is where he leaves it.[12]

What Wolterstorff has done is to sketch the metaphysical requirements for a doctrine of God corresponding to the biblical rendering of God. God "deputizes individuals" to speak in his behalf. All three of our texts exemplify such transactions; at Sinai God also speaks to all Israel. Moreover, there is no question but that God interacts with humans, accepting responsibilities along with assuming power. Wolterstorff has defended the main features of the biblical view of God, humans, and the transactions between them.

The question that Wolterstorff's analysis prompts is whether the interpreter of Scripture must subscribe to a particular metaphysic to enter into transactions with the God who addresses the interpretive community from the text. God has accommodated to the capacity of the human mind by offering access through a persona established by and maintained in the collective imagination of ancient Israel. The question is: Is God's identification

11. Wolterstorff, *Divine Discourse*, 95–113.
12. Ibid., 114–29.

with YHWH, the God of Israel, an identification with the particular intellectual horizon of this ancient Near Eastern people?

Wolterstorff himself struggles with some aspects of this question. He
must reclassify as metaphorical the biblical discourse about the physical
cosmos. He also records with approval the church's tendency to consider
the ascription of emotions to God to be "figurative," in other words, not
really applicable to God but to the human experience of God. We might say
that his strategy is to pick and choose between which aspects of the biblical rendering of God he will take literally and which he will not. Undoubtedly, this strategy has been the interpretive practice of the Jewish and
Christian religious communities through the centuries.

I propose that we leave the biblical rendering of God intact and recognize
that the challenge is to fuse the horizons of the textual world and the worlds
of the interpretive communities. It is a case of translating the divine accommodation to contemporary audiences, of recovering the rhetorical power of
a text for the audience that recognizes its authority. This hermeneutical
model does not preclude metaphysical reasoning, but it does not require a
metaphysics as a precondition for encounter with the text of Scripture.

The First and Second Hermeneutic. Wolterstorff's concepts are in place for
a final assault. The Bible is a collection of human acts of discourse that can
be read and studied in their own right, but within the religious communities that constitute its primary interpretive communities these human
words are divine discourse as well.

Scholarship is indispensable for the discernment of the human discourse. The first level of textual interpretation is for the noetic content of
the discourse. It is a good rule to seek to understand statements literally. If
the unit of discourse makes sense at that level, one can infer that the author
intended to say just that. However, sentences frequently have several possible meanings, and then one must make a judgment as to which was intended. When the literal sense does not seem to make sense, one seeks to discern
some "figurative" meaning.

Wolterstorff offers a theory of metaphor based upon sentences rather
than words. A word that has a denotative meaning can become a metaphor
by being placed in a sentence in which its denotation yields a sense the
interpreter cannot imagine the author to have said.

In addition to conceptual content, discourse has designative content,
that is, it refers to persons, places, and things located "outside" the text. History and geography play an essential role in understanding a text.[13]

---

13. I cannot tell how broadly Wolterstorff would extend designative content. Would the
reconstruction of the socioeconomic structures and processes of ancient Israel have any

Wolterstorff has taken recourse to authorial intention as the guide to interpretation. Whatever else a text may mean, it begins with the illocutionary action—the act of inscription that counts as an assertion, promise, plea, and so on. Discourse, though, is too rich and indeterminate to restrict it to the author's own conscious intention. A text is, thus, open to figural uses, with the proviso that these not be divorced from authorial intention.[14]

Wolterstorff provides an example of how he would apply his first hermeneutic in a later chapter on "the illocutionary stance of biblical narrative." Because his discussion is not germane to the issues at hand, we can dispense with it.

The human discourse of the Bible becomes divine discourse by appropriation. Some discourse is deputized, but hardly all. For logical reasons, Wolterstorff needs a category broad enough to include all of the Bible. If God has appropriated this discourse, the task for the interpreter who seeks to find God's message for a religious community is to question each passage for what in its human discourse God would be intending to say to the particular contemporary audience and occasion.[15]

To judge what God would be intending to say, one needs certain rules or principles deriving from the nature of God. The Bible is to be regarded as *one* book, with each passage read against the background of the whole, because God does not speak in contradictions. One can trust that God does not lie or assert falsehood, so whatever text (or aspect of a text) does seem to be false or dishonest is to be discounted as an untrustworthy or misinformed witness. There are rules of content: God intends to instill the love of God and neighbor and transmit sound doctrine, so any text that instills hate or speaks foolishness lacks divine authorization. Finally, the church has held that the purpose of God's speaking is to communicate on matters of faith and morals, not physics, biology, or city planning.

A biblical text may not coincide with divine discourse in a number of ways. Some of these are purely formal. Discourse addressed to God or describing God must be converted into the conceptual content conveyed by God. The point of a text must be distinguished from its means of expression, and the latter may not be true, for example, prescientific cosmology used to praise the power and providence of God. Sometimes the human

positive contribution to make to the text's designative content? A similar question might be asked of noematic content: Can one employ ancient Near Eastern concepts and images to decide what the biblical text meant?

14. Wolterstorff, *Divine Discourse*, 130–52, 153–70, 183–201.

15. Ibid., 202–22. The contemporary aspect is categorized as presentation, and Wolterstorff only discusses that aspect briefly here and there. So his hermeneutics deals with what God said and how it might apply to us.

author may have meant something literally, but it can only be considered appropriate to God in a figurative sense. The church has generally considered statements about God's emotions to be in that category. Finally, the text may have been addressed to particular people with a particular problem or issue before them, and it is necessary to abstract something of general import from the specifics.[16]

Wolterstorff foresees an objection to his hermeneutical model: it rests the decision as to what God is intending to communicate upon the judgment of the interpreter as to what is appropriate to God. The obvious danger is that the interpreter will discover God saying in a particular text what the interpreter already believes, expects, or wants to hear. After expounding and critiquing several attempts to avert this subjectivism, he concludes that we—if we adopt his hermeneutics—must accept the responsibility of judgment and guard against subjectivism by presuming initially a congruence between what the text says and what God means to communicate, and be open to the possibility that the beliefs with which one approached the text are mistaken. In addition, it is important to discuss the text in community, cultivate knowledge of ourselves and our world, and practice a religious regimen.[17]

Wolterstorff's account of what he calls the "first hermeneutic" is unexceptionable, though it is not particularly well fitted to many of the topics and methods of current critical biblical scholarship. A composite text, for example, raises a question as to whose authorial intention is to be taken as normative. Multiple layers of intention are at issue as well as authorship/editorship. If the rhetorical transaction between text and audience is an essential ingredient in communication, the reception and application of the text by the audience must condition the authority of authorship. Despite these qualifications, Wolterstorff rightly grants autonomy to critical scholarship and historical reconstruction. Questions as to what a text means to say and what it means to say it about are hashed out by a scholarly community that has no investment in the theological consequences of its findings.

I actually concur with Wolterstorff that theology is or can legitimately be by and for the religious communities that accord Scripture normative authority. However, biblical theology is a child of a mixed marriage. The church and synagogue did not distinguish between the message of the Bible and the living faith of the religious community. It was critical scholarship that forced Jews and Christians—often against their will—to recognize discontinuity and outright disagreement. Once the difference was acknowl-

16. Ibid., 202–22.
17. Ibid., 223–39.

edged, however, it was the interest of believers in the message of Scripture that generated biblical theology.

Some practitioners of the theology of Hebrew Scriptures hold that the ideal is a purely descriptive account of what these texts say about God and humanity and nature. One might say that this type of biblical theology considers autonomous reason the only legitimate reason. However, if the Scriptures are designed to elicit faith and obedience, there should be an alternative that seeks the message of the text by becoming the reader the text seeks to engender. This conclusion is what I take Levinas to mean by "obedient reason." A biblical theology so grounded would also grant those interpretive traditions in which faith was seeking understanding the status of witness alongside the critical reconstruction of the original meaning.

Perhaps a common meeting ground can be found for autonomous and obedient exegesis and synthesis in the maxim my colleague Allen Scult and I proposed: "Interpret the text as the best text it can be."[18] Both believer and neutral scholar should be able to agree in principle on criteria for a best text reading and assess readings on this basis. Consensus should not be expected, but the conflict of interpretations could sort out the viable and strengthen them.

Wolterstorff's application of Austin's speech-act theory is a disappointment to me. By seeking out a common category for all Scripture, he set aside the distinctive way each type of discourse engages the interpretive community. He does note the existence of "deputized discourse," but evidently would apply the same "second hermeneutic" to it as to the rest of Scripture. The only difference is that the interpreter must distinguish the "rhetorical-conceptual structure" of statements by God from those of narrative or prayer.[19]

My argument has been that the performative utterances of God require responses from the addressee, which differ in kind from those that do not. The performative creates the knowledge it communicates and constructs a relationship between speaker and addressee. To know the truth of the utterance, the addressee must enter into the relationship and play the role specified by the illocutionary force of the utterance.

The effort of another philosopher to apply Austin to scriptural discourse, Donald Evans, comes closer to my approach than Wolterstorff's. It should prove instructive to review his treatment of the Sinaitic narrative; it may lend a certain degree of support to what I have been doing.

18. See A. Scult and D. Patrick, *Rhetoric and Biblical Interpretation*, 21–23, 84–88.
19. *Divine Discourse*, 208-9

Evans's *"Creation as a Performative Action."* The title of Evans's book, *The Logic of Self-Involvement*, derives from another strand in Evans's thought, one that he drew from Ian Ramsey. Self-involving language is discourse that requires the speaker to adopt a stance toward what she says.[20] One might say that the speaker is invested in what is said, though he may be speaking insincerely. According to Evans, only two categories of performative utterance have this reflexive force, commissive (promisory) and behabitive (expression of attitude). However, he adds a category—expressions of feeling.[20] In these kinds of discourse, the speaker is taking a stand on a question that cannot be answered by an appeal to the facts. Many of these questions involve values which Evans, along with most theorists of his time, considers to be autonomous.[21]

The book is divided into philosophical and theological halves, with the first chapter in the philosophical half applied to biblical materials in the first chapter of the theological, and so forth. Only chapter 4 actually explores the attribution of performative discourse to God. Evans begins by examining texts depicting the creation of Israel, particularly the exodus and covenant, extrapolates from that to world creation, and concludes with New Testament teaching on creation.

YHWH's demonstration of miraculous power falls outside performative discourse, according to Evans, but the inauguration of a covenant does involve the exercise of authority. YHWH created Israel with a subordinate status, making him Lord, with a role, making him Appointer, and with a value, making him Evaluator. These belong to the performative category of exercitive, but YHWH also commits himself to preserve Israel in this status, that is, he is its Guarantor.[22]

The same performative acts are ascribed to God as Creator of the world, particularly in the tradition ascribing creation to the word. Creation receives subordinate status, is given a role and value, and God commits himself to its maintenance; these acts call for human correlative responses of gratitude, trust, and submission.[23]

> The efficacious word of God in Creation has not only supernatural causal power but also Exercitive, Verdictive and Commissive force; and man's word concerning the Creator who is Lord, Appointer,

---

20. I. Ramsey, *Religious Language: An Empirical Placing of Theological Phrases* (New York: Macmillan, 1957), 11–54; D. Evans, *The Logic of Self-Involvement*, 11–15, and elsewhere.

21. These can overlap with commissive and behabitive. He puts expression of feeling on a scale from symptom to manifestation to expression to report of feeling: see *The Logic of Self-Involvement*, 116–24.

22. See Evans, *Self-Involvement*, 64–66, 135–37.

23. Ibid., 145–51.

Evaluator and Guarantor is self-involving acknowledgment. . . . This act of acknowledgment includes both Behabitive and Commissive elements.[24]

Here Evans introduces his category of the "on-look": "In his utterance concerning Creation, biblical man implies that he must take the divine action to be performative; that is, he *looks on* Creation *as* a performative action."[25] Evans is going to add the adjective *parabolic* to the term *on-look* to distinguish it from the *analogical on-look*.

This is the extent to which Evans explores the performative language of Hebrew Scripture. He complements it with a study of expressive discourse (he so terms *glory* and *holiness*) and concludes with an argument regarding the reference of creation language. Because these arguments are not directly germane to our concern and do not seem to affect his statements about performatives materially, we can leave off here.

Evans's discussion of God's performative acts has taken an odd turn. He clearly appreciates the different illocutionary forces of the divine utterances establishing the covenant with Israel, and notes that these utterances entail a correlative from the addressees. However, he leaves the transactions behind for a set of abstractions characterizing the deity and a corresponding set characterizing the human community. I suspect that he is under the influence of those biblical theologies that divide the subject along the lines of God, humans, and the interaction between them.[26]

In my exposition of the covenant and commandments, I sought to understand how the text creates the community it depicts. The commandments address the interpretive community along with the people within the textual world. A relationship between YHWH, the Law-giver, and the readers is elicited from the text. That relationship is one of responsibility and accountability to the divine speaker. The reader should accept this responsibility in trust and affection for the One who shows care for us by giving us the way of life and righteousness.

The account of covenant making and theophany is intended, I argued, to persuade the audience that they, as members of this people, are under an obligation to recognize and obey YHWH. It not only legitimizes the theocratic structure of the community, it seeks to persuade readers that they too would have chosen as their ancestors did. By concurring in this decision,

24. Ibid., 151–58.
25. Ibid., 159.
26. For example, L. Köhler, *Old Testament Theology*, trans. D. S. Todd (Philadelphia: Westminster, 1957): Part I, God; Part II, Man; Part III, Judgment and Salvation.

the interpretive community in a sense renews the covenant. According to other narratives, actual renewals took place at various critical junctures of Israelite history.

The perlocutionary effect intended by the commands is, of course, obedience. However, obedience is not required to put the commandments into force. The community recognizes the obligation of its members to obey what YHWH commands. The individual members of the community are henceforth accountable to YHWH for their compliance, and failure to do so brings judgment. Without the commandments, there would be no disobedience and judgment: the performative force of the commandments is upheld in both obedience and disobedience.

Evans's application of speech-act theory does construct the knowledge of God from the performative transactions depicted in the text, but he does not consider that the text might actually elicit transactions with the readers. The creation texts are quite different from the Sinaitic narrative in this respect (cf. Gen. 2:1-3, a blessing, and Exod. 20:8-11, a commandment). I suspect, though, that a close reading would uncover the performative force of divine discourse for the readers. Evans's insensitivity to the transactional character of divine discourse requires a separate theory—"on-looks"— to explain how the teaching is appropriated.

While we are searching for analogies for the ontological status of divine discourse, we might look in the direction of religious liturgy. How are the words "This is my body . . . blood" understood in Christian tradition? If the words are regarded as descriptive of the elements, theologians have to devise theories as to how they can be something else. If the words and elements are understood as a performative act of God, the celebrant receives them as the word of God made flesh. Perhaps the divine performative discourse in Scripture and preaching is sacramental, involving "real presence." Certainly the Talmudic discussion of Torah invests the words with the same illocutionary force as they had for the people assembled at the foot of the mountain.

John Climacus's Thought-Experiment

The first question that must be asked is why *Philosophical Fragments* should even be included in a discussion of the hermeneutics of revelation. The book does not purport to be an interpretation of the Bible and does not draw on the Bible for its formulations. When it alludes to Scripture, it is Christian Scripture, not the Hebrew Bible. Moreover, it is something of a hall of mirrors. The author of record is a creation of Kierkegaard, but not a pseudonym: Kierkegaard disowns the writings of his characters/authors, as any honest writer of fiction would.[27] And that is just a beginning. Christian revelation is formulated in language appropriate to Greek polytheism, and everything said about it is a counterimage to Socratic teaching. It is all presented hypothetically, as though such a type of teaching is only an interesting conceptual possibility, not a historical claim. Surely such an intellectual game should be ignored by any serious discussion of the interpretation of the Bible. And if that were not enough, the book is more than 150 years old.

Aside from the fact that I have deep affection for the book, I offer the following apologia for my inclusion of it. Through most of the history of the church, apologists with a philosophical bent have been concerned to tone down the claims of revelation.[28] It has been common to establish analogies between revelation and philosophical knowledge or to employ philosophical metaphors to explicate the meaning of revelation.

In religious eras, the assimilation of revelation to natural knowledge did not seem to undercut the distinctive claims of revelation too seriously, but at least since the Enlightenment there has been an erosion of the claims to know God through God. Christian apologetics in this era is a story of retreat after retreat in the face of triumphal science and math, autonomous ethics, and individualistic sensibility. The concept of revelation has faded away like the Cheshire cat. Kierkegaard's intellectual environment included Kant, who had restricted religious knowledge to the postulates of moral reason, and Hegel, who had demythologized the images of revelation into the universal concepts of an immanent divine mind.

Dogmatic theologians, to be sure, continued to defend a supernatural knowledge communicated miraculously in the Bible to the church. They constituted, however, a cultural backwater. They had retreated, to employ another metaphor, into the castle of the church, leaving the field of cultural conflict to religious liberals and secularists. They would venture into battle periodically, taking their stand on their most vulnerable claims— miracles and prophecy; the intellectual culture could ignore them or ridicule them as anachronisms.

Kierkegaard decided to call a halt to the erosion of the concept of revelation in apologetics by formulating a model of revelation that was incommensurable with the philosophical and scientific understanding of truth and knowledge. The knowledge of God is available only in a life-transforming relationship to God. It is an existential knowledge, not an objective body of concepts or moral precepts.

---

27. See Appendix to *Concluding Unscientific Postscript to the Philosophical Fragments*; Kierkegaard's Writings, XII.1 (Princeton: Princeton Univ. Press, 1992), 617–23, 25–30.

28. I am using the word *revelation* in the medieval theological sense here.

Note that Kierkegaard did not take his stand in the protective confines of orthodox dogmatics, but on the modern cultural battlefield. He formulated the concept of revelation in terms neither dogmaticians nor philosophers would recognize. The reader of *Philosophical Fragments* recognizes, of course, that Climacus is speaking about Christ, but the way Christ is spoken of departs from the terms of the debate between the orthodox, the apologists, and the secularists. One could not rehearse the old put-downs, or defenses, of revelation. The oddity of this exposition of revelation was increased by its hypothetical formulation and the presentation of Christ as an anti-Socrates. The era was infatuated with Socrates, with Kierkegaard at the head, but it would not recognize its own philosophical positions in Socrates. Kierkegaard's "target" is thus hidden behind a teaching no nineteenth-century reader would subscribe to.

I propose to take the reader on a relaxed tour of the argument of *Philosophical Fragments*. Some of Kierkegaard's philosophical arguments can be left aside because they are tangential to our interest. I will not follow the text too woodenly, and will interject some supporting thoughts along the way. When I have set forth Climacus's construct, I will try its fit on divine performative discourse.

Socrates. Climacus proposes to describe revelation in comparison to Socratic teaching.[29] The focus will be on teacher and learner, and the relationship of these roles to what is taught. It will give no consideration of the content of knowledge, only the transmission of it and the presuppositions of that transmission. The Socratic teacher wants to transmit knowledge, not opinion. That is, the teacher desires that the learner not take what she says on authority, but know why the knowledge is true. A math teacher seeks to teach students the axioms and rules of mathematical thinking, not to rote-memorize answers to problems—not only the axioms and rules, but their rational cogency.

If the learner can grasp these, he must already be in possession of them. Otherwise, at some point the knowledge would rest upon authority, which is opinion. Socrates concludes that humans must be born with the form or idea of truth. The teacher's task is to prompt the learner to recall what she already knows, but has forgotten. Hence the well-known "Socratic method" depicted in the *Meno*: an uneducated slave comes to a sophisticated mathematical concept by a series of leading questions. More typical of the Platonic dialogues, however, is a questioning that exposes opinion

---

29. Discussed in *Philosophical Fragments;* Kierkegaard's Writings, VII (Princeton: Princeton Univ. Press, 1985), 9–13, 23–24, 25–30.

and prompts the person being interrogated to search for the principles and concepts that would yield knowledge.

The teacher in this process is a "midwife," one who helps the learner to deliver the knowledge with which she is pregnant. Moreover, the transaction between teacher and learner is only the occasion for learning, perhaps the stimulus. Once the student has learned the truth that he had "forgotten," perhaps to judge perception and opinion according to true principles and concepts, the transaction can be forgotten. Neither the teacher nor the exchange between teacher and student is relevant to the truth that has been uncovered.

Why have humans forgotten what they know, or become unsure in their judgment regarding what is true and what is false? Socrates—or Plato— entertained the idea that the rational soul exists in a state of truth before it enters the body, and the trauma of being born and the distractions of the coming and going of finite things makes it forget. The world of sense experience and opinion eclipses the innate knowledge of eternal ideas or forms. Perhaps one can sense the kinship of this idea to the Hindu concept of *maya* (illusion).

A close reading of the dialogs hints at a dissatisfaction with this account of ignorance. In dialog after dialog, the one interrogated gets angry at having his ignorance exposed, and does not follow Socrates willingly in a dialectical quest for truth. Moreover, some of Socrates' auditors used his method of arousing doubt as a means for the cynical quest for power, or as a reason to abandon themselves to debauchery. He was condemned and executed by the Athenian court as an atheist and corrupter of the youth.

If Socrates or Plato were to admit that "ignorance" was willful, their conception of education would have to be modified. The will would have to be changed, or redeemed, for the learner to be able to recognize the truth. This notion will be one of the entry points for revelation.

Before we leave Socrates, we should observe that he professed to be a pious man. An oracle prompted his quest for wisdom, and he showed a deference to the gods. Typical of his piety was the way he went about discovering the truth of the oracle: by setting out to disprove it. According to Kierkegaard, Socrates' religion was a "religion of immanence." That is, the *knowledge* of the gods can be ascertained by the rational evaluation of all opinion, basing all theology on knowledge of first principles. One might say that he was the first philosopher of religion.

The God. Climacus's thought-experiment is to imagine a transaction between teacher and learner that inverts Socrates' educational scheme.[30]

---

30. Discussed in *Philosophical Fragments*, 13–20, 24–30, 31–35.

The trick is to avoid reverting to the conception of education Socrates is opposing, namely, the passing on of opinion on the basis of authority. Christian revelation, unfortunately, has often been so conceived, and it produces a kind of immature dependency of the believer on the arbitrary authority of God in exchange for the promised rewards, namely, eternal salvation. Kierkegaard sets out a model of a transaction in which the temporal factor, the event in time, is essential to the truth that is communicated, and the teacher's relationship to the learner is the relation of the learner to the truth.

The temporality of the transaction is what we might call Kierkegaard's wedge issue. Socrates—indeed, all of Greek philosophy—could find little "truth" in history. The truth must transcend the coming to be and passing away of temporal process. That the learner came to a realization of the truth at one time rather than another is accidental or incidental. One may remember it fondly, but if one forgot it, nothing would be lost. Physical science has often regarded its history in this fashion.

To make the events of history significant, the truth must come into being in them. How can timeless truth come into being in time? Kierkegaard proposes the concept of the "moment," the temporal event in which the eternal "comes into" time, or actually comes into being in time in such a way that the learner cannot abstract a timeless truth from the event and then forget the event as an occasion. Though the moment occurs in temporal process, it cannot be in a cause-and-effect relationship with the sequence of events, for then the temporal would give birth to the eternal and the eternal would only have the timelessness of continuing influence in its effects.[31] Thus, the moment escapes the notice of the historian and the Hegelian philosopher of history.

Now comes the teacher. How can the teacher be made essential to the truth that the teacher communicates? The Socratic teacher is in fact essential in one sense: the better the midwife, the better the chance of successful delivery. Socrates was so good at asking questions, exposing opinion, and probing for the foundations of knowledge that philosophical studies still reenact the dialogs as an exercise in philosophical thinking. Yet, what one seeks to discover in the Socratic dialogs is a truth that in no way depends upon Socrates' authority.

How can the teacher be made more than the occasion and stimulus to discovery of truth? Only if the teacher so embodies the truth that what the teacher teaches cannot be abstracted from who the teacher is. The teacher

---

31. Theologians in the twentieth century who developed the concept of history-making event into a theological concept may have thought they were following Kierkegaard's lead, but in fact it is a version of the concept he was opposing.

must be, Climacus says, "the god." A human teacher may, indeed should, embody the qualities he hopes to instill in his students, even inspire a certain degree of imitation; but in the end he seeks to bring his students into relationship with a truth, a subject matter, or virtue that transcends him. The god, however, is the embodiment of the truth in such a way that what is taught is how to be in relationship to the teacher.

This relationship still has the potential for being authoritarian, though no longer a communication of opinion. How can the authoritarian potential be removed? Only if the learner is so constituted that she needs to be in relationship to the teacher to be complete. It can only be true if the teacher is also the creator, and the creature can only be complete by relation to others and to the source of self and others. In this sense, the learner is already in possession of the truth: she is constituted to be in relationship.

If this is so, why do humans need to learn? Why are we ignorant? Kierkegaard follows biblical tradition in ascribing the condition of ignorance to the willfulness of the learners. While humans are so constituted that they are complete only in relationship to the creator and others, they are free to seek completion autonomously. In freedom, humans squander their freedom. They fall into a condition of "untruth," of autonomous fulfillment, and cannot extricate themselves. Indeed, though they may be anxious and lonely and in despair, they do not know what is wrong. To be healed, they must first of all realize their condition. They cannot be taught it as fact or objective truth; they must recognize it in themselves. Yet it requires the act of the teacher, who does know their condition, to reveal their condition to them. The teacher not only communicates the truth to the learner but provides the condition for knowing that it is true.

The relationship still has the potential of immature dependence. Kierkegaard introduces another concept to avoid that: the relationship of teacher to learner must be one of equality. Here he introduces (hypothetically, of course) the doctrine of the incarnation: the god comes to humans not in majesty and power, but as a servant, a human among humans, not even as a powerful or spectacular human, but one of the "common people" who suffers and dies as one of them. What distinguishes the god is that he is the god in human form, and elicits relationship with himself to complete the lives of his brothers and sisters.

Performative Transactions. Kierkegaard's thought-experiment is a transparent formulation of the Christian kerygma, and he underscores this formulation by introducing classical theological terms to name various concepts in his model, and jokes with the audience about whether he is plagiarizing. On the other hand, the way Kierkegaard has set up his thought-experiment allows him to cast Christian doctrine in a parabolic light. Everything seems to fall into place so nicely because he is constructing an ideal possibility. If we treat it as parabolic, and not demand a doctrine from it, it illuminates the type of rhetorical transaction we have identified in God's utterances to Moses at the burning bush, to all Israel at Sinai, and to the Northern Kingdom in Amos's prophecies of judgment.

The promises, commands, and verdicts issued in these utterances create the knowledge they communicate. The moment of communication is more than an occasion; the transaction between God and human recipient(s) puts the command, promise, or verdict into effect. Without the utterance, the "idea" does not exist. The textual audience must relate to the transaction as defining its existence as well. It is through the performative utterance of God to the human addressee of the textual world that what is said comes into time, into existence. The utterance becomes a source of hope and responsibility for readers through their response to the performative addressed to them.

God the "teacher" is indispensable to the truth of the utterance. To trust in a promise is to trust the person who made it. To obey a command is to acknowledge the authority of the speaker and to trust in the speaker's wisdom and goodwill. To accept the judgment uttered in prophecy is to acknowledge the authority, integrity, and wisdom of the judge. The textual audience makes these same movements in relationship to the performative force of each text. The language of performative utterances involves not only the act of the speaker, but a transaction between speaker and audience that creates a particular relationship between them.

Climacus's point that the ignorance of the learner is a state of untruth for which the learner is responsible[32] would not seem to fit either the exodus or covenant making. The Israelites in Egypt were the victims of oppression, of the sin of others. They are themselves innocent—though not innocents— and the revelation of God is a rendering of justice. The commandments do presuppose the capacity, even penchant, of addressees to act wrongly, but they create the responsibilities whose violation are wrongful acts and where enforcement maintains justice, holiness, and peace within the community. Only the prophecy of judgment holds the audience responsible for its ignorance. And in this case, it is not the individual learner whose acts are judged, but the community in its collective life.

We must expand the definition of sin to include corporate evil and even "sinful" situations. The Egyptians do not enslave the Israelites out of innocent ignorance, and when they refuse to release them God is justified in

32. *Philosophical Fragments*, 15.

coercing compliance. When the pharaoh says, "Who is YHWH, that I should heed his voice and let Israel go?" (Exod. 5:2), we could understand it as the ignorance of one people respecting another people's gods, but it is tinged with the arrogance of an imperial power toward subject peoples. The pharaoh should recognize the truth of this deity in the justice of the request.

The Hebrew Bible holds humans responsible for their ignorance. To be sure, it is quite aware of the limits of human knowledge due to finitude, but it is most suspicious of the willful element in ignorance. All humans are accountable to the Creator for adherence to a moral order and for piety toward the transcendent. Nor are the Israelites rendered ontologically innocent by their victim status; they are responsible to God and for each other.

The Pentateuchal narrative does not assume that humans have an innate capacity to be just and faithful, though they are held responsible. Even before their final deliverance at the sea, the people begin to grumble at the leadership of God and Moses, and rebellion breaks out several times during the wilderness sojourn. Obviously the people cannot sustain a relationship with YHWH by their own willpower; YHWH conducts and compels them along a way that they could not go on their own. In this sense, the scriptural text confirms Kierkegaard's assertion that the teacher not only brings the truth to the learner, but "provides the condition for understanding [it],"[33] which is to say, existing according to it.

Amos's pronouncement of national judgment does address eighth-century Israel as mired in sin—oppression, exploitation, and false religious consciousness. Indeed, the people are so enmeshed in the oppressive pattern of behavior and institutional corruption, and so bent on justifying themselves, that they are incapable of recognizing the truth of the divine decision. Amos must inaugurate the judgment to dislodge them from their false, defensive consciousness and allow the course of human events to reshape their knowledge of God's will. Only when the people have come to accept the truth of their judgment can they be restored and healed.

It seems to me that Climacus's description of the learner's condition of being in untruth most resembles the prophetic message. Amos's audience was in a condition of willful ignorance, and it must not only be brought face-to-face with the truth, it must undergo a transformation in order to know it to be true. If the prophet's message describes a perennial feature of human character and its historical enactment, Climacus's position does have biblical roots.

33. Ibid., 14.

Kierkegaard develops his concept of revelation in the strongest incarnational terms, and it would seem that this aspect of his presentation would be totally out of keeping with the Old Testament. But appearances can be deceiving. Kierkegaard's well-known work *Fear and Trembling* expounds the divine command to Abraham to sacrifice his son.[34] Departing from a long figural tradition in the church, Kierkegaard expounds it as a paradigm of faith without reference to Christ.[35] Clearly, for him, the God of Israel is the true God.

The poetics and rhetoric of Hebrew Scripture clearly do provide a basis for an understanding between God and God's people. First of all, God is rendered as a persona in interaction with creatures, particularly with members of God's people. God is addressed by name, and has an inner life of thoughts and emotions, exemplifying a particular character. The rendering itself confronts the reader with a presence. God intervenes in the course of human events, and responds to human actions. The divine attributes are embodied in the character of God, they are not empty abstractions. If sophisticated readers regard this language as naive, they miss precisely the power of the language to establish an equality between God and humans allowing for understanding.

The rhetoric of the biblical text engages the audience in its maturity. The promises, commandments, and judgments of God are designed to persuade the audience of the truth of what is communicated. When the readers are commanded to honor no god but YHWH, they have the account of creation and primordial history, the stories of the acts of God in the lives of the patriarchs and matriarchs, and the deliverance of Israel by God from Egyptian slavery and conveyance through the wilderness "chronologically behind them" and the story of Israel from the wilderness to the exile before them as an argument for the commandment's truth. When Amos announces the verdict of God, the decision is given reason in powerful accusations of oppression and decadence. It is not an authoritarian text.

Finally, there is the record of protest. The people are virtually authorized by the communal laments to stand up to God's judgment, to insist that their perspective be taken into account, to insist that God demonstrate his worthiness of praise by delivering a maltreated people. An authoritarian text would silence such dissent. Even if the decisions all go with the house of Hillel, the opinions of the house of Shammai must be respected.

---

34. *Fear and Trembling/Repetition*; Kierkegaard's Writings, VI (Princeton: Princeton Univ. Press, 1983), 1–123.

35. There are plenty of references to gospel and epistle teaching, but that is not the same as typology.

Postscript

Numerous types of discourse fill Hebrew Scripture. Many would not count as revelation according to either of the definitions we have been using in this book. Communal laments, for example, are not depictions of events in which God is manifested in the visual world nor do they communicate knowledge of God at God's initiative. A variety of revelational discourses is presented as well. Depictions of theophanies manifest God to the mind's eye but do not communicate the knowledge of the biblical God apart from the discourse that takes place within them. This book has concentrated on the latter. How is divine discourse related to other scriptural discourses?

It depends upon how much unity the interpreter is willing to ascribe to Scripture. It is common in current theological thinking to celebrate the theological diversity of Scripture. A kind of nominalism is definitely in ascendancy. I subscribe to the view that this is extreme, and the Scripture is designed to be synthesized—to be read as a whole.[36]

If the Old Testament is taken to be a whole, if some passages engage readers in a particular, distinctive way, this way of engagement applies to the whole. If divine performative discourse requires readers to trust in commissives and obey exercitives, this type of transaction is communicated to discourses that build on reason and experience. If one is trying to jump across a ditch fifteen feet wide, a leap of twelve feet doesn't do it.

The passages that we expounded, moreover, are by any account among the most prominent and powerful in Scripture. They have the capacity to shape the identity of the interpretive community far beyond their textual magnitude, and to set the terms for reading others. The burning bush and the burning mountain are inscribed deeply on the minds of every reader of the Bible, and what was said there has a power to condition the message of any other passage.[37] Finally, the pattern of engagement characteristic of these three passages is repeated in most divine discourse in Hebrew Scripture. When God speaks, the illocutionary force is generally of a performative character. God promises, commands, issues verdicts, and supports them with behabitives, self-identification, and the like. If one observes closely, one will discover that the accounts of these performatives usually breach the proscenium arch; the reader is brought into the performative transaction depicted in the text.

Do these performative transactions really have anything in common

---

36. See chapter 7, "The Bible says . . ." in *Rhetoric and Biblical Interpretation*, 127–39.
37. It also shaped the writing of the literature: the proclamation of the first commandment at Mount Sinai is a major structuring device in the Pentateuch: see my "The First Commandment in the Structure of the Pentateuch," *VT* 45 (1995): 107–18.

besides being performative discourse? Actually, falling under the category of performative discourse brings a certain theological unity with it. What is said, and hence to be known, comes into existence in the act of saying and receiving. Its truth cannot be known apart from the correlative response of the recipient(s). It is this type of discourse that marks faith, obedience, and contrition off as primary virtues of the faithful. It is this type of discourse that makes the historical moment of decisive significance. It is this type of discourse that makes the speaker essential to what is communicated. It is this type of discourse that makes sin and redemption the heart and soul of the biblical story. It is this type of discourse that seeks to make reason obedient.

It would, however, be an egregious mistake to elevate these commonalities into an overriding principle of biblical theology. It is the nature of performative utterances to be particular and useful. If God's performative utterances have a tendency to expand, as they do, they remain contingent and each new application requires divine authorization. A biblical theology that grasps the logic of these utterances will attend to the distinctive force of each and be aware of the divergences as well as the convergences of God's "many and various" acts of speaking (cf. Heb. 1:1).

INDEX OF ANCIENT SOURCES

INDEX OF AUTHORS